£2

THE RELIGIOUS IDEAS

OF THE

OLD TESTAMENT

THE RELIGIOUS IDEAS

OF THE

OLD TESTAMENT

BY

H. WHEELER ROBINSON. M.A.

Second Edition, revised by

L. H. BROCKINGTON, M.A., B.D.

Senior Lecturer in Aramaic and Syriac
in the University of Oxford

GERALD DUCKWORTH & CO. LTD.

3 HENRIETTA STREET, LONDON, W.C. 2

First published in September 1913.

Reprinted 1923, 1926, 1930, 1934,
1938, 1947, 1949, 1952

Second Edition 1956

Printed in Great Britain
by T. and A. CONSTABLE LTD., Hopetoun Street
Printers to the University of Edinburgh

PREFACE

BEHIND the shifting scenes and crowded stage of Old Testament history, and expressed in the varied literature of a thousand years, there are a few simple, yet profound, ideas which are fundamental to the religion of Israel. It is the aim of this book,[1] within the limits of the series to which it belongs, to present these leading ideas in their historical setting, with some indication of their theological and philosophical value, and of their significance for Christianity. The method of treatment is therefore distinct from that which would naturally be adopted for a history of the religion as a whole through successive periods, though the historical development is more or less followed in the discussion of each topic, and in the order of treatment. Archæological detail is given only to the extent necessary for the illustration of the forms assumed by the ideas. The general point of view is that of one who believes critical study of the Old Testament to be no obstacle but a great help to the progress of the Gospel of the New Testament. The interest felt during recent years in the literature of the period between the two parts of Scripture, and in the Judaism of the time of Christ, has perhaps tended to obscure the elementary truth that the Gospel of the New Testament after all springs from the dominant ideas of the Old Testament. The unity of

[1] A summary of the argument is given in the closing paragraph of the first chapter.

Scripture is shown by its fundamental conception of religion as the personal fellowship of God and man. Prior to the New Testament, and judged simply from the standpoint of comparative religion, the Old Testament offers the purest and noblest example of that conception. The proof of the reality of that fellowship is the moral emphasis which characterises the religion of Israel.

The author of this book is much indebted to Dr. G. Buchanan Gray and the Rev. David Stewart, M.A., who have read it in manuscript, and rendered valuable help by their numerous criticisms and suggestions. He has also to thank the Rev. H. C. Rowse, M.A., for assistance in the correction of the proofs.

PREFACE TO SECOND EDITION

A GLANCE through the pages of *Inspiration and Revelation in the Old Testament*, which was prepared during the closing years of Wheeler Robinson's life and published in 1946, a year after his death, will show that if he himself had revised this book for a new edition the main alterations might well have been made in the closing chapter rather than in the body of the book. That chapter was written at a time when the critical view of the Old Testament was still held in grave suspicion because it seemed to many to undermine the authority of the Scriptures. To-day the suspicion is not that the critical study has undermined the authority but rather that it has caused scholars to lose sight of the theological significance of the Old Testament. The last chapter, therefore, if re-written by Wheeler Robinson, might well have had much to say about the value of historical criticism and exegesis to the theologian. The main conclusions of the chapter would have remained the same, however, namely, those of the abiding worth and intrinsic truth of the Old Testament Scripture and of its significance in preparing the way to a better understanding of the Christian truths.

It may reasonably be claimed that he would not find much to re-write in the body of the book. The religious ideas of the Old Testament remain the same, however differently they may be spoken of and interpreted in succeeding generations. Wheeler Robinson was rightly insistent that every generation must accept the duty of restating ancient ideas in the light of its own characteristic thought. For him the study of the Old Testament was the handmaid of his Christian faith. His use of it was essentially theological and his writing about it always constructive. In many ways he anticipated thereby the more recent demand for theological study and interpretation of the Old Testament. It is this theological interest, coupled with his clear constructive thinking, that puts his book beyond the reach of the reviser and makes it of lasting value in the form in which he himself wrote it.

A number of minor changes have been made in the text, many footnotes have been altered and a few pages of Additional Notes added to indicate where knowledge and opinion have changed since the book was first written, more than forty years ago.

The Bibliography has been considerably altered, but much of the old Bibliography remains in the references to literary works in the footnotes.

L. H. BROCKINGTON.

June 1956

CONTENTS

CHAPTER I

CHAPTER II

CHAPTER III

CHAPTER IV

CHAPTER V

CHAPTER VI

CHAPTER VII

CHAPTER VIII

CHAPTER IX

THE RELIGIOUS IDEAS OF THE OLD TESTAMENT

CHAPTER I

THE HISTORY AS THE SOURCE OF THE IDEAS

THE difference between conventional impressions of the Old Testament and the attitude of the serious student towards it, may be compared with that between two views of the same landscape, as seen by the casual spectator and by the geologist respectively. Both are gazing on the same fertile valley, set in its framework of lofty hills, through the verdure of which can be seen here and there the course of the streams that feed the river below. The one gratefully accepts the whole scene as it lies before him, in its abiding majesty and grace. The other, not necessarily less responsive to its beauty, looks beneath the thin covering of soil on the hills to the limestone that makes them, thinks of the buried fossils that tell the story of successive ages, traces the slow creation of that far-stretching plain through the soil washed down from the crumbling rock, to be carried onwards and deposited afresh by the ceaseless ministry of the river. His mind's eye rests, not on the result alone, but on the interaction of forces, the successive processes, the evolving work of uncounted centuries that have made this result. He understands better what he sees, because he knows how it came to be what it is.

It is not otherwise with the Old Testament. We know

and love its sunlit peaks and shadowed valleys, its green
pastures and still waters, the familiar unity of the whole
as it lies outstretched from Genesis to Malachi. Sinai
frowns upon it from the background, and its river runs
onward to that city of God which hath no need of the sun.
Patriarchs and prophets, whose names are household
words, have made this scene their familiar habitation ;
here kings have gone to battle, and saints of God have
won better victories, lifting their eyes to these hills. When
we think what all this has meant to unnumbered lives,
which have drawn so much spiritual strength from its
influence, we need not wonder at the passion of resent-
ment that the critical study of the Old Testament has
often aroused in those without sufficient faith to realise
that beauty is only enriched by a deeper truth. But the
critical study of the Old Testament has simply done for
it what geology has done for natural landscape. Under-
neath the conventional form of the Old Testament literature, critical scholarship has taught us to recognise the
successive strata that have built up the mountain peaks
of faith and vision, each with its own fossil survivals
from the past. The classic utterances of prophetic
morality, the penetrating disclosures of the soul's deep
secrets, which have borne so goodly a harvest, were only
possible because of more primitive elements and cruder
material transformed from forbidding rock into fruitful
plain. To learn all this, we must first unlearn many things
we have taken for granted. We must be patient enough
to let the evidence overcome our prejudices. Critical
study can be a moral as well as an intellectual test, and
it is perilously easy to deny what we have never laboured
to understand. But of one thing we can be certain from
the outset. Critical study of the Old Testament can no
more rob us of its spiritual and religious value than geo-
logical study can make any landscape less beautiful, or
its soil less fruitful. The Old Testament is the permanent

possession of the human race, and the more we know of
the nature and history of its great ideas, the more powerful
ought to be their influence upon us.

The book we have to study has been conventionalised
both by the Christian and by the Jew, and we must in
both cases penetrate beyond commonly accepted theories
in order to reach historic truth. The task is easier in
the former case, because we possess the Jewish Scriptures
practically in the form in which they existed when they were
appropriated by the Christian Church,[1] and are not compelled first to eliminate Christian alterations. Christian
traditionalism in regard to the Old Testament belongs wholly
to the realm of interpretation.[2] In the earlier centuries
this was allegorical, and admitted of the wildest fancies.
At a later date, as the dogmatic system of the Church
developed, the whole Bible became a uniform text-book
of dogma, which could be cited with little or no recognition
of the development between its first page and its last. As
such, it passed from the Catholic to the Protestant Church,
and acquired a new significance, because the traditions
of the Church as a parallel authority were explicitly
rejected. Protestant dogma confidently interpreted the
Old Testament according to its ' plan of salvation ', and,
until the comparatively recent historical study of Scripture, the Bible was read with the conviction that it would
give throughout a consistent and uniform statement of
Protestant doctrine, if its various utterances were systemati-
cally collected and combined. From such an assumption
we are not yet free, and it affects men often unconsciously
in their exegesis of the Old Testament.

[1] But the earlier Christian Scriptures were in the Greek version (the
Septuagint), which contained, in addition to the Hebrew Canon, a number
of other books circulating amongst Greek-speaking Jews. These books,
broadly speaking, are now known as the Apocrypha, and form part of the
Roman Catholic Canon (the Vulgate). The Protestant Canon is identical
in contents, though not in order, with the Hebrew.

[2] Of course, including translation, as in the retention of ' virgin ' in A.V.
and R.V. of Isaiah vii. 14, against the meaning of the Hebrew.

Jewish traditionalism is more difficult to deal with, because it is inwrought into the texture of the Old Testament itself. The literature was divided into three groups, in the general order of their supposed antiquity and value, viz. 'the Law, the Prophets, and the Writings'.[1] On these three terraces, one below another, lay revealed the supposed history of Israel, with the golden age of the patriarchs on the crest of the hill. God was worshipped from the beginning, but His full revelation was not given until Moses. From that divine Law Israel fell away, to be rebuked and vainly recalled to obedience through the prophets. For this disobedience the Exile was the punishment ; to the penitent faithful the restoration was the reward, though they still waited through the centuries for the hope of Israel, its full re-establishment as the people of God. This dogmatic framework shaped not only the Jewish interpretation of the Old Testament, but even the literary form in which it was allowed to reach the Christian Church. The actual history, it was naïvely felt, must have corresponded with this theory.[2] So earlier records were pressed into the service of the later ideas of the religion. The literary documents of the history of Israel are not, in our present Old Testament, arranged in the historical order of their composition, nor preserved in their original integrity. The narrator's aim was not the scientific accuracy which we desiderate in the historian of to-day ; the ancient writer felt free to mould the traditions of the past into an illustration of the convictions of his own time. Yet we must be grateful to these writers for one thing ; they have often incorporated older documents into their own writings, with comparatively little change. It is the presence of

---

[1] The 'Prophets' also included Joshua, Judges, 1 and 2 Samuel, 1 and 2 Kings, but not Daniel, which is assigned to the 'Writings'.

[2] The way in which the history was re-written in accordance with the ideas of a later age may be seen by comparing 1 Chronicles xv. with 2 Samuel vi. (the ark brought to Jerusalem).

these older strata that has enabled Old Testament scholarship, within the last century, to reach a view of the history which is doubtless incomplete and sometimes faulty, but which brings us much nearer to the truth than did the conventional view.

The evidence for these statements belongs to that department of Old Testament study which is technically known as ' Introduction '.[1]   It is partly philological, consisting in the examination of Hebrew words, phrases, and styles of composition ; these reveal, as in all languages, a development of usage in successive generations.[2]   In part, also, the evidence is derived from the subject-matter ; ideas and customs appear in professedly the same document, which cannot be reconciled on the assumption that they are really contemporaneous, though they admit of natural explanation on the assumption that they,

[1] See H. W. Robinson, *The Old Testament, its Making and Meaning*, 1937, J. E. McFadyen, *Introduction to the Old Testament*, New Ed., 1932, or the larger introductions of S. R. Driver, 9th ed., 1913, R. H. Pfeiffer, 1948, and A. Bentzen, 1948. Almost all Old Testament scholars would agree on the following summary of conclusions. The earliest Hebrew literature we possess consists of songs or other poetry, of which the oldest is probably the Song of Deborah ; this goes back to the twelfth century B.C. Stories of the heroes who are now classed as ' judges ', and of the first two kings, were composed a century or two later, as was also the earliest code of Hebrew law, known as the ' Book of the Covenant ' (Ex. xx. 22-xxiii. 19). This has been incorporated into one of the two oldest strata of the Hexateuch (Genesis-Joshua), which are usually assigned to the ninth (J) and to the eighth (E) centuries respectively. The prophets of the eighth century (Amos, Hosea, Isaiah, and Micah) profoundly influenced the second code of Hebrew law, which underlies our present Deuteronomy. This code was promulgated in the last quarter of the seventh century ; the history of the later kings came to be written under the influence of a Deuteronomic interpretation. Another code dating from the Exile is found in Leviticus xvii.-xxvi. ; it is closely dependent on the work of the prophet Ezekiel. The fourth code was that accepted by the post-exilic community at the initiative of Ezra (who returned in 458 or 397 according to which Artaxerxes is meant in Ezra vii. 7) ; it is known as the ' Priestly Code ', and we owe to writers of this school the present form of the Hexateuch, Many of the Psalms and some other works of developed religious thought, such as Job, belong to the post-exilic period ; Chronicles belongs to the third, Daniel and possibly Ecclesiastes to the second century B.C.

[2] Thus the syntax and vocabulary of Ecclesiastes—one of the latest books of the Old Testament—show many points of contact with post-Biblical Hebrew, and many differences from the Hebrew of the early monarchy.

and the original documents in which they appear, belong to different periods.[1]

This rearrangement of the documents is not, as is often supposed by those who are unacquainted with the evidence, an arbitrary reconstruction ; it is simply a result of the science of historical criticism working on the actual documents. The facts which characterise them have to be explained, and this is the explanation of the facts which has gradually approved itself to the overwhelming majority of competent scholars. If any one still wishes to employ the documents for historical purposes in the conventional way, he ought first to be ready with a better explanation of the facts, such as the different conceptions of priest and sacrifice in what is alleged to be the same document, or the complete ignorance of the Deuteronomic law of a single sanctuary, which prevails before the seventh century B.C. On the other hand, the critical rearrangement of the documents which their own characteristics compel us to make, yields a view of the history of Israel which is natural without being naturalistic. The final evidence for the conclusions of this critical study is the resultant organic view of Israel's history, revealing the same principles of development throughout its course as we find in all other human history.

According to Rabbinic legend, Moses saw from Pisgah not only Israel's future land, but also Israel's future history, unrolled in swift panorama before his eyes. Some such outline of events is necessary for us, in order that the characteristic features of the history may appear. The most remarkable of them all is the issue from that history of the religious ideas which will claim our attention.

[1] *E.g.*, all Levites are priests according to Deuteronomy xviii. 1, but the (later) law of Leviticus i. 5 confines the priesthood to Aaron's sons.

1. *The History in the Literature*

The history of Israel began with the migration of certain nomadic tribes, of Semitic origin, from the Egyptian borders and control, and with their invasion of Palestine. The date at which this invasion occurred is approximately settled by evidence independent of the Old Testament. The glimpse of Palestine afforded in the Tell-el-Amarna Letters of about 1400 B.C. shows that the Hebrews of the Bible were not yet settled there; but an Egyptian inscription in the latter half of the thirteenth century refers to Israel in such a way as to suggest that it was then one element in the mixed population of Palestine. At some time, therefore, not long prior to 1200 B.C., we may suppose the Israelites to have gained an entrance into Palestine, as a group of tribes more or less united for purposes of warfare under the name of their God, Yahweh. Nothing is known of the previous history of these tribes and of their religion, though something may be conjectured from the traditions of their ancestors which were written down centuries after the settlement in Palestine.[1] We have no documents contemporary with Israel's nomadic period; the story of the Exodus from Egypt is first told by writers separated by many generations from the days of the desert.[2] Much of that story clearly throws back the conditions of settled life in Palestine into the very different life of wandering tribes. But with every allowance for these later accretions, inevitable in the case of oral tradition, there must have been a nucleus of historic fact in the tradition that so powerfully influenced the later course of the history—the tradi-

---

[1] For a fair statement of the present degree of our knowledge, see S. H. Hooke, *In the Beginning* (Clarendon Bible), 1947.

[2] 'The Egyptian monuments give no information as to the sojourn of the Israelites in Egypt, and as to the Exodus' (Jeremias, *Das Alte Testament im Lichte des Alten Orients*, p. 400).

B

tion that these tribes had a most remarkable escape from the pursuit of their Egyptian over-lords, that their leader, Moses, taught them to see in this escape the hand of Yahweh, and that from that time onward these tribes believed that Yahweh was their God, and that they were Yahweh's people. The later history requires such a deliverance, such a prophet-leader, and such a faith to explain its course, and there is no sufficient reason for rejecting the later belief that this relation between Yahweh and the tribes gathered at Sinai was formally expressed by some kind of 'covenant'.[1] On the other hand, we have no reliable knowledge of the explicit conditions or requirements of that 'covenant'; all that the history of the following centuries warrants us in saying is that Yahweh became primarily the war-god of His people. But it would be perfectly natural for tribal customs, especially tribal justice, to pass under the protection of the war-god, even from the earliest days.[2] The one unquestionable fact, in a realm of conjecture and infer- ence, is that the Hebrew tribes which advanced from the desert to the conquest of Palestine brought with them a faith in their God, Yahweh, which became the dominant factor in their history.

The traditional account of the conquest of Palestine describes its completion in a single generation.[3] But the earliest sources, imbedded in the Books of Joshua and Judges, show that the conquest was gradual and piece- meal.[4] Some tribes seem to have effected an entrance from the south, and to have secured a settlement there, whilst others crossed the Jordan from the east, so that the division of Israel into a southern and a northern portion belongs to its earliest days. At first the Israelites secured

---

[1] On the history of this important term, see chap. viii. § 1.

[2] Cf. Exodus xviii.

[3] E.g., Joshua xi. 23 ; contrast xiii. 13, xv. 14-19, xv. 63, xvi. 10, xvii. 11- 13, 14-18, xix. 47 ; Judges i. 1-ii. 5 ; these all belong to a much earlier document.   [4] See Additional Notes.

little more than settlement in the hill country, whilst the
richer plain lands remained in the occupation of the
Canaanites. The consequent isolation of these scattered
groups of Israelites encouraged the Canaanites to a combined attack, which has left its record in the earliest piece
of literature which the Old Testament contains, the Song
of Deborah. It was not until the time of Solomon that
the gradual absorption of the weaker Canaanites by the
hardier Israelites was completed. But, just as Greece,
a thousand years later, conquered her conqueror Rome,
so Canaanite culture proved more perilous to Israel than
Canaanite chariots. Palestine was a fertile and civilised
country long before the Israelite invasion. The transition from the pastoral life of the desert to the more developed
agricultural life of Palestine had important consequences
for the religion of Israel. Just as Israel's tribal life was
under the protection of Yahweh, so the civilisation of
Palestine was linked to the local Baalim. To adopt a
new mode of life was, in those days, to be committed to
a new religious development. The issue before Israel was,
therefore, the choice between the worship of these Baalim,
in addition to their war-god, Yahweh, and the transference to Him of the attributes of the gods of the land. The
latter alternative prevailed, and from this transference
arise the chief problems and crises in the earlier period
of Israel's religion. The political unity of the nation
was not achieved until about 1000 B.C., under David.
For the first two and a half centuries of Israel's life in
Canaan we have little more than the records of local
heroes—the so-called 'Judges'—who became prominent
in this or that section of the people. It was the hostile
pressure of the Philistines [1] which finally welded the
people together, as that of the Canaanites might have

---

[1] This people is probably to be identified with the non-Semitic *Purusati*,
who invaded Syria in the time of Rameses III. (c. 1200 B.C.). Their original
home, 'Caphtor' (Am. ix. 7), is usually taken to be Crete.

done had it been more effective. The kingship emerges in Israel as a military function, and Saul is primarily Israel's leader against the Philistines. (It is significant that here again, as in the desert, we find a prophetic personality, that of Samuel, prominent in this new departure.) Saul failed to accomplish the purpose of his kingship, and was defeated and slain by the Philistines. But David, who followed him, was successful, and his success brought other consequences for national development, in the extension of the territorial borders, and in the union of the northern and southern elements under a single ruler. This union did not continue further than the reign of Solomon—a reign chiefly noticeable for the inner development and organisation of the nation; under his son Rehoboam the super-imposed bond uniting north and south was broken, and the original grouping that went back to the first invasion of Canaan asserted itself. But the memory of this brief period of the undivided kingdom, and of its real political independence, became one of the most potent of religious influences. Its brevity found compensation in the intensity with which, through many centuries, the nation was inspired with the hope of a return of the Davidic kingship, and of the glory of that idealised past.[1] One important result of the kingship was the establishment at Jerusalem of the royal temple, destined to become, after many generations, the concrete centre and embodiment of Israel's religion.

The history of the divided kingdoms of Israel and Judah is really the history of the northern kingdom, Israel. The centre of power and interest lies in the north, and Judah is of negligible political significance so long as the northern kingdom lasts. The relation of Judah to Israel was practically that of a vassal kingdom, as is shown by the service of Judæan troops in the campaigns of the northern kings. In the course of the two centuries (933-722), during which

[1] See chap. viii.

the northern kingdom existed, there were two dynasties of importance, that of Omri (887-843), and that of Jehu (843-745). Under Ahab, the son of Omri, came the inevitable conflict between the religion of Canaan, as expressed in the cult and culture of Phœnicia, and the religion of Israel as the worship of Yahweh alone. The immediate causes which made the northern kingdom the arena of ultimate and fundamental issues were Ahab's political marriage with a princess of Tyre, and Elijah's passionate devotion to the God of Sinai. The full strength of the nationalistic movement was revealed in the reign of Ahab's son and second successor, Jehoram. A conspiracy in which Jehu was the hand and Elisha the heart, overthrew the dynasty of Omri in the interests of the religion of Yahweh. The dynasty of Jehu, thus introduced, lasted until the shadow of Assyria fell across throne and people in the eighth century B.C. Prior to this, Israel's foreign relations had been chiefly with the neighbouring state of Damascus, which was the one foe to be feared.[1] But, in fact, Damascus was really the protector of Israel from Assyrian attack. The combined forces of Damascus and Israel were defeated by Assyria in 855, but it was not until a century later that the absorption of Israel by the great world-power became imminent. This new element in the history of Israel explains the most characteristic feature in the religious development of this period. Just as the pressure of Philistia had created the military kingship of Saul and David to replace the clan-leadership of the ' Judges ', so that of Assyria created a new type of what may be called ' international ' prophecy, in place of the older nationalistic type represented by Elijah. Amos and Hosea, discerning a spiritual law in the natural world, interpret the foreign peril as a divine judgment. The breadth of their application of this principle corresponds with their enlarged conception of Yahweh

[1] Cf. the story of Naaman and the captive Hebrew maid (2 Kings v.).

Himself as the ruler of the nations. This moral interpretation of history by the prophets of the eighth century, together with the idea of God which it implies, is the most important religious event of this period. It was the more influential because history itself confirmed the principles they laid down. When Samaria finally fell to the Assyrians (722), the new prophecy was vindicated, for it had continuously threatened national disaster as a divine judgment on social unrighteousness. A most impressive object-lesson was given to the sister-kingdom of the south, which, though still politically insignificant, now became the centre of religious interest.

Already, before the fall of Samaria, Judah had accepted the position of a tributary state to Assyria; Ahaz had been led to take this step in 732, as a means of protection against the united forces of Damascus and Israel, though against the advice of Isaiah. The influence of this prophet was exerted more successfully upon Hezekiah, the son and successor of Ahaz, to the extent, apparently, of some reformation in the existent worship of Yahweh. But Isaiah was not able to prevent Hezekiah from alliance with Egypt against Assyria, a policy which finally brought Sennacherib's army against Jerusalem (701). It was either in this, or in a later campaign, that a pestilence broke out in Sennacherib's army, and saved the city, so offering confirmation of Isaiah's faith in Yahweh, and a new ground for the growing confidence of the people in the inviolability of Jerusalem. Under Manasseh (692-638) political dependence on Assyria brought with it a great influx of Assyrian religion, which prevailed until the time of the Deuteronomic Reformation (621) under Josiah. The fall of the Assyrian capital, Nineveh, to the united Medes and Babylonians (612) merely changed the hand by which the last blows were to be struck. In 597 Nebuchadrezzar captured Jerusalem, and deported some of its principal inhabitants; ten years later, provoked by a new revolt, he destroyed the city. Throughout this closing generation in the history of the southern kingdom the prominent figure for the history of religion is Jeremiah. His apparently unpatriotic counsel of submission to Babylon was but the husk for the kernel of a deeper patriotism. That patriotism was united with a new recognition of the place and value of the individual in religion, which is expressed both in his own vividly described personal experience, and in the prophecy of the ' new covenant' which Yahweh will make with each Israelite.[1] Such spiritual ideas, however, were too far in advance of the times for their full influence yet to be felt. It was rather the idea of the old covenant, as elaborated in the Book of Deuteronomy, which was the immediate legacy of this period. In this book, for the first time, the religion of Israel was linked to a written code of law, publicly accepted.[2] Here was a book, inspired by the teaching of the eighth-century prophets, yet destined to become the nucleus of a priestly and legalistic literature—that of the Pentateuch. Here was the prophetic philosophy of history enforcing the moral demands of Yahweh so powerfully as to influence all subsequent historians in their judgment of the past. The Deuteronomic Law was therefore of the first importance, though its immediate (pre-exilic) operation was so transient, and its measure of immediate success so limited. The primary demand which it made for a single sanctuary was enforced by the Exile; the local sanctuaries, with all their Canaanite associations, were never revived.

The influence of the Exile on the future life of the nation was profound and far-reaching. What it destroyed of

[1] Jeremiah xxxi. 31 f.
[2] 2 Kings xxiii. 1-3.   The discovered book, which king and people covenanted to obey, is shown by the details of the actual reformation (verses 4 f.) to have been identical with the central part of Deuteronomy (see Additional Notes).

political ambition, it more than repaid in religious intensity. On the one hand, it nurtured the priestly conception of a community wholly devoted to the service of God, with the ritual of the temple as the living centre of that service. On the other, contact with a larger world widened the horizon of Yahweh's activity, and the conception of Yahweh's purposes. These two influences are best seen in the two great prophets of the Exile, viz. Ezekiel and Deutero-Isaiah (Is. xl.-lv.). Both are agreed in throwing themselves on God for the needs of the future ; the new worship and the new life will spring from Him. But Ezekiel sees the climax of divine intervention in the restoration of religion as the priest naturally conceives it, religion as it takes visible form in a reorganised cult, and in the customs of a people ceremonially 'holy'. Ezekiel, in fact, promotes the codification of priestly law by his vision of a priestly Utopia. In him begins the spirit of the post-exilic Judaism ; he marks the beginning of the second half of Israel's history, as did Moses that of the first. The vision of Deutero-Isaiah is of an altogether different kind, though, like that of Ezekiel, it awaits the activity of God for the introduction of the new era. This prophet, like Amos and Hosea, is kindled by the sight of new political movements, yet not to condemnation, but to consolation. He does not, like Ezekiel, draw his strength from memories of the temple that was, but from the hope of the people that shall be, when Cyrus shall have accomplished the work of liberation, to which Yahweh has anointed him. As a matter of history, Cyrus conquered Babylon in 539, and is said to have permitted the return of Jews under Sheshbazzar in the following year.

It is clear that the circumstances of this so-called 'Return' were in sharp and painful contrast with the glowing prophetic anticipations of it. The Temple was not rebuilt until eighteen years afterwards, when the prophets

Haggai and Zechariah, stimulated by political events in the Persian kingdom, aroused the depressed and dis-illusioned settlers to their task. This was accomplished by 516. But its completion brought no such revival of the glories of the past as these prophets had promised. Perhaps the peculiar mission of Israel was never in greater peril of abandonment than during the interval between the rebuilding of the second Temple and the arrival of Nehemiah in 444 B.C.[1] Through his energies, the ruined walls of the city were rebuilt, notwithstanding the jealous opposition of those who surrounded the Jewish com-munity. It was the reforming zeal of Nehemiah which made the religious reform of Ezra possible. Ezra's activity resulted in the solemn acceptance of the Priestly Law, which now forms the chief element in the Pentateuch. This was the second great step in the transference of the idea of revelation from oral prophecy to the written word. The first had been made with the acceptance of the Deuteronomic Code two centuries earlier. Thus was introduced that 'legalism' which characterises Judaism, the post-exilic religion of Israel.[2] The nation had lost its political independence, and had become an ecclesiastical community, gathered within a small district around its one Temple.

When we seek to trace the inner history of the Jewish community through the following centuries, it is almost as though we were writing the history of a local Church, with no direct outline of events available, but simply its successive hymn-books, the magazines that circulated amongst its members, and the report of an occasional sermon. The literature of the period is not scanty, but

[1] If the earlier date (458) be accepted for Ezra, then his earlier arrival seems to have produced no result until he was reinforced by Nehemiah.

[2] The term 'Judaism' will be used strictly in this sense throughout the book. 'Hebrew' is generally used to denote the pre-exilic religion, in contrast with Judaism, though it may also be used of features common to the whole religion of Israel, before and after the Exile, when there is no ambiguity.

it is difficult to discover the course of events in which it originated. The Jewish community remained politically dependent on the Persian kingdom until the conquest of that kingdom by Alexander the Great in 332. In the division of his kingdom, Palestine fell to the control of Egypt; after more than a century of Egyptian control it passed into the hands of the (Syrian) Seleucidæ. In the second century began that fierce conflict between Judaism and Hellenism, of which the Book of Daniel is one literary product, and the First Book of the Maccabees is another. The suppression of the Temple worship by Antiochus Epiphanes in 168, and his attempts to Hellenise the Jewish community, provoked a successful revolt, which for a time lifted Judaism once more into the political arena. The freedom secured by the Maccabees lasted until the capture of Jerusalem by Pompey in 63 B.C. So the Jewish nation became part of the Roman Empire, until the outbreak of the fiercer nationalism led to the destruction of Jerusalem in A.D. 70. The religious development of this post-exilic period is far too complex to be summed up in a sentence. To it belong not only the devotional religion of much of the Psalter and the problem of the Book of Job, but also a most remarkable growth in eschatological speculation, the literature of which lies, for the most part, outside the Canon of the Old Testament, and beyond the scope of this book. We measure the religious significance of these centuries best when we remember that, whilst the casuistry of the Mishnah is one of their results, the unfettered life of the New Testament is another.

2. *The Salient Features of the History*

The history which has been outlined is remarkable both in itself and in its product, the religious ideas of the Old Testament. How far, it may be asked, does the history enable us to explain that product? In other words, what are the most characteristic features of the history, and what have they contributed to the resultant literature ? In the first place, the nation was exposed to *a remarkable series of foreign influences*. This was due partly to the geographical position of Palestine, lying as it did on the high-road from East to West and West to East, and between Egypt and Assyria, the great world-powers of antiquity, partly to the comparatively rapid succession of political changes in these world-powers, and in the surrounding nations, which marked the thousand years of Old Testament history. The alleged influence of Assyrio-Babylonian ' monotheism ' on the nomadic religion of Israel may be left out of account, as a speculation without definite proof or probability. But when the Israelites entered Canaan, and passed from nomadic to agricultural life, they were brought into a new world just because of the relatively high civilisation of Palestine. Even the mere change of occupation would have affected their religious conceptions, for ancient life and ancient religion were very closely interwoven. In course of time Yahweh came to be conceived as the giver of the produce of the land conquered through His aid. It was natural, therefore, for them to suppose that He ought to be worshipped somewhat as the former inhabitants had worshipped their dispossessed Baalim. The institutions of Israelite worship, its religious festivals, and sacrificial customs, appear to have been drawn largely from the practices of Canaan. The holy places of the land, each with its sacred stone and wooden post, passed over to the victorious invaders, and became the sanctuaries of Yahweh. The same relation holds of the three great festivals of the Jewish year. The Feast of Unleavened Bread, the Feast of Weeks, the Feast of Booths are all shown by the details of their observance to be agricul- tural in character—*i.e.* they could not have belonged to a period prior to settlement in Canaan, and were most probably adopted from the Canaanites. Even the prophets themselves, who afterwards become so distinctive a feature of Hebrew history and religion, are genetically related to an older non-moral type of *Nebi'im*, who are, perhaps, like the holy places, the festivals, and the general details of sacrifice,[1] a contribution of Canaan to Israel's development. All this was the more natural because the inhabitants of Canaan belonged to the same division of the Semitic races as did the Israelites; the language of the Canaanites was practically the same as that of their Hebrew invaders.[2] But, besides this positive influence of religious *custom*, there was a negative influence of contrasted *principle*, which had a profound effect on the religious leaders of Israel. Baalism, as a form of sensual nature-worship, stood in direct opposition to the sterner Yahwism of mountain and camp. In Canaan these antithetical types of religion were brought face to face, and there is often no profounder influence on any religion than that in which it recognises its own antithesis. In addition, however, to this contact with the local worship of the Canaanites, Israel was now increasingly brought into relation with the far-reaching Assyrio-Babylonian world of thought. For the Tell-el-Amarna Letters, written about 1400 B.C. in cuneiform writing, prove that the Assyrio-Babylonian influence had been dominant in Palestine at an earlier period. When Hebrew thought did, at length, advance to speculation on the origin and early history of the world, as in the first eleven chapters of Genesis, it was as much influenced by Babylonian myth and legend as we are to-day by evolutionary science.

---

[1] Cf. the Ugaritic sacrifices mentioned in the Ras Shamra texts and the Phœnician sacrifices named in the Marseilles inscription. There are evidences even of human sacrifice amongst the Hebrews (cf. that of Jephthah's daughter) as well as amongst the surrounding peoples (Mesha's son to the god Kemōsh). On the significance of the story of the sacrifice of Isaac (Gen. xxii.), see chap. vi. § 2 (esp. p. 147).

[2] This is seen from Canaanite words occurring in the Tell-el-Amarna Letters, and from the names of places mentioned there, and in Egyptian inscriptions.

How far the idea of Yahweh as supreme God of the world was the result of Babylonian influence in Palestine, must remain matter of conjecture; the evidence here points rather to independent development than to direct borrowing.[1] The Code of Hammurabi, dating from about 1750 B.C., provides many parallels to the 'Laws of Moses', and the resemblance in the form of the laws is specially remarkable. We may also trace the influence of Babylon in a number of other directions, such as the architecture and furniture of the Temple, and the Jewish calendar. Renewed contact with the Assyrio-Babylonian Empire from the ninth to the sixth centuries B.C., resulted in the absorption of the northern kingdom, and in the introduction of foreign cults into the southern. But the still closer contact of the Exile, under prophetic guidance, enlarged the outlook of that remnant of the nation which maintained its distinctive religious life—a life effectively distinguished by the practice of circumcision and the observance of the Sabbath. Foreign influence is less apparent in the customs of the post-exilic community, because the institutions of Judaism were now more or less fixed, and this isolated society, gathered around the Holy City and conscious of its peculiar mission, was less plastic to the moulding hand. But in the realm of thought the Persian period was hardly less influential than the Babylonian. The new problems of human destiny and of the possibilities of life beyond death, the rise of the conception of Satan as the enemy of God, the doctrine of many angels, through whom the transcendent God mediated His rule of the world—these developments must certainly have been influenced, if not occasioned, by Persian

[1] 'The kernel and true meaning of the monotheistic conception of the universe, as unfolded by the prophets, is lost by any endeavour to place the conception on a level with the monotheistic strain that is vaguely but unquestionably present in the speculations of the Babylonian-Assyrian priests' (Jastrow, *Aspects of Religious Belief and Practice in Babylonia and Assyria*, p. 417).

religion. The influences of Greek religious thought were sharply arrested in Palestinian Judaism by the success of the Maccabæan revolt, and the Old Testament shows less of their direct effect than we might have expected. But those influences produced a copious literature amongst the Jewish Dispersion, and culminated in the philosophic work of Philo. Truly, though in a sense other than the prophet's, it might be said that the desirable things of all nations were brought to fill the Jewish Temple with glory.

A second striking feature of the history of Israel is *the scope it afforded to individual initiative*. Side by side with the remarkable series of foreign influences acting on Israel from without, there is an equally remarkable series of prominent personalities guiding Israel's life and thought from within. When we look down the line of Israel's leaders from Moses to Ezra, and consider how each contributes to the shaping of Old Testament religion; when we notice how each fresh crisis, in what we should call the secular history, finds a spiritual interpreter; when we remember how such men as Moses, Samuel, Elijah, Elisha, Isaiah, Jeremiah, Nehemiah become protagonists in the arena of national life, and others like Amos, Hosea, Ezekiel, Deutero-Isaiah, Ezra, stamp their personal convictions on the religion of the generations that follow them, we may justly say that, to a unique degree, this is a history of dominating personalities. Every nation, of course, has had its outstanding men, and some nations might offer, at select periods of their history, a fair parallel to Israel in this respect. But the age of Pericles at Athens, or the last century of the Roman Republic, is not typical of Greek or Roman history as a whole. The life of Greek cities doubtless offered abundant scope to the free play of individuality, but the divided life of those cities limited its influence, and the absence of an exalted national religion meant the loss of the highest source of inspiration. Roman life, under both Republic and Empire, was a unity in a sense in which Greek never was; but Republican patriotism, and the majesty of the Empire, alike demanded the repression of the individual. Israel, however, at least during the greatest periods of its religion, combined liberty of personal action with the unity of an intense national faith. Owing to its relatively narrow compass and concentrated position, the whole nation could be reached, and its life shaped, by the influence of one man, to a degree impossible in Greek and Roman civilisation. Through the continuity of the idea of God, the influence of the successive individuals was concentrated on a single end, and devoted to the guidance or interpretation of a singularly varied history, in the light of moral principle. The combination of such events and of such personalities, and their product in the prophetic consciousness, is doubly remarkable. We are justified in saying that Israel was in a peculiarly favourable position to assimilate the most varied elements from the culture of the ancient world, and also to give them, through its leaders and teachers, the highest moral and spiritual interpretation.

A third important aspect of Israel's history is *the self-consciousness of the nation as being the bearer of a unique religion*. Perhaps the most significant fact in regard to any nation is the idea it cherishes of its own destiny. National ideals, subtle in their composition, profound in their effect, are influences shaping successive generations. In the case of Israel, the national ideal became predominantly religious. The nation as a unit was pledged to Yahweh, and Yahweh to the nation. The prophets through whom the national self-consciousness became articulate, recognised that Israel's religious experience was a solemn trust and a great responsibility. Israel, as a nation, became conscious through its prophetic leaders that it possessed a religion intrinsically unique. That consciousness was neither so early nor so universal within Israel as has often been supposed. But the narrow intensity of devotion to Judaism which has made the Jew conspicuous throughout all the centuries is already visible in the post-exilic community of the Old Testament. Behind it lies a proud consciousness of spiritual superiority. The Roman could not understand the exclusive attitude of the Jew, who rejected the working compromises of religious syncretism, and would not show tolerance for any other creed. But Christianity understood it, and in her victorious contest with Gnosticism by this sign conquered. The tenacity of the Jewish self-consciousness is seen in the continuity of the nation through many disasters and misfortunes. It is seen especially in the elasticity of hope, by which Israel's sorrows were transformed and taken up into the vision of a higher purpose. The self-consciousness of Israel shows its strength in the constant renewal of the Messianic hope, and in the picture of Israel as the suffering Servant of Yahweh, humbled for a season the more gloriously to atone for the sins of the world. In fact, without this peculiar self-consciousness of Israel, we could not explain its resistless vitality, and its striking power to appropriate and transform the most alien elements. But how can the self-consciousness itself be explained ? In the *form* of the relationship between Yahweh and Israel there is nothing peculiar. To find a parallel belief, there is no need to go further than Israel's kinsfolk and next-door neighbours, the Moabites, who (on the Moabite Stone) write of their god Kemōsh, as the Israelite at first writes of Yahweh.[1] But there is no parallel to the inner nature of that relationship. Its claim to be unique has been acknowledged by history. The religion of Israel, in fact, made fuller demands on human nature (morality), and gave fuller opportunity

---

[1] When Moab has been conquered by Omri of Israel, it is 'because Kemōsh was angry with his land'. It is Kemōsh who says to Mesha, the Moabite king, 'Go, take Nebo against Israel'.

to divine revelation (ethical monotheism) than any other. Both features are seen most clearly in the prophetic consciousness of Israel, which is the nation's self-consciousness at its highest. Beyond Israel's 'men of the Spirit', as has well been said, we cannot press for further explanation of Israel's unique religion—unless we believe, with Israel, that they were indeed men of God.[1] If divine truth were uniquely given to any nation, then we might expect just such a pride in its possession, based on the reality of an experiential knowledge of God, as characterised the self-consciousness of Israel.

The three features of the history already indicated belong to its intrinsic nature, and are independent of any judgment we may form of the value of its results, the religious ideas of the Old Testament. There is, however, a fourth deserving to be noticed, which becomes apparent in the light of those results and of their incorporation in Christianity. From this standpoint, perfectly legitimate to the general historian, we may say that there is *a remarkable teleological or 'providential' aspect of the history of Israel*.[2] From stage to stage of that history there is a continuous narrowing of the arena, a condensation of issues, a bringing to focus, as it were, of the national experience.[3] The loose relationship of nomads passes into the more settled life of tribal groups, and common perils bring these groups into the unity of a state. Israel in the north becomes an object-lesson in the ways and thoughts of Yahweh, from which Judah profits. The 'righteous remnant' of Judah returns from the Exile with definitely religious ideals, and practically becomes the single city of Jerusalem,

[1] Wellhausen, in *Die Kultur der Gegenwart*,[2] (I.) iv. 1, p. 15.

[2] This statement is not meant to imply that the history of, say, Greece or Rome does not also possess a teleological aspect, but simply to show the extent and nature of this feature in the case of Israel. If God controls history to rational ends, we may trace the working of His purpose in the means by which those ends are reached.

[3] The gradual concentration of the patriarchal stories on Jacob is a reflection of this historic truth.

with its one Temple spiritualised by passionate devotion into the vestibule of the unseen world. This political poverty finds compensation in ever-increasing spiritual wealth. The stereotyped ritual becomes the backbone of a living and vigorous faith, strong enough to defy the bitterest persecution. The ideas create a literature destined to become fundamental to the religion of many peoples in many lands. Those who in any real sense respond to the message of that literature to-day are bound to feel that a uniting purpose runs through the history which created it, and that the spirits of Israel's prophets were not finely touched but to fine issues. Each stage in the process lasted long enough to contribute something vital to those issues. National freedom, before it was lost, created a nation's self-consciousness. Prophetic teaching, before its voices fell to silence, created the Old Testament. The Temple-cult nourished the piety of far-off synagogues till they had prepared the world for a new and progressive faith. The earthly Jerusalem did not suffer destruction until it had created the ideal of the heavenly. If that final result be indeed thought worthy of a divine purpose, then the purpose is surely traceable in the history that leads up to it in so remarkable a manner. For it is a history progressively creative of the great ideas which are the foundation of the Christian faith.

The final chapter of this book will discuss the claim that these ideas constitute part of a divine revelation. But this at least may be said at the outset, in view of the salient features of Israel's history—that no other history known to us is more fitted to be the channel of such a revelation. A modern philosophy of revelation will certainly demand that there be the genuine interplay of divine and human personality, *both active*.[1] It will seek to relate the ' chosen ' nation so vitally to its

[1] See chap. ix. § 1.

historical environment that the contribution of other nations is real, and the measure of truth they possessed is fully recognised. Its ultimate proof will rest on the experiential and intrinsic worth of the religion, the same evidence that created the faith of Israel. It will ask for the inter-relation of the ideas with the past and with the future, in such a way that the unity of all human history is established. All these requirements are to be found in the history of Israel when it is critically studied. The issue is not as to the presence here or there of a ' supernatural ' element amid ' natural ' conditions. That distinction, so used, is a legacy from the categories of the eighteenth century. We gain a much richer idea of revelation, a much deeper insight into the divine activity, when we conceive the evolution of the nation's life as both natural and supernatural throughout, and not as a mosaic of both. Instead of a series of interruptive invasions and interjected commands, in a more or less alien environment, we see that both environment and personality are themselves in the hands of God, however fully He grants the exercise of personal freedom. He manifests Himself in the contour lines of Palestine and the influences of racial kinship, in the pressure of surrounding nations and the course of national politics, not less truly than in the prophetic consciousness which is guided to the interpretation of these phenomena. No purely naturalistic formula will ever explain Israel's history. It is true that in the national life, as in the individual, personality often seems to shade off into the physical organism and material environment below, as well as to touch the divine being above. But the environment simply draws the limits within which the personality of the nation or the individual ultimately exercises its freedom. The essence of religion, and therefore of revelation, lies in the real spiritual intercourse of God and man, which human freedom and divine grace make possible. God is concerned with all human life, not with that of Israel alone. Yet Israel's history becomes fully intelligible only when we construe it as the articulation of divine ideas to a unique end through the fellowship of God and man.

The religious ideas of the Old Testament are studied most naturally when they are regarded as organic elements in the one comprehensive idea of religion. They were slowly developed in closest relation to the history, and in response to the successive demands of Israel's experience. The religion of Israel underwent many changes, but faith in the fellowship of God and man gave unity to its eventful history, and supplied that inner continuity which is the mark of a true development. The most characteristic feature of the religion was its moral emphasis. Under the influence of that emphasis, the ideas of God and of man gained in meaning and majesty, until they demanded a wider arena than the political history of a single nation. The God of Israel was recognised as the one God of all the world on whom human nature and destiny everywhere depended. Religion brought the divine personality into such effective relation with the human, and the human with the divine, that the fellowship of God and man became a living fact of experience. God made Himself known to man, particularly through the spoken word of the prophet and the written law of the priest. Man could venture to approach God through particular places, times, persons, and offerings. But two disturbing elements were felt within this fellowship of God and man. There were human acts which were believed to alienate God ; there was human suffering, regarded as the evidence of His alienation. Here lay the peculiar problems of Israel's religion. But the hope of Israel rose beyond sin and suffering into confidence in the covenanted help of God, into the vision of His effective intervention in the affairs of Israel and the world, into the consciousness of a divine purpose to be realised even through human sorrows. These are the ideas which are embodied in the religion of Israel. If their intrinsic worth, their permanent value, their universal application, can be maintained against all possible objections, then the history of Israel which created these ideas constitutes a revelation of divine truth.

CHAPTER II

THE IDEA OF RELIGION

THERE have been many attempts at framing a definition of religion, and probably no single formula will ever command universal assent. To the theist this difficulty is rather a confirmation of his faith than a hindrance to it. If there be a real fellowship between God and man, a superhuman Personality in active relationship of helpfulness towards the dependent human personality, religion is a reality so full of life that it is as hard to define as life itself. A man's religion is constantly growing with his life, and a nation's religion comprehends the experience of many generations. In God's sight, the thousand years of Israel's history reflected in the successive contemporary records of the Old Testament are but as a single day; but in a man's, they are centuries crowded with the rich development of human experience. The Israelite of post-exilic times, worshipping in the Temple at Jerusalem, might confess his kinship with that far-off wandering Aramæan who had been his ancestor,[1] but the nomadic religion had been absorbed into the worship of an agricultural community, and quickened with the life-blood of prophetic morality, long before the religion of the Old Testament assumed its final, legalistic stage.[2] The impression of that religion frequently gathered from the Old Testament in its present form is inadequate to the

[1] Deut. xxvi. 5.
[2] See A. Causse, *Du Groupe Ethnique à la Communauté Religieuse*, 1937.

historic truth. The covenantal relation between Yahweh and Israel is often represented as a sort of commercial bargain—so much for so much—made explicit from the very beginning. The most characteristic feature of the religion seems to be its elaborate ritual, a ritual remote, in many of its ideas, from modern thought. On the other hand, the prophets seem to be continually insisting on familiar moral truths, often so obvious as to seem unnecessary when we have translated poetic metaphor into homely prose. But this general impression does the Old Testament great injustice. The real expression of its religion is not a written Law—that, however important, is but one of its later phases; the permanent record of the religion is a history, brought before our eyes in a very varied literature. Religion is always related to history, even when it claims a horizon as wide as humanity, and builds on data of universal significance. The ethical discipline of the Buddha cannot be explained except through the Hindu religion it reformed, and the Hindu doctrine of transmigration which it incorporated. The theology of the Kur'ān reflects the personal fortunes of Muhammed, and the social and religious conditions of Arabia in the seventh century after Christ. Thus, the religions of history become intelligible to the student only as he follows their footsteps to ruined shrines, and their thoughts to abandoned philosophies. But a religion may be related to history more closely than through the circumstances of its birth. History may itself be made the divine revelation. The foundation of the temple of religion will then be found, not in the psychological analysis of human nature, as is the case with Buddhism, nor in a theological conviction of the divine, as is the case with Muhammedanism, but in the fortunes of a whole people, interpreted as the work of God. It is this which is characteristic of the religion of the Old Testament. The emphasis on moral discipline which it finally achieves is certainly not less than that of Buddhism. The place it gives to prophetic personality is as prominent as that claimed by Muhammed. But the constant and underlying strength of the Old Testament religion is its conviction that God is revealing Himself in the history of a family, a people, a community. To a peculiar degree, therefore, we have here to do with a *historical* religion.[1] Even the ideals of the Old Testament take a quasi-historical form. In the full noon-tide of the actual history Israel threw back its developed consciousness into the twilight that went before the dawn. The patriarchal stories, from this standpoint, are the picture of that gradual providence of Yahweh which prepared a people for His possession. Their value does not depend upon their historicity, but rather on the simple beauty of the narratives themselves, and on the religious idea they convey, the idea that Yahweh was with His chosen people from the beginning.[2] But Israel was not content with finding support for this great and profound idea in the pre-Mosaic past, by an intuition that penetrated beyond the vision of the historian. It projected the same faith into the future, and created the Messianic Hope, the light of Israel's dark days, the inspiration of its later history, its immediate point of contact with its greater successor. The Messianic consciousness of Israel, the confidence in the re-establishment of a Davidic king and kingdom, the faith in the supernatural restoration of the future, the increasing emphasis on the eschatological side of religion, already begun within the Old Testament—these are due to the same instinct which created the story of Israel's pre-Mosaic past. The

---

[1] 'From the beginning onwards, the Old Testament religion and its development are distinguished from the other ancient religions by their conspicuously historical character' (Stade, *Biblische Theologie des A.T.*, p. 12).

[2] Yahweh is said to have 'elected' Abraham from a heathen environment. 'Your fathers dwelt of old time beyond the River . . . and they served other gods. And I took your father Abraham from beyond the River, and led him throughout all the land of Canaan' (Josh. xxiv. 2, 3).

truth behind both is not the truth of petty detail, the existence at some remote period of a sheikh called Abraham, or the success at some future day of the Zionistic movement of Judaism. It is rather the same truth which is sufficiently confirmed from that period of Israel's story which does lie in the partial light of history—the truth that Israel was not only the people of Yahweh, but that Yahweh was the living and ever-active God of Israel, visible in history as its Saviour and Redeemer as well as its Judge.

In the religious interpretation of this history the emphasis should fall on the grace of God in helping Israel, the redemptive attitude which spontaneously prompts Him to come to Israel's need. As is elsewhere said, the idea of a ' covenant ' is apt to be misleading. Whatever may have been the Pharisaic conception of the relation between man and God, there can be no doubt that the Old Testament religion as a whole rests on faith in the divine grace. Yahweh is constantly revealing Himself in historic acts which show Him as Israel's God. ' A manifest work of God, a prophet of God to interpret it, a community of men who had experienced it and understood it—such were the conditions under which the new religion arose '.[1] The religion of Israel begins with a divine deliverance from Egypt, and it constantly expects deliverance from all other foes. It rises to the great idea that the service of God needs the gift of His Spirit for its fulfilment. It conceives Him as keeping in constant touch with His people through the prophets. All this is quite distinct from such a commercial relation between God and man as characterises the religion of Rome, at least on its public side.[2] It is no exaggeration to say that the religion of

[1] Guthe, *E. Bi.*, col. 2221.
[2] This must not be regarded as an adequate characterisation of Roman religion as a whole. Warde Fowler (*The Religious Experience of the Roman People*, pp. 200 f.) has pointed out the significance of the private vows.

the Old Testament is, in its own way, as truly a religion of redemption as that of the New, though the redemption is differently conceived and nationalistically applied. The Decalogue is prefaced by the words ' I am Yahweh thy God, which brought thee out of the land of Egypt, out of the house of bondage '.[1]   The Book of Deuteronomy calls for a grateful and responsive love to God as the ultimate spring and source of obedience to His commandments.[2]

It is this conception of moral obedience to God as the supreme sacrifice, and not the elaborate ritual of the later days, which is really the characteristic feature of the worship of the people of Yahweh. ' Thus their beliefs about the origin and early history of the world, their social usages, their code of civil and criminal law, their religious institutions, can no longer be viewed, as was once possible, as differing in kind from those of other nations, and determined in every detail by a direct revelation from heaven : all, it is now known, have substantial analogies among other peoples—the distinctive character which they exhibit among the Hebrews consisting in the spirit with which they are infused, and the deep religious truths of which they are made the exponents '.[3]

1. *The Unity within the Development*

The period of religious development which can be traced most clearly in the Old Testament, extends from the foundation of the national faith under Moses to the establishment of the religion of the law under Ezra.   There are literary products of a later, and traditions of an earlier

But he admits that ' in the *vota publica* . . . we undoubtedly find something in the nature of a bargain—covenant would be a more graceful word—with a deity in the name of the State ' (*op. cit.*, p. 202).
  [1] Ex. xx. 2, Deut. v. 6.   [2] Deut. vi. 5.
  [3] Driver, *Modern Research as Illustrating the Bible*, p. 16.

period, but none of them afford the materials for confident historical reconstruction. Within the central period indicated, we may most easily realise the fact and the nature of the development by taking cross-sections, as it were, at convenient points. These are given by three such representative documents as the Song of Deborah (Jud. v.), the Book of Amos, and the narrative of Nehemiah viii.-x. They are short enough to be read in rapid succession; their approximate dates are beyond question; they are characteristic illustrations of the spirit and nature of the religion of Israel at the beginning, middle, and end of its most plastic period.

The Song of Deborah shows the position of affairs in the north of Palestine, within a generation or two of its invasion by Israel. A number of Hebrew tribes settled around the Great Plain are aroused to united action against the pressure of the unconquered Canaanites who occupy it. Yahweh is the common war-God of these tribes; they are brought together through their loyalty to Him, and their confidence in His aid on the field of battle. He dwells afar in the southern desert of their former nomadic life; but He comes at their need, and manifests Himself especially in the storm and the swollen river which contribute to the defeat of the foe. Because Israel is ' the people of Yahweh ', the battle is His, and those who fight come to the help of Yahweh. The battle is consequently both a moral and a religious act; tribes are praised or blamed as they do or do not meet their obligation to share in it, and the highest praise is given to the Kenite woman, Jael, who slew (as we should say, treacherously) the fugitive general of the enemy, Sisera. Here, then, is a concrete example of the earliest religion of Israel as a united people. The vivid poem shows the intensity of the national religion; it also suggests the moral potentialities of a faith capable of becoming the centre of common action and social obligation. Neither the religion nor the morality is

Christian. But without the energy and intensity of their effective union on the battlefield of the Plain, it would be much harder to understand the subsequent developments.

The Book of Amos, four centuries later, records the convictions of an individual thinker which are not yet the faith of a nation. His denunciations also reveal the general character of the contemporary religion of Israel. The people no longer think of Yahweh as coming from Sinai to help Israel in battle; He has become the God of Canaan, worshipped at Canaan's holy places, and with Canaan's often licentious rites. Yahweh is the sufficient guarantee of the nation's safety from foreign attack; ' the day of Yahweh' will deliver Israel from all her foes. But He is not concerned with the social and moral conditions within the nation; the luxury of the wealthy and their oppression of the poor can go on side by side with zealous worship at Bethel and Gilgal. Against these popular ideas the prophet's message stands out in clearest contrast. Yahweh is not simply the God of Canaan, nor is He linked to Israel in so purely mechanical a fashion that His intervention must necessarily be in Israel's favour. On the contrary, He who stands above all nations, and judges them all, will assuredly judge most rigorously the people to whom He has given exceptional privileges. The standard of His judgment is not ritual devotion but moral conduct : ' I hate, I despise your feasts, and I will take no delight in your solemn assemblies. . . . But let judgment roll down as waters, and righteousness as an ever-flowing stream '. In such words, contemporary religion is directly challenged by Amos; the sanctions to which he appeals are the warnings already given by Yahweh through agricultural and other disasters, and above all, through the appearance of Assyria on the political horizon. The downfall of the northern kingdom in the course of the next generation confirmed his words, and largely helped to make his convictions an essential part of the national religion.

The narrative of Nehemiah viii.-x. describes events little more than three centuries later than Amos, but it pictures quite another world of religious life—that of the post-exilic community. The kingdoms of North and South have shrunk into a small religious community, clustered around the rebuilt Temple of Jerusalem, as its one and only religious centre. The emphasis naturally falls on the sacred past, and the story significantly begins with the request of the people for ' Ezra the scribe to bring the book of the law of Moses, which Yahweh had commanded to Israel '. Reverence for the sacred roll is expressed by the account of its solemn reception ; the people rise, Ezra utters a blessing, the people say ' Amen, Amen ', and bow to the ground, when he opens the roll. This voice from the past makes a deep impression on them ; ' all the people wept when they heard the words of the law '. Their leaders begin on the very next day to carry out its details. Within the same month, after an address reviewing the providence of God in Israel's history, a covenant is made and sealed by the leaders, and adopted by ' all them that had separated themselves from the peoples of the lands unto the law of God '. This separation is secured by abstinence from all inter-marriage with them, by the observance of the Sabbath, and by other distinctively Jewish ordinances. The closing words of the narrative may stand as the fitting motto for post-exilic Judaism : ' we will not forsake the house of our God '.

None reading these portions of scripture attentively can fail to see how profoundly and materially the religion of Israel has developed from the twelfth to the fifth centuries B.C. The contrasts in the succession of warrior, prophet, and scribe, of sword, living voice, and written word, are significant of far deeper changes in the conception of what religion itself is. Yet there must be some unifying principle that links these stages together, and comprehends them all, and, with them, all the intervening minor changes. The unity is that of a continuous faith that Yahweh is Israel's God, that His personality is as real and living as man's, that the relation between the corporate personality of Israel and the divine Person is moral, and that no other deity counts at all.

This conclusion will be confirmed and illuminated if we gather up the prominent religious features in the three cross-sections that have been taken. In the life revealed by the Song of Deborah there is a national relation to Yahweh ; we might indeed say that these scattered tribes are constituted a nation by their common relation to Him. Religion is not something individualistic, the private intercourse of a man with his God ; the individual is related to God through the nation, and his worth appraised by reference to the national life and interests. It is apparent that there is no question of any other God for Israel. Whatever may be true of other nations, Israel stands in a peculiar and exclusive relation to Yahweh, one which may rightly be called moral, though the Song is concerned with the battlefield. For the battlefield is the centre of the national life and interests, and the God who controls it will not fail to prove adequate in other spheres. The warrior's loyalty to his fellow-Israelites and to Yahweh implies a relationship no less moral than that which is demanded in the social and civic intercourse of daily life. This moral relationship, however, becomes much more prominent in Amos, where it gains a wider application and a new estimate of its worth. It is applied to the whole range of the social life of Israel, as well as to the battle-field. It is explicitly contrasted with the ritual worship, and is declared to be the one essential offering. The moral experience of man is here made the interpretative prin-ciple in the conception of God, a step of the most profound significance for religion. Human personality, as represented in the prophetic consciousness, becomes the channel of revelation of the divine morality. The great sanction of this morality is the whole course of the history of Israel and its neighbours. Morality is no private attitude, no merely social or tribal custom ; it becomes the law of the world, as God governs it. Events have a meaning, and that meaning is moral. The moral consciousness of man is thus made the sufficient clue to the fortunes of the peoples. In the religion of the Law, as introduced by Nehemiah and Ezra, we have lost the freshness and informality of this appeal, but the principles it represents are made accessible to those who are not prophets. The written Law is Yahweh's sufficient revelation of His will. It becomes the explicit statement of the covenant between Him and His people. Loyalty to it is loyalty to Him, and such loyalty means separation from the uncleanness of those who do not know Him, as Israel knows Him, with that intimacy of knowledge which His grace has made possible.

It is clear that the emphasis falls on Yahweh in this continuous relation of fellowship between man and God. He is active both in history and in human consciousness. He is to be interpreted by the highest attribute of human personality, its moral consciousness. Such a faith in the moral and exclusive relation between Israel and Yahweh is the nucleus around which many elements from without gather and crystallise in the course of the generations. Such a faith is also the condition for the development of the ideas of God and man. For these ideas become what they are in the Old Testament through their inter-relation—the idea of God as actively gracious and self-revealing, and the idea of man as ultimately dependent on God.

2. *The Moral Emphasis*

The most important feature of the Old Testament fellowship of God and man, *i.e.* its moral emphasis, is obviously related to the clear conception of personality, human and divine, in Israel's religion. Personality always implies moral obligation, and finds its highest expression through morality. Where personality is adequately recognised, there will necessarily be the recognition of morality. The parent who wisely respects the personality of his child provides the only environment in which the moral consciousness of the child will properly develop. When Israel was a child, Yahweh loved him, and called His son out of Egypt into those conditions of freedom which made moral development possible. From the earliest days, therefore, at which the national history can be said to have begun, *i.e.* from Sinai, it is justifiable to claim that a moral relation existed between Yahweh and Israel. However limited in its original scope, and crude in its applications, that moral relation was certain to develop with the advance in the knowledge of Yahweh's personality, and with Israel's experience of relationship, as a corporate personality, to Him. The 'legislation' of Moses in the nomadic period[1] must have been very different from the elaborate structure of the Pentateuch. But the recognition of an obligation to Him who had delivered Israel from Pharaoh would itself be a moral nucleus for all subsequent development; sooner or later, the customs of the tribe, the 'things that were done in Israel', would gain a new significance as 'laws of Yahweh'. The exact extent and nature of the earlier morality is of quite secondary importance as compared with the fact that the religion of Yahweh was essentially moral in principle. This has been traced with

[1] Ex. xviii. ; cf. Doughty's description of the administration of justice in the desert in more recent times (*Arabia Deserta*, i. p. 249).

some reason to the circumstances of its origin : ' Israel's religion became ethical because it was a religion of choice and not of nature, because it rested on a voluntary decision which established an ethical relation between the people and its God for all time '.[1]

The Old Testament is undoubtedly the most profoundly moral book which antiquity can offer. Its moral emphasis cannot be adequately represented by the quotation of a number of striking verses, such as Micah's ' What doth Yahweh require of thee, but to do justly, and to love mercy, and to walk humbly with thy God ? ' Similar utterances selected from the literatures of other religions would not prove that they possessed Israel's emphasis on morality. This is shown rather by the part which moral ideas have taken in the development of the religion, notably in the prophetic teaching of the eighth century, which has already been illustrated in the case of Amos. But before this moral development culminates in the great prophets, its course can be traced in such words as those of Nathan to David concerning Bathsheba, and those of Elijah to Ahab concerning Naboth's vineyard. The ideas which underlie the earlier narratives of the Pentateuch also, show that the prophets of the eighth century were not without like-minded predecessors. Nor could we explain the success of the prophets as shown in the pervasive influence of their principles in almost every branch of the literature of the Old Testament, unless some general sympathy with those ideas already existed. We see that influence alike in the codes of law [2] and in the philosophy of history,[3] in the confessions of personal religion [4] and in the practical precepts of every-day life.[5]

[1] Budde, *The Religion of Israel to the Exile*, p. 38.
[2] Cf. Deut. v. 14, 15 with Ex. xx. 10, 11 ; in the Deuteronomic code the Sabbath law acquires a philanthropic instead of a purely religious motive.
[3] It is widely recognised that the historical books have been edited by writers who share the Deuteronomic point of view and have come under the influence of prophetic teaching.
[4] *E.g.*, Pss. xv., xxiv.   [5] As in the Book of Proverbs.

One of the most striking examples of this moral emphasis is afforded by the chapter in which Job challenges the justice of God by the review of his past life. It is significant of the degree to which, at all events, the later religion is 'moralised', that all except one [1] of the numerous misdeeds Job repudiates would be condemned from the standpoint of universal morality. Nothing could more forcibly express the fact that morality is the heart of Old Testament religion. Even the Priestly Code, with all its elaborate precautions for ceremonial 'holiness', is still in large measure a moral document, the outcome of a passion for perfection that shall be worthy of Yahweh. [2]

This vital union of morality and religion had important consequences for both, as it always must have. Morality gained new and powerful sources of inspiration and support. The consciousness of personal fellowship with God, and of the presence of His Spirit, reinforced the moral aspirations, and created a new confidence that they might be realised. The moral interpretation of history brought support from without to the moral loyalty within; for He who spoke in the demands of private conscience was the God who humbled or exalted nations. Not less was religion exalted and enlarged by the projection of moral experience into the unseen world. When Hosea argued from the moral relations between his adulterous wife and himself to those between Israel and Yahweh, the principle involved was more important than that which Newton discovered when he linked a falling apple to a moving star. It made a spiritual pathway along which thought could and did move with confidence. It is not an accident that the first explicit demand for faith in God [3] should

---

[1] xxxi. 26 f. ; see, further, the discussion of 'Moral Holiness' (chap. vi. § 4).

[2] Lev. xi. 44.

[3] Isaiah to Ahaz : 'If ye will not believe, surely ye shall not be established' (Is. vii. 9) ; but the great example of Abraham's faith (Gen. xv.), if not the remark that Yahweh 'counted it for righteousness' (verse 6), appears a century earlier.

come to us from the eighth century, when religion was
seen to deal with a realm in which moral experience held
true. Morality and religion strengthened each other, and
their union in the Old Testament prepared for their more
majestic union in the New Testament, where the concentration of a powerful religious dynamic on the homeliest
duties and relationships of men has for its background
a moral judgment that is chronicled in history. The
greater detail and more limited area of the New Testament make these characteristics more immediately impressive. Yet they are really the continuation, refined
through the personality of Jesus, of the moral emphasis
of the Old Testament.

The Old Testament has also taught the world one of
the two great ways of conceiving what morality essentially is. As we owe ' ideals ' to Greece, so we owe ' laws
of God ' to Israel. The enlightenment of the conscience
of the prophets as to the social and moral life of their
age was for them a divine revelation, as it may still remain
for us, whatever be the psychological analysis of the conviction. Ultimately, the living conscience was replaced
by the written Law, which owed its moral energy and
religious outlook, though not its contents, largely to the
work of the prophets themselves. But whether the
immediate authority was primary or secondary, whether
men listened to the prophet as he spoke, or to the Law
which the scribe had written, they were taught to regard
morality as the ordinance of God for man, and duty as
essentially the obedience of the human will to the expressed
and revealed will of God. To the ordinary reader of
the Bible this way of conceiving morality has become
so familiar that it seems obvious ; he is hardly conscious
that any other is possible. But even the most cursory
study of ethical systems will show that this is but one
way amongst many, and that the dominance of this idea
in our ordinary religious thinking is part of our debt to

Israel. In Greece, for example, the trend of thought was very different. Morality was conceived in relation to the human rather than to the divine personality. Its characteristic note was not obedience, but harmony; the realisation of an ideal of due proportion, a conformity to nature as against convention. In fact, some of the most striking differences between Greek and Hebrew-Jewish religious ideas can be traced to the distinction between morality and religion in the former case, and their union in the latter.

Two qualifications must be made to any favourable estimate of the moral emphasis in the religion of the Old Testament, apart from the obvious fact that the morality is itself progressive, and is always to be judged in relation to its own age. The first of these relates to the presence of so large a non-moral element in the Law which Judaism canonised. From the time of Ezra the Priestly Code was accepted as a divine revelation. Not long after his time, apparently, this was combined with Deuteronomy and the narratives known as J and E to form our present Pentateuch, which became the primary basis of the Jewish religion, as it remains until the present time. There is much in the Pentateuch of permanent moral worth, capable of continuing the ministry of the prophets whom it overshadowed in the popular estimation. But there is also much that is simply a survival from pre-prophetic days, such as the laws of purification, and the distinction between clean and unclean. As mere survivals in a literary record, they would not detract from the intrinsic value of the moral teaching. But, by the canonisation of the Law, these survivals are all placed on the same level of authority as the moral elements. In general, that ceremonial expression of religion which the great prophets condemned as in itself valueless is given a place of honour equal to that of morality in the divine revelation. 'It is clear', admits a sympathetic Jewish exponent of the Law,[1] 'that the drawback or misfortune of such a code was its equal accentuation of the ceremonial and the moral'. But, whilst this qualification is a serious one for the Judaism which is based on that Law, it is of much less account when we can afford to regard the Law itself as one phase of a long development, admitting of retrogression as well as of progress. Besides, in any estimate of the Jewish religion, we must not forget the passionate loyalty and the fine devotional spirit which the religion of the Law could evoke. Their memorials are written for all to read in the First Book of the Maccabees, and in the canonical Book of Psalms.

The second qualification relates to the utilitarianism of Jewish morality, especially noticeable in the 'Wisdom' literature (e.g. the Book of Proverbs). 'If the fear of Jehovah is the first part of the instruction which it gives, the art of getting on in the world is the second'.[2] 'No Wisdom book finds a source of happiness in man's love to God and communion with Him'.[3] In regard to the obvious limitations of the Wisdom literature, it must not be forgotten that its principal aim is the application of morality to the practical circumstances of life, and that it does not claim to be a complete or typical statement of the whole religious outlook of the 'wise men'.[4] If these books are silent, as they are, in regard to the contemporaneous ritual of the Temple, they may equally be silent as to the more spiritual motives and religious experiences which clustered around it. Still, it remains true that the doctrine of strict retribution, which the prophets and Deuteronomy enunciate, has its own perils. There is a difference of tone in the Book of Proverbs,

[1] Montefiore, *The Origin and Growth of Religion as illustrated by the Religion of the Ancient Hebrews*, 2nd Ed., 1893, p. 478.
[2] Cheyne, *Jewish Religious Life after the Exile*, p. 137.
[3] Toy, *E. Bi.*, col. 5335.
[4] A similar reminder is necessary in regard to the Christianity of the second-century Apologists.

as compared with the moral teaching of Deuteronomy, which suggests that whole-hearted love for Yahweh is no longer the primary motive to obedience, and that it is now overshadowed by the secondary motive, the appeal to material rewards and penalties. The highest moral emphasis of the Old Testament is that which makes morality not so much a means to the end of obtaining reward, as an offering to Yahweh, prompted by the sense of His gracious help and favour.

Some would add a further criticism of the moral emphasis of the Old Testament, viz. that ethical values, after all, are not the only values, and that the Old Testament religion is impoverished, both by its comparative disregard of artistic beauty,[1] and by its comparative lack of interest in speculative truth. Does not Greece claim a place in the revelation of the divine, and does not this almost exclusive moral emphasis in the religion of Israel constitute an ultimate weakness rather than a strength ? In answer to this objection, it may be said that there is no intention in this volume to suggest a philosophy of revelation which would not make room for all the contributions of all the peoples, as well as of Israel. But morality is uniquely related to religion, and the peculiar strength of Israel's religion, at times of crisis and grave peril, lay in just the intensity and concentration which sprang from its blending with morality. We may speak with truth of a Puritanic element in the religion of Israel, conspicuous long before devotion to the written word became its centre. In the earliest days, it is seen in the protest of the nomadic conscience against the culture of Canaan, one of Israel's legacies from the desert. When Israel settled down to the life of agriculture in Canaan, and almost necessarily to its forms of religion, there were some whose loyalty to Yahweh urged them to condemn the

---

[1] The charm of Old Testament narrative, and of its lyric poetry, must not, however, be forgotten.

culture which had such an accompaniment. Accordingly, we find them, under the name of Rechabites, refusing, even down to the days of Jeremiah, to abandon the old nomadic ways of life. They would have nothing to do with vineyard or field or seed ; they drank no wine, they lived in tents. The religious significance of their protest is seen in the close relation of their 'father', Jonadab the son of Rechab, to Jehu, the destroyer of Omri's dynasty and of the Baal-worshippers.[1] They were opponents of the foreign culture (necessarily bringing with it, in ancient civilisation, a foreign religion) which Omri and Ahab had introduced ; their protest was at once moral and religious ; its intensity led them to denounce the new life which seemed to them entangled with the new religion. The great prophets did not join them in such a protest, though Jeremiah clearly honoured them for their convictions. But even the prophets look back to the days of the desert as characterised by a simplicity of worship and a loyalty of devotion in painful contrast with their own time.[2] The same consciousness of what is often the moral and religious cost of culture appears in Jeremiah's contrast of the plain life of Josiah with the greater luxury of his son.[3] The whole relation of the Old Testament religion to art is but a wider application of the same principle. Such limitation was the price paid for moral intensity, a price often, though not always, paid by the spirit of Puritanism.

It is this moral intensity, then, which, more than anything else, lifted the religion of Israel above that of all its contemporaries, and gave it the power to assimilate foreign contributions without loss of its native strength

[1] 2 Kings x. 15-28. With the Rechabite attitude towards the vineyard of the Canaanites, cf. the story of Noah's drunkenness (Gen ix. 20 f.) and the vow of the Nazirites (Num. vi. 3 ; cf. Jud. xiii. 7, Amos ii. 11).

[2] *E.g.*, Hos. ii. 14, 15. The nomadic seems to be preferred to the agricultural life in the story of Cain and Abel, and in the pictures of patriarchal times.

[3] Jer. xxii. 14, 15.

and continuity. As was indicated in the opening chapter, Israel's history is remarkable for the number of influences operating upon it from without. Had it not been for this moral intensity, the nature-worship of Canaan might easily have permanently degraded the religion of Israel to its own low level of sensuality. But the moral instinct of the nation was guided by its religious leaders to ' take the precious from the vile ' ; the necessary forms of worship were borrowed, whilst the immoral features of the Baal-cult, such as religious prostitution, were, at least ultimately, rejected. The same selective moral sense worked on both the legislation and mythology derived from Babylon, and gave them a new value and meaning. No better proof of the inherent vitality and moral strength of the faith of Israel could be given, than this power it possessed to assimilate and transform the various elements due to its historical environment.

3. *The Contribution of Semitic Animism*

The great ideas of God and of man which we owe to the Old Testament, emerge from a religious experience in which the eternal God gradually revealed Himself to Israel under the name of Yahweh. Through this divine fellowship, in which the thoughts and feelings of the inner man were confirmed by the moral lessons of history, there was awakened in the hearts of the receptive a deep sense of obligation, and a deeper trust. But the chief forms in which this fellowship came to be conceived, the ways in which the more personal side of the religion found expression, are the direct continuation of primitive beliefs common to the Semitic peoples. These may be classed together under the general name of Semitic animism. Obviously, they stand in a much closer relation to the subsequent religious development of Israel than those external influences—Canaanite, Babylonian, Persian, and

Greek—which have already been noticed. The condition of their survival was that they could be assimilated or reconciled to the religion of Yahweh. Of this order are the general ideas of human life and death, and of existence beyond death. We can easily parallel from other peoples, non-Semitic as well as Semitic, the idea of the breath or the blood as identical with the soul, and the attribution of psychical characteristics to the heart, liver, eye, bones; the funeral customs, such as the mourners' meal and the mutilation for the dead, are by no means peculiar to the Hebrews; their conception of Sheol, the abode of the dead, has many points of resemblance to the Greek Hades.[1] The demonology of the Old Testament is peculiarly scanty,[2] as compared with the luxuriant growth of Babylonian beliefs, and the universal idea of the *jinn* among the Arabs; but this is explained by the character of Yahwism, which would tolerate no rivals. Many ideas and practices have undergone considerable change in the process of adoption, but their relationship to general animism is unmistakable. Such are those of the ban, or taboo, the ' devotion ' of a city, a person, or a thing; the importance attached to the spoken word, as seen in the significance of blessings and curses and oaths; the use of ephod and teraphim, especially for oracular purposes; even the practice of circumcision, which became so distinctive a mark of Judaism, is shown by comparative anthropology to be originally a form of mutilation, preparatory to marriage, practised by many peoples.

These survivals of primitive belief and practice do not, as has been said, materially affect the cardinal ideas of the Old Testament. Interesting as they are to the anthropologist, they are still but petrified growths in comparison with the living faith of the prophets. But the Hebrew

---

[1] See chap. iv. § 4.

[2] As it is, we have references to *se'īrim, lilith* (Is. xxxiv. 14, xiii. 21), *shedim* (Deut. xxxii. 17, Ps. cvi. 37), *'Alūkah* (Prov. xxx. 15) and possibly *rabītzu* (Gen. iv. 7); perhaps *'Azā'zel* (Lev. xvi. 8) belongs here.

psychology which was directly developed from Semitic animism provides the cardinal conception of God's means of contact with man—the idea of the Spirit of God, together with the idea of human personality as a unity of soul and body, entirely dependent upon God. Both ideas will receive fuller discussion in their proper places ; they are briefly noticed here because, without them, the general idea of the Old Testament religion would be very incomplete.

As for the first, the animistic conception of invasive spirits (which flourishes so abundantly, without marked difference, in the atmosphere of Babylonian polytheism and demonology) is transformed amongst the Hebrews into the idea that peculiar and abnormal phenomena in human life and character must all be traced to one source, Yahweh (e.g. Samson's strength and Saul's madness). An important consequence of this unification is that the idea of the Spirit of Yahweh develops step by step with the idea of Yahweh's character, and ultimately becomes ethical and spiritual in the full sense. The highest ranges of spiritual experience are thus conceived to depend on the co-operation of Yahweh ; the suppliant's supreme appeal is that Yahweh take not His holy Spirit from him. That remarkable and unique feature of Hebrew religion which we call the prophetic consciousness is thus profoundly conditioned by Hebrew psychology.[1]

In contrast with the dualistic idea of body and soul which is characteristic of Greek thought as a whole, the Hebrew emphasis falls on the unity of personality. The soul does not continue an immortal life after the death of the body ; it goes out or dies with the body, and all that is left is the shadowy semblance of the former self, body and soul, which is gathered into Sheol. The result of this limitation for Hebrew thought is a remarkable concentration of attention on the present life. The

[1] See note 5 on p. 117.

problems of Hebrew religion call for present solution. The
escape from their pressure by a doctrine of prior existence
or future adjustment is not open. Consequently, the
Hebrew thinker is driven in on himself, and on his present
relation to Yahweh. It is Yahweh, and Yahweh alone,
who besets him behind and before. He is compelled
to fling himself on Yahweh, because he is wholly dependent
on Him. This explains why the Hebrew religion can rise
to such heights of spiritual splendour as characterise the
Book of Job and some of the Psalms ; it also explains,
or helps to explain, the rich spiritual content of the doctrine
of a future life, when at length (beyond the range of the
Old Testament, except for some tentative beginnings) that
doctrine is evolved.

Such is the general idea of religion which the Old Testament presents. Through the successive phases of a long
development it displays the unity of an ever resurgent
faith that Yahweh will not abandon His people, and that
none other god can claim a place beside Him. In the
experience of that faith, the conviction is begotten that
nothing can be good in Him which is evil in man, and that
mercy is more than sacrifice.[1] This moral emphasis fills
with new meaning the Hebrew ideas of divine activity
and human dependence. ' In the case of no other people
of the ancient East ', it has been said, ' do we find the conception that the whole sacrificial ritual lies on the circumference of religion, and is not religion itself, but has within
it merely the significance of a symbol '.[2] We must not
make the mistake of thinking that every Israelite who
participated in the Temple ritual rose to this height of
spiritual outlook. But none who reads attentively the
Psalter of that Temple can doubt its presence in the
case of some. Its significance is the more profound
because it escapes the perils of Deism on the one hand,

[1] See Additional Notes.   [2] Sellin, *Die alttest. Religion*, p. 17.

and of some doctrines of divine immanence on the other. This is a feature of Old Testament religion which is often missed. The elaborate cult, taken by itself, left man and God over against each other, negotiating through transactions on a plane below their own spiritual nature. But just as mediæval mysticism learnt to transcend the worst features of mediæval sacerdotalism, so this Hebrew ' mysticism ', as we may call it, rose above the perils of its own forms into the personal society of God. On the other hand, the clear-cut ideas of human and divine personality made impossible such an inclusion of the human within the divine as would have robbed man's life of its freedom and reality. The mutual fellowship of God and man was so real, so intimate, so dramatically conceived, that it boldly expressed itself in terms and figures drawn from the common life of the home. The prophetic ideas of God as Father and Husband are derived from the simplest, deepest, and most universal forms of human fellowship. With such thoughts of God, Israel set forth on its spiritual pilgrimage into the world of things unseen, and through them it became the pioneer of religion. So, at least, it may seem to us. But to Israel the truth was rather that Yahweh had entered the world of things seen, and that His presence was manifested in the activities of providence without, and the energies of the Spirit within, the life of His people.

CHAPTER III

THE IDEA OF GOD

THE nearest approach of the Hebrew mind to the definition of God is given in the words, ' I am Yahweh thy God,
who brought thee out of the land of Egypt '.[1] In other
words, the God of Israel is identified as the agent in a
historical event intimately affecting the fortunes of Israel.
This conception holds good for the whole development
of the idea of God. He is conceived not as abstracted
from human life but as revealed within it. He is not
Brahman, comprehensive of the universe, which issued
from him and returns to him, when the cosmic illusion has
run its course ; He is not the Prime Mover of Aristotle,
attracting the evolving life of the world ; He is not a deity
of Olympus, occasionally interfering with human lives
when the line of his pleasures crosses them, or one of the
gods of Epicurus, dwelling afar in supreme indifference
to human affairs, where

> ' Nor ever lowest roll of thunder moans,
>   Nor sound of human sorrow mounts to mar
>   Their sacred everlasting calm '.

He is Yahweh, the God of Israel, known for what He is
by what He does. He is the unseen partner in Israel's
fortunes, afflicted in all their afflictions. Their interests
are His, and His ought to be theirs.

The most obvious result of this relation is seen in the

---

[1] Ex. xx. 2.

experiential character [1] of the conceptions it affords. They keep close to experience, are warm with the blood of human life, definite with the outline of the visible event, capable of moving men to emotional response, because never divorced from their original human setting. The Old Testament idea of God has the freshness of personal experience, in contrast with the generalisations of abstract thought. The religions of the surrounding nations are more or less conventionalised nature-religions. The religion of the Old Testament kept the unconventionality of life, because its roots struck ever deeper in the soil of history. The speculative monotheism ascribed to Babylon and Egypt is dead, because it was never much more than an esoteric theory. The religion of Israel, in its most essential features, still lives within the larger arena of Christian civilisation, because it came into being to meet the actual needs of men, and can still meet them.

In comparison with the history of this experience, the various Hebrew names of God would tell little about Him, even if their etymologies were certain. Almost the only statement about the Hebrew names of God which would command general acceptance from modern scholars is that their original meaning is unknown. The general terms 'El and 'Elohim may possibly be connected with the idea of 'strength'; of the epithets, Shaddai and 'Elyon, the former is cognate with an Accadian word *shadu*, mountain, and the latter means 'lofty'; the personal name, Yahweh, is explained in the well-known passage in the Book of Exodus either as 'He is' (*i.e.* 'becomes') or 'He will be' the suggestion apparently being that the God of Israel actively manifests Himself as, or will show Himself to be, what He is.[2] Even if this meaning were original,

---

[1] The appeal to experience is, of course, found in every religion, but its value lies in the idea which is thus elucidated. In the Babylonian religion, for example, resort to experience issues in an elaborate system of divination and astrology, instead of a moral monotheism.

[2] Ex. iii. 13 f. If this difficult passage means rather that God will

it would obviously throw us back on actual history for the unfolding of Yahweh's character; but in all probability the original meaning had been forgotten when the passage came to be written, and this interpretation was suggested, as is frequently the case with Hebrew proper names in the Old Testament, because it seemed appropriate to the context. It would be of more service to us to know the early history of the name Yahweh than its original etymology. It is characteristic of one of the early documents of Genesis (J) to employ this name from the Creation onwards;[1] but no certain evidence for the pre-Mosaic use of the form Yahweh (as distinct from Ya(h)u, which is well attested) seems yet to have been brought forward from extra-Biblical sources.[2] It may be assumed that the new religion of Israel was not linked to an entirely new divine name. Some have conjectured that the name was traditional in the tribal group with which Moses was connected. Perhaps the most likely hypothesis is that which regards Yahweh as the God of the Kenites, with which tribe Moses became connected by marriage. This does not indeed tell us anything more about the pre-Mosaic conception of Yahweh. But it helps to explain why Moses should have become His prophet, as it does other incidents in the Exodus narrative. In any case, however, all these questions are of secondary importance compared with the development of the idea of God, under the name of Yahweh, as historically manifested in intimate relation to Israel.

continue to be in the future what He has been in the past (cf. Procksch, *Das Nordhebräische Sagenbuch*, p. 199), the reference will still be to the experience of history, not to metaphysical existence.

[1] Cf. Gen. iv. 26. The other early document (E), which begins with the story of Abraham (Gen. xv., xx. f.), uses the general term 'Elohim', which is also employed by the Priestly Code until the revelation of the name 'Yahweh' to Moses (Ex. vi. 3).

[2] The alleged *Yahwe-ilu* of the Hammurabi period is doubtful, but *Yaubani* (Yau has created) implies the worship of a god Yau about 1500 B.C. A useful summary of the facts is given by Paton, in *E.R.E.*, iii. p. 183; see also A. Lods, *Israel* (Eng. tr.), pp. 320 ff.

This relation began at a time when the existence of supernatural beings was unquestioned. They were as real a part of the environment within which they operated as the earth men trod, or the sky that roofed them in. Consequently, the Hebrew religion does not offer any elaborate reasonings to demonstrate the being of Yahweh; it accepts Him, just as the Moabites accepted Kemōsh.[1] A modern mind would instinctively gather the facts of experience, natural or spiritual, and then proceed to argue that God must exist as their explanation. But this is the reverse of the procedure which characterises Hebrew and Jewish thought in the Old Testament. Yahweh is taken for granted; Job, in his keenest mental anguish, denies not the existence of God but simply His goodness. It is only in the silent thoughts of the heart that the profane or churlish man dares to say to himself, 'There is no God',[2] and even then his thought relates to God's activity, not to His existence. Thus the Israelite comes to the interpretation of history, and, eventually, of nature, with an axiomatic faith in Yahweh. When he found, as he so often did, that his idea of the character and attitude of Yahweh did not adequately explain what happened, he had to revise the contents of the idea itself, thus taking a step forward in religious development.

1. *The Scope of Yahweh's Sovereignty*

This enlargement in the idea of God may be first considered in regard to the area over which the power of Yahweh[3] is conceived to extend. The development proceeds from the idea of the nomadic war-god of the Mosaic

---

[1] Ultimately, of course, belief in the supernatural involved some sort of inference from special experience. See the first paragraph of chap. v.

[2] Pss. x. 4, xiv. 1. Cf. also the 'scepticism' of the author of *Ecclesiastes.* 'His faith in a personal God is never shaken; atheism or materialism is not conceivable in an ancient Oriental mind' (Davidson, *E. Bi.*, col. 1160).

[3] 'The true content of the idea of God among the Semites in general is lordship' (Wellhausen, *Reste arabischen Heidentums,*[2] p. 145).

period, through that of the agricultural land-god of Canaan,
into that of the world-god, and up to the absolute monotheism reached by the time of the Exile.   The expansion
takes place always in response to new needs and problems.
As Robertson Smith has said of Semitic religion in general,
' the help of the gods was sought in all matters, without
distinction, that were objects of desire and could not
certainly be attained by the worshipper's unaided efforts
. . . the really vital question is not what a god has power
to do, but whether I can get him to do it for me, and this
depends on the relation in which he stands to me '.[1]   The
glory of Israel's religion was that this relation was capable
of standing every strain that was put upon it, though this
capacity was disclosed to Israel only as the successive
strains were actually felt.   We have already seen—e.g. in the
Song of Deborah—that the power of Yahweh is primarily
realised on the battlefield.   It must be remembered
that war is usually part of religion in early times and
among primitive peoples.   Warriors are consecrated by
special rites and taboos for the battle ; the invisible forces
of the spiritual world form a very real part of their allies.
This is illustrated by the early narrative of Joshua's
vision before the attack on Jericho.[2]   He sees a supernatural being with a drawn sword, who announces himself as captain of Yahweh's host—in this case, probably
the angels who will assist Israel in the coming battle.
From time to time, in such ways as this, Yahweh brings
or sends help to His people in their warfare.   Examples
are the victory over Egypt under the leadership of Moses,
over Canaan under that of Barak, the repulse of the
Midianites through the local ' judges ', and the final overthrow of the Philistines through David.   Careful study
of the narratives will show how closely Yahweh is identified
with the victory in each case.   The human leaders are
His agents, controlled by His Spirit.   The kingship in

---

[1] *Religion of the Semites*, pp. 82, 83.   [2] Josh. v. 13 f.

E

Israel was called into existence in the first place for military purposes, and to this end the prophet Samuel anointed Saul as the first king. By this time the idea of Yahweh was much more than that of a mere war-god ; but so long as Israel was struggling towards political establishment and consolidation, the idea of Him as the helper in battle is primary. It is no accident that amongst the earliest literature of Israel reference is made in the Old Testament to ' The Book of the Wars of Yahweh ' ; [1] such a title would cover His most important aspect for Israel. Equally characteristic of the earlier ideas of Yahweh are the fortunes of the Ark in the war with the Philistines.[2] It is at one and the same time the primitive sanctuary and the battle standard.[3] Whatever were the associations that first gathered round the name of Yahweh, it is as the giver of victory over other peoples that He first appears in the literature of Israel.

It was natural, indeed almost inevitable, that the national God whose presence and power were revealed in such victories should eventually have ascribed to Him a larger sovereignty than that of the battlefield. This extension into other realms of national interest would be the tendency from the very beginning, even though clan and family cults may have maintained themselves for a long time.[4] But they would be tolerated just because they were not felt to challenge the exclusive claims of Yahweh to the worship and devotion of Israel. In this sense the commandment which occupies the first place in both the earlier (Ex. xxxiv. 14 f.) and the later (Ex. xx. 3 f.) Decalogue states a principal characteristic of Yahwism from the first. The ' jealousy ' of Yahweh against all rivals[5] was an important feature of the idea of God, and

---

[1] Num. xxi. 14.   [2] 1 Sam. iv.-vii.; cf. Num. x. 35, 36.   [3] See Add. Notes.
[4] The use of the *teraphim* perhaps illustrates this ; cf. Budde, *The Religion of Israel to the Exile*, pp. 59 f.
[5] Cf. *e.g.* Ex. xxxiv. 14, Num. xxv. 11; cf. Pedersen, *Israel*, III-IV. pp. 619 ff.

an effective safeguard against the perils of syncretism. To the principle it represents Hosea especially appeals; 'thou shalt know no god but me, and beside me there is no saviour'.[1] Its most dramatic illustration in the history of Israel is found in the story of Elijah. The introduction of the foreign cult of Melkart of Tyre under Ahab was a direct challenge of Yahweh's claims, to be clearly distinguished from the slower and more insidious influences of the local cults of Canaan. The revolution accomplished by Jehu in the Northern Kingdom,[2] and the related movement under Jehoiada some years later in the Southern Kingdom,[3] were inspired by religious zeal for the exclusive claims of Yahweh. Even the heathen reaction under Manasseh may have been plausibly reconciled with the supremacy of Yahweh within Israel, by the subordination of other deities to Him.

The conquest of Canaan by the Israelites did not merely change their manner of life from the nomadic to the agricultural; it also exercised a profound influence on their religion, and opened a realm, quite distinct from the battlefield, into which the sovereignty of Yahweh might be extended. Agriculture had its religion, not less than warfare, in the ancient world. Isaiah says of the farmer's skill, 'His God doth instruct him aright, and doth teach him'.[4] The Canaanites worshipped the various local deities (Baalim) as the givers of their agricultural produce. When the Israelites came to settle down beside them in the portions successfully occupied, it may have been the case that the loyalty of Israel to the war-god, Yahweh, did not seem infringed by worship rendered at the same time to the local gods of the harvest and the vineyard.[5] But the completer occupation of the land, and the absorption of the Canaanites, meant the absorption of their

---

[1] xiii. 4.
[2] 2 Kings ix. f.
[3] 2 Kings xi.
[4] Is. xxviii. 26.
[5] Cf. *E. Bi.*, *s.v.* 'Baal', col. 403 and W. F. Albright, *Archaeology and the Religion of Israel*, 1942.

deities. The attributes of the local Baalim, the supernatural lords of each district, passed to Yahweh, who was
worshipped at the various local sanctuaries, and probably
without much change of ceremony. There was here a
great peril for the religion of Yahweh, a peril which was
recognised by what has been already called the Puritanic
element in Yahwism. Subtly yet unmistakably, the idea
of Yahweh as a Person standing in moral relation to Israel
was in danger of being transformed into that of a nature-
god, with none of the sterner virtues of the battlefield,
and with many sensuous and degrading associations.
Hence the attack of Amos and Hosea on the religious
ritual of their time. Hosea refuses to recognise as the true
God of Israel the Yahweh locally worshipped, and would
discard the name ' Baal ', which has been transferred to
Him (ii. 16). It is the Yahweh who brought His son
Israel out of Egypt, the God of history, who is really the
giver of all the good things of Canaan, its corn and wine
and oil, its wool and its flax (ii. 8, 9). Yahweh has become
the land-god, equally for Hosea and for those he is criti-
cising. But, for Hosea, Yahweh is much more than the
land-god, the giver of every good and perfect gift the land
affords ; He is the God of the desert and the battlefield,
who has revealed to the mind and heart of the nation
His moral attributes of righteousness and love. In other
words, the eighth-century prophets are contending for a
moral against a physical idea of God. We see in their
protest the real supremacy of the religion of Yahweh over
the alternative nature-cults. That protest was continued
in the Book of Deuteronomy, which aimed at meeting
the peril by transferring the whole worship of Yahweh
from the old local sanctuaries, with all their powerful
associations, to the Temple at Jerusalem. The reformation of Josiah on these lines in 621 was perhaps too drastic
to have been permanently successful, had it not been for
the Exile which followed shortly after it. It was the Exile

which made possible a new beginning, with the Deuteronomic principle of the single sanctuary for its accepted
basis ; it was the fact that the returned Israel was a small
community settled within a single long day's walk from
Jerusalem which made the principle practicable.

The third and final stage in the expansion of Yahweh's
sovereignty marks the extension of that sovereignty to
include the whole world. The original claims of Yahweh
were for *Israel's* service. Even down to the Exile, Israel
continued to admit the existence of other gods *for other
nations*. Jephthah believes that Kemōsh gives his people
a territory through victory, in just the same way as Yahweh
gave Amorite territory to Israel.[1] David complains that
banishment from ' the inheritance of Yahweh ' will mean
the necessary worship of other gods in other lands.[2]
Naaman is represented as asking for ' two mules' burden
of earth ' from Yahweh's land, that he may continue to
worship Him, by a sort of legal fiction, when back in Syria.[3]
There is thus no formal or *a priori* denial of the existence
of other gods in their proper realms. That which actually
happened was the gradual appropriation of those realms
by Yahweh, and the victorious extension of His sovereignty over other countries, until their gods become as
colourless as shades in Sheol, and Isaiah can call them by
a mocking term that denotes their worthlessness.[4] At
first, the victory of Yahweh over the gods of other nations
depended on the victory of Israel over the nations themselves. But, ultimately, theology outran politics, and
Yahweh was recognised as the one and only God of all the
world, to whom belonged that unique and supreme place,
even from the very beginning of all. It is in the anonymous prophet of the Exile that we first meet with the
clear assertion that other gods do not exist at all : ' Is

[1] Jud. xi. 23, 24 ; cf. Num. xxi. 29.   [2] 1 Sam. xxvi. 19.
[3] 2 Kings v. 17 ; cf. xvii. 33 (the foreign colonists in Samaria).
[4] Is. ii. 8, etc. ('elīlim).

there a god beside me ? . . . I know not any'.[1] But, centuries before this, the practical 'henotheism' which underlies this explicit monotheism was already operative. It appears in the earlier story of the creation of man (J), in which all human life and history are made to begin from Yahweh, although as yet He moves within nature, rather than stands transcendently above it. We see the same position more explicitly asserted when Amos represents Yahweh as ruling the surrounding nations, and saying to this nation ' Go ', and to another ' Come ' ; [2] or when Isaiah treats the might of Assyria as a mere instrument in the hand of Yahweh.[3] But even the classic formulation of Israel's ' monotheism ' in Deuteronomy, ' Yahweh is our God, Yahweh alone ',[4] carries with it in the same chapter the *theoretical* recognition of other gods. Jeremiah might consistently have denied the existence of other gods ; Deutero-Isaiah, as a matter of fact, does this, and drops the keystone of the monotheistic arch into its place, for all the future of Israel.[5]

2. *The Personality of Yahweh*

The personal name, Yahweh, denotes a personality and character which are, in many respects, as distinct and clear-cut as those of any human figure in the Old Testament. The attributes of a storm-god are frequently ascribed to Yahweh, but, within the historic period, these are no more than favourite forms of His manifestation. Behind the thunder which is His voice, the cloud which is His chariot, the hail and lightning which are His weapons,

[1] Is. xliv. 8.   [2] Amos i., ii. ; cf. ix. 7.   [3] Is. x. 5.
[4] Cf. Deut. vi. 4 and 14. For the above rendering, see the present writer's note in the *Century Bible*. (See also Additional Notes.)
[5] The Jews at Elephantine seem to have associated a female deity with the worship of Yahweh (Cowley, *Aramaic Papyri of the Fifth Century B.C.*, p. xix.), a fact which must be explained as a survival of the (subordinative) polytheism of Manasseh's time.

there stands a personal being whose thought, feelings and
will are as real as those of men. The divine personality
has, of course, a range of activity, with modes of percep-
tion and operation, which far surpass those of human
personality. But, at the centre of this activity, according to the faith of the earlier centuries at least, there is a
personal nature so much like man's that it can be expected
to manifest itself like his. That is why the Old Testament affords so vivid a portrait of Yahweh. He sets
about making the first man as a human potter would,
though the life-giving breath He imparts differentiates
the result from any work of man. He walks in the garden
He has planted, just as a man would, to enjoy the cool
of the evening, and His suspicions are aroused by the con-
cealment of the man and woman, and confirmed by ques-
tioning, in human fashion ; but He has a far-reaching
power to punish the guilty. He ' comes down ' to see the
tower which men, in their presumption, are building, and
He scatters them from the same motives that would actuate
some human king, whose sovereignty was imperilled by
the doings of his subjects ; but the action He takes has
results that extend beyond the power of men. Yahweh
even repents of having made man, and takes measures to
destroy him, but the smell of Noah's sacrifice is so sweet
in His nostrils that He never repeats the Flood. These
statements [1] and others like them in the earliest literature are not figures of speech. They show just that
imaginative mingling of human and superhuman characteristics which is ever found on the palette of the man
who is trying to paint a picture of God. The warmth and
vitality of this crude and naïve anthropomorphism survive

[1] They are taken from the document known as J, which uses the personal
name, Yahweh, and makes Him visible to the human eye, as in the visit paid to
the tent of Abraham (Gen. xviii. 1 f.). The somewhat later narrative known
as E, which characteristically employs the general term, ' Elohim ', instead
of the personal name, Yahweh, does not allow Him to be visible to the
waking eye. But even so late as the second century B.C., when God is seen
in vision He is an aged, white-haired man (Dan. vii. 9).

from these earlier days into the more exalted idea of God found in a later age. In the post-exilic period, Yahweh the intimate and familiar friend of the patriarchs becomes the transcendent God with the unspeakable name, who has created the world simply by a series of majestic commands (Gen. i.). But this later idea of God is still far from being a mere metaphysical abstraction. The more physical elements in the earlier anthropomorphism are, indeed, either abandoned, or resolved into conscious imagery. We cannot suppose, for example, that the dramatic figure of Yahweh as a blood-stained warrior coming from Edom (Is. lxiii.) is meant by the prophet to be taken literally. Yet the psychical side of the anthropomorphism—the ascription of human thoughts, feelings and desires to Yahweh—is still largely unconscious and uncriticised. Thus, whilst that laughter of Yahweh at the plans of earthly kings which the Psalmist describes may be in part metaphor, the wrath with which He gives His representative on earth the power to destroy them is to be taken literally. The prophetic and devotional literature of Israel owes much of its unique power to the intensity of this personalisation (not personification) of Yahweh, which expresses so vividly, and yet so naturally, the corresponding intensity of religious experience.

This growth in spirituality of the idea of God, through which the emphasis falls on the inner side of personality, and the physical or quasi-physical reference is minimised, would have been seriously retarded, if not wholly prevented, by the use of images in the worship of Yahweh. But, from the prophets of the eighth century onwards, there is emphatic rejection of such material representations. This first appears in Hosea, in criticism of what he calls ' the calf of Samaria '.[1] He is clearly referring to the bull-images erected by Jeroboam I. at Bethel and

---

[1] viii. 6 ; cf. xiii. 2. Amos viii. 14 is uncertain. In Deut. iv. 12, idolatry is condemned on the ground that He who was *heard* on Horeb was not *seen.*

Dan, when the kingdom was divided.[1] The narrative
describing this incident shows that the worship associated
with these images was offered to Yahweh, not to some
rival god, and further, that Jeroboam is probably returning to some well-established precedent, and is not intro-
ducing a dangerous innovation that would have defeated
the very object he had in view. The story of the golden
calf made by Aaron (Ex. xxxii.) throws back this precedent as far as the nomadic period. It is, however,
much more probable that the use of this particular emblem
is due to the Canaanites : the bull is the natural incarna-
tion of strength amongst an agricultural and pastoral
people,[2] and many pottery models of cows have been found
in recent excavations at Gezer. We have no evidence as
to the existence or non-existence of images of Yahweh,
prior to the settlement in Canaan ; the prohibition in
the Second Commandment [3] is probably due to the influence of the prophetic teaching. Elijah, Elisha, and Jehu
show no disapproval of the image-worship practised in
the Northern Kingdom. The presence of the Ark in the
Temple may doubtless have helped to keep the Southern
Kingdom more free from image-worship. Many scholars
regard the ephod, frequently used for oracular purposes,
as a form of image of Yahweh. The teraphim were apparently of human form, since David escaped through the
substitution of one of these for himself ; [4] but they seem
rather to belong to the class of household gods than to be
images of the God of the national cult. Nor are we
justified in asserting that the 'brazen serpent' ascribed
to Moses, and retained until the reformation of Hezekiah,[5]

[1] 1 Kings xii. 28-33.
[2] Cf. the terra-cotta bull-heads from the neighbourhood of Ascalon, reproduced by Vincent, *Canaan d'après l'exploration récente*, p. 169.
[3] Ex. xx. 4. In the 'ritual Decalogue' contained in Ex. xxxiv., the
prohibition seems to be of the peculiar variety of images called 'molten'
(verse 17); the older form of 'graven' images may have been allowed.
[4] 1 Sam. xix. 13 f.
[5] Num. xxi. 9 ; 2 Kings xviii. 4.

was more than the centre of some demon-cult.[1] But whatever be the facts for the earlier centuries, the attitude of the full-grown religion of Israel towards images is unmistakable. The imageless shrine of the Holy of Holies, on which Pompey and his officers came to gaze,[2] is no accident of the worship of Yahweh. It marks the growing spirituality of the idea of God, by the elimination of the material symbol as inadequate. The principle of the imageless shrine was carried to its full development when the worship of God who is Spirit was lifted into a realm of personal relationship independent of the mountains of Jerusalem or Samaria.

It is to the instinctive and unchallenged idea of divine personality that we owe the vivid and dramatic conception of God which characterises the Old Testament. No religious literature gives so graphic and ample a portrait of divine personality, and the anthropomorphism is inseparable from it. As already stated, the earlier anthropomorphism was felt to be unworthy of God. There is a growing consciousness of the inadequacy and incongruity of what may be called physical anthropomorphism, which culminates in the post-exilic doctrine of the divine transcendence, with its complementary idea of angelic mediation between God and man. But to the modern mind there is a deeper difficulty, a difficulty often felt in regard to psychical, as keenly as in regard to physical, anthropomorphism. Personality has been held to mean limitation, and limitation to involve such a doctrine of God as makes Him only a greater man, and really puts Him outside human life. Obviously, this is no place to discuss the purely philosophic question whether personality in God implies limitation inconsistent with His deity. But several truths should be remembered, lest the term ' anthropomorphism ' raise a quite unwarranted prejudice against the Old Testament idea of God. In the

[1] See Additional Notes.   [2] Tacitus, *Hist.*, v. 9 ; *Antiquities*, xiv. 4. 4.

first place the question is really one of degree ; we cannot think or speak of God at all, unless in the language of our human experience. To dismiss all anthropomorphism is to dismiss all possibility of the knowledge of God. In the second place, however difficult it may be to frame a doctrine of divine personality that shall be wholly consistent, we are using, in 'personality', the highest category of our experience to interpret our highest faith. The philosophical problem was not present to the minds of Biblical writers, but there is a solution implicit in the Old Testament, and more clearly articulated in the New—the idea of the Fatherhood of God, which links Him in spiritual kinship to men, and makes it possible for them to be 'partakers of the divine nature'. Finally, if anthropomorphism be not ruled out of court altogether, it may be claimed that the form of it which the Old Testament offers is on the whole noble and exalted. Its phraseology still dominates our devotional vocabulary. The highest idea of God is still, like Yahweh Himself, enthroned on the praises of Israel. Philosophical theism has not always recognised its debt to the Hebrew religion for the deepest realisation of divine personality.

3. *The Moral Character of Yahweh*

The central place of the eighth-century prophets in the interpretation of the character of God must not be allowed to obscure the truth that they are themselves the result of a long development. The relation between Israel and Yahweh did not begin to be moral in the eighth century ; it began to be moral when it began to exist. The great fact for the future was not the precise scope of the original idea of Yahweh, but the recognition that Israel had to do with a powerful person, who was morally interested in its welfare. The relation between Yahweh and Israel was like a friendship between two men, beginning in some act of generous help rendered by the stronger to the weaker, behind which act the larger heart and mind are gradually discerned. Such a relationship could not fail to grow in moral significance with the moral growth of the nation itself. The literature and history of what is called the ' pre-prophetic ' period sufficiently reveal the manner of this. The prophet Nathan, speaking in the name of Yahweh, boldly rebukes David for a moral fault.[1] The prophet Elijah, also speaking in the name of Yahweh, is not less severe concerning the appropriation of Naboth's vineyard than concerning the favour shown to a rival religion.[2] The impression we gain of Yahweh's moral character as conceived by these two prophets is confirmed by the contemporary legal and narrative literature. It is true that the ' ritual Decalogue ', as it is called, the series of ten brief rules for religion which may be extracted from Exodus xxxiv., is concerned with ritual, not with morality, and that the ' moral Decalogue ', our familiar ' ten commandments ', is to be regarded rather as a compendium of eighth-century prophetical teaching than as an anticipation of it. But the Book of the Covenant (Ex. xx. 22–xxiii. 19), which may fairly be placed under the early monarchy, is far from being simply a ritualistic code of laws. It is indeed surprising to find how many of the moral demands of the great prophets are here, in principle, already required by Yahweh from Israel : the generous treatment of the slave, the ' stranger ', the widow and orphan, the debtor and the poor ; impartial and incorruptible equity in the administration of justice ; proper regard for parents ; even the duty of driving back an enemy's stray cattle. Clearly the God who requires such conduct from His people is already possessed in their eyes of a pronounced moral character. The social life of a settled and agricultural people (for whom alone the Book of the Covenant is

[1] 2 Sam. xii. 1 f.   [2] 1 Kings xxi. 17 f.

suitable) has produced a remarkable growth in the idea
of Yahweh within little more than a couple of centuries of
the invasion of Palestine. Nathan's condemnation of
David may well accompany the Book of the Covenant
as a more or less contemporary footnote to it, showing
morality and theology together in the making. The
two 'prophetic' narratives of the pre-Mosaic period,
known as J and E, to which most of the light and colour
of the earlier pages of the Bible are due, similarly show a
moral conception of Yahweh that effectually links the
period of David with the eighth century. The patriarchal
stories do not only reveal man and God as so intimately
related that they almost walk the earth together; they
just as strikingly declare the moral conditions of that
fellowship, and none the less because the morality is not
always Christian.[1]

The advancing moralisation of the idea of God is, however, chiefly brought home to us in the 'writing' prophets
of the eighth century, especially Amos, Hosea, and Isaiah.
These three prophets are all concerned with the moral
relation existing between Yahweh and Israel, but each
of them emphasises a different aspect of that relation,
and consequently presents a characteristic idea of God.
The thought of Amos centres in the absolute justice of
the divine sovereignty. Yahweh, the God of Israel, is a
great ruler, governing beyond as well as within Israel on
moral principles (i., ii.). The divine election of Israel
was a purposive moral act, always subject to moral criticism and control: 'You only have I known of all the
families of the earth, therefore I will visit upon you all
your iniquities'.[2] These iniquities are chiefly social
injustice, e.g. the oppression of the poor through exaction
and bribery,[3] together with commercial dishonesty [4] with

---

[1] E.g., the support given by Yahweh to Abraham in his deception of
Pharaoh.
[2] iii. 2.   [3] ii. 6, 7; v. 11, 12.   [4] viii. 4-6.

a view to luxurious and idle self-indulgence.[1] Whilst
these go on, elaborate acts of worship at the sanctuaries
are a mockery to Yahweh; [2] the only true offering to
a moral ruler is morality.[3]   Just as Yahweh punishes the
iniquities of other nations on moral grounds, so will He
punish those of Israel; the special relation that exists
between the nation and Himself carries with it a higher
moral demand, and severer penalties. The idea of God
that dominates the prophet's mind is clear and unmistakable. Yahweh is righteous, and has both will and power
to administer the government of the world by the standard
of His own character. The moral revulsion of Amos from
the immoral religion and the religious immorality of the
Northern Kingdom became his divine call to prophesy.
His contribution to the idea of God is essentially the faith
that the divine personality is not less moral than the
human heart of the prophet.

The emphasis of Amos necessarily neglects the other
side of the relation between Yahweh and Israel, the bond
of 'loving-kindness' which unites God to His chosen
people. This was brought out by Hosea, writing some
fifteen years later than Amos. Hosea stands within the
Northern Kingdom, not without it, like Amos; personal
experience of the faithlessness of a still loved wife has
opened his eyes to the deeper meaning of the bond between
Yahweh and Israel. Accordingly, he came to conceive
Yahweh not simply or chiefly as a moral ruler, but as a
Father and a Husband,[4] and his emphasis falls on the
religious, as much as on the social, faults of Israel. In
other words, his idea of God is interpreted through the
deepest relationships of human life, those of the family,
and it is the wounded, yet surviving, love of God for Israel
which is central in his thought, as the offended righteousness of God was central in the thought of Amos.   The

[1] iii. 10, 12, 15 ; iv. 1 ; v. 11 ; vi. 4 f.   [2] iv. 4, 5.
[3] v. 21-25.   [4] xi. 1 f. ; ii. 16.

deepest moral conception of God which the Old Testament contains are implied in the two figures of marriage and parentage which Hosea employs. On the one hand, the passionate love of Yahweh for His bride seeks for her the truest life : ' I will betroth thee unto me in righteousness, and in judgment, and in loving-kindness,[1] and in mercies. I will even betroth thee unto me in faithfulness, and thou shalt know Yahweh ' ; on the other, the tender patience of the father is seen in Yahweh's readiness to take into His arms the stumbling child, learning to walk, and to carry it when it is weary.[2] Israel is perishing because it does not *know* Yahweh,[3] its Husband and its Father.

These two great ideas of God, as righteous, and as loving, spring from the fundamental thought of the personal relation which unites Him to His people, and are both needed to reveal its content. But when these two are recognised, all other moral ' attributes ' are implicitly given. Consequently, we do not find that the third great prophet of this century is able to add any further attribute which we can place beside the fundamental qualities of love and righteousness. What Isaiah does is, however, to lift the idea of the righteous and loving God of Israel to a new majesty of conception by his repeated emphasis on the divine *holiness*. The familiar details of the vision in the Temple which constituted the prophet's call sufficiently illustrate this, as does his favourite title for Yahweh —the ' Holy One of Israel '. We must not make ' holy ' here a mere synonym of moral righteousness, or we lose the force of Isaiah's conception of God. The earlier idea of ' holiness '[4]—which, etymologically, may mean ' separation '—is that of inaccessiblity, perilous and unknown power, involving mysterious taboos, and superstitious fears. The idea is common to many peoples in their primitive stage, and has no essential connection with the moral development of the idea of God. But

[1] See Add. Notes.   [2] ii. 19, 20 ; xi. 1-4.   [3] iv. 6.   [4] See chap. vi.

when the moral ideas of divine righteousness and love were firmly grasped, as they were by Amos and Hosea, the recognition of the transcendent majesty of God by Isaiah gave them a wider range and fuller meaning. It reminded men that the Personality with which man had to do was divine, not human. Men were men, not gods, as the boasted cavalry of Egypt were flesh, not spirit.[1] The idea of God thus reached in the eighth century became the permanent and underlying idea of the highest religion of Israel. The transcendent holiness of God was the majesty of a righteous and loving Person. In that unity, all the deeper religious ideas of Israel find their source. We must not forget that they are a unity. ' The antithesis which in dogmatics we are familiar with is a righteous or just God and *yet* a Saviour. The Old Testament puts it differently,—a righteous God and *therefore* a Saviour. . . . To say that Jehovah is a transcendent moral person is to express the whole doctrine of God '.[2]

4. *The Divine Purpose in Creation and Providence*

At the outset of this survey of the Old Testament idea of God, it was said that the proper starting-point was Israel's experience of the historical relation in which it stood to Yahweh. This experience has shown (1) the gradual expansion in the idea of Yahweh's sovereignty from the tribal war-god to the one Ruler of the whole world; (2) the recognition of a very distinct personality, conceived along the lines of human nature, at the centre of this sovereignty; (3) faith in the moral character of this personality. There remains to be considered the practical outcome of the relation of this moral personality to Nature and man. What was His purpose in creation ? what aims were conceived to control His attitude and general procedure throughout the history of Israel ?

[1] Is. xxxi. 3 ; cf. Job x. 4.
[2] Davidson, *Theology of the Old Testament*, pp. 144, 161.

It is highly significant for the answers to these questions that the movement of Israel's thought is from the grace of God experienced in history to the interpretation of Nature, and not *vice versa*. The advance of Hebrew religion from the spiritual to the natural realm [1] stands in direct contrast with the advance of Greek thought from the natural to the spiritual. [2] The extension of Yahweh's power into the realm of Nature was a consequence of the worth and vigour of the idea of Yahweh as moral personality. In the original form of that idea, so far as we can trace it, Yahweh's function as the tribal war-god is that of one power among many others. He operates from within Nature, not from a transcendent position above it. Yet from the beginning, Yahweh is not *of* Nature. He belongs to the realm of personal life. He is not a mere expression of natural phenomena, like the Baalim, and He cannot be naturalistically explained. But His power is felt to be operative in one new sphere after another, in the early and latter rains of the cornfield, as well as in the storm that hurled the swollen Kishon upon the Canaanites, until all the phenomena of the natural world are eventually subordinated to Him. Thus Nature gained its unity by the relation of its various elements to Yahweh. [3] It became, in fact, one vast illustration of His power and proof of His majestic wisdom, just as it comes at length to be portrayed in the nature-poetry of the Book of Job, the worship of the Psalter, or the philosophy of the Wisdom literature. [4]

[1] This is the real significance of the frequent remark that the interest of the Old Testament is not 'scientific'. But it must also be remembered that the Old Testament is written according to the 'science' of its times and horizon, which admits of no reconciliation with modern science.

[2] This remains true of Greek philosophy as a whole, even if the cosmologies are shown to be related to earlier mythological ideas. (See Cornford, *From Religion to Philosophy*.)

[3] Cf. Koeberle, *Natur und Geist*, p. 233.

[4] Job xxxviii.-xli. ; Pss. xix., civ. ; Prov. viii. 22-31 ; Job xxviii. So, often, in Deutero-Isaiah (*e.g.* xl. 28, xliv. 24). The doctrine of divine creation thus becomes the great confirmation of the sufficiency of Yahweh to carry through His purposes.

But, although there is appeal to the wonder and majesty of Nature as God's work, in order to humble man, and although the glory of God in the natural world and His joy in it owe nothing to man, it is no exaggeration to say that the Old Testament regards Nature, in the last resort, simply as the arena for the moral issues of human life. This is apparent in the stories of creation, both the earlier and the later. In the earlier (Gen. ii. 4 f.), the interest is focused on the fateful exercise of freedom on man's part, through which are changed even the natural phenomena of human life and work [1] (e.g. child-bearing and the tilling of the ground). In the later (Gen. i.), though the transcendent God now stands outside of and above Nature, as its absolute disposer, His work still culminates in the creation of man, made in His image, i.e. set in a similar relation of authority in regard to all other creatures.[2] This proud place of man is explicitly stated in the well-known words of the eighth Psalm, which marvel at the glory and honour with which God has crowned man. Amid the glories of the earth by day,[3] or beneath the wonder of the stars by night,[4] man plays his part, and that no small one, in the purposes of Yahweh. The omnipotence of Yahweh, displayed in the desert or the dungeon, on the bed of sickness or the storm-tossed ship,[5] is concentrated on man's religious development. The omniscience of Yahweh penetrates to the very secrets of the heart of the being so marvellously fashioned in the womb by His hand.[6] The unchanging purpose of Yahweh is accomplished in and through man, as surely as the purpose of the potter on the revolving clay.[7] This complete control of human life is the more easily accepted by Hebrew thought, because of the Hebrew conception of Nature. In the conservation or maintenance of Nature,

---

[1] Contrast the change of nature for the better, in sympathy with human fortunes, as in Is. xxxv., and in Ezek. xlvii.   [2] See Additional Notes.
[3] Ps. civ. 23.   [4] Ps. viii. 3 f.   [5] Ps. cvii.
[6] Ps. cxxxix.   [7] Jer. xviii. 6.

as in its transformation in the Messianic age, Yahweh's
relation to it is conceived to be direct and immediate.
The chain of what we should call natural causation is
indeed recognised. For example, in the promise of agricultural prosperity to Israel, the corn and wine and oil
are traced to the fertility of the earth, and this, again, to
the rain from heaven. But these links are not second
causes in our sense of the term ; at the end of the series,
as always in Hebrew thought, stands Yahweh, setting
it in motion.[1]   Palestine is indeed naïvely contrasted with
Egypt, as being superior because it 'drinketh water of
the rain of heaven', and not from the artificial irrigation
of the land of the Nile ; [2] *i.e.* in the former land the personal attention of Yahweh is more manifest. Thus, in
the realm of Nature, 'everything is supernatural, that is,
direct divine operation'.[3]   The supreme purpose of
Yahweh, which has controlled His activity in the creation
and conservation of Nature, and in the direction of human
history, is made articulate again and again in the rebukes
and appeals of the prophets. 'The ox knoweth his owner,
and the ass his master's crib : but Israel doth not know,
my people doth not consider'.[4]   Yahweh's purpose is
that man should learn to say 'I delight to do Thy will,
O my God'.[5]   This will of God, springing as it does from
His moral character, is itself moral. He seeks a social
end, the fellowship of man with Him through moral
obedience. This is salvation in the deeper and more
spiritual sense of the Old Testament. True, it is crossed
by the consciousness of Israel's central place in the grace

---

[1] Hos. ii. 21, 22.
[2] Deut. xi. 10-12. A 'rain theology' was 'as important for Israel as the
Homousia for Christian councils' (Duhm, *Jeremia*, p. 131).
[3] Davidson, *D. B.*, ii. p. 198. 'Two beliefs characterise the Hebrew mind
from the beginning : first, the strong belief in causation—every change on
the face of nature, or in the life of men or nations, must be due to a cause ;
and, secondly, the only conceivable causality is a personal agent' (*l.c.*). A
good example is the annual cycle of the seasons (Gen. viii. 22).
[4] Is. i. 3.   [5] Ps. xl. 8.

and purpose of God, with the result that the universalism implicit in the moral purpose is variously limited by the nationalism. But even in the religion of the Law, when the nationalism has assumed its most stringent aspect, obedience to the revealed will of Yahweh is recognised as the supreme end of man, and the supreme glory of God. The attitude of Jesus to the will of God, and His emphasis on the absolute worth of obedience as the supreme ' value ' of human life, are the best illustration of what the Old Testament indicates as the purpose of Yahweh in creation and Providence. Thus, as an Old Testament prophet might have said, is the glory of Yahweh's self-manifestation in human history [1] to find its complement in the voluntary surrender of human life to His holy will. As the difficult problems of human character and destiny were realised by Israel's finest minds, the emphasis was thrown more and more on the divine resources, the supernatural power of the Spirit of God to bring life out of a dead nation,[2] the willingness of Yahweh to make a new covenant, and so write it on the hearts of men that they can no more forget or refuse its claims.[3] Here, as so often in the history of the idea we have reviewed, the new demand arouses the new faith that maketh not ashamed. The resources of Yahweh are called into action like the hidden reserves of a battlefield, but they are never exhausted.

The Old Testament idea of God satisfies the deepest demands of religion by bringing God and man face to face in a moral relation. Calvin begins the *Institutes* with the characteristic remark that ' Almost the whole sum of our wisdom, which ought to be judged really true and solid wisdom, consists of two elements, the knowledge of God and of ourselves '. Newman's conversion, under Calvinistic influences, in his fifteenth year, reproduced

---

[1] Num. xiv. 21, 22 ; cf. Is. vi. 3.
[2] Ezek. xxxvii.   [3] Jer. xxxi. 31 f.

the same conviction, 'making me', he says 'rest in the thought of two and two only absolute and luminously self-evident beings, myself and my Creator'.[1] In these two widely differing men, there is the same ultimate debt to the religion of the Old Testament, which brings God so near to human life, and makes Him more real than one's neighbour. The contrast of this idea of God with all forms of pantheism is obvious. Yahweh, as we have seen, is not derived from Nature, or linked to Nature. His affinities are with human personality. He stands above the chaos (apparently conceived already to exist[2]) from which He fashions His world. Problems enough for philosophical theism remain in such an idea of God, but at least it makes impossible that lower pantheism, or rather materialism, which would explain the highest things from the lowest. The higher pantheism of the Jew, Spinoza, was impossible to his ancient kinsmen, through their strong hold on the reality of human freedom and moral experience, even had such a doctrine of divine immanence been historically conceivable in Israel. The Old Testament idea of God, moreover, though it so clearly separates Yahweh from the world He created and rules, gives no real support to quasi-dualistic ideas of a power working against difficulties, to somewhat doubtful ends,—ideas which have a certain popularity at the present time, as they had when Gnosticism flourished. Whatever may be true of the earlier idea of Yahweh, the monotheistic doctrine of the prophets places all things in His hands. His final triumph is secure. The faith of Israel in its own future shows absolute confidence that the ultimate victory is in the hands of its God. Some of the limitations in the Old Testament idea of God are apparent enough, but they are limitations of form, not of ultimate principle. They may be compared with

[1] *Apologia*, p. 4 ; cf. *Parochial and Plain Sermons*, i. p. 90.
[2] Cf. Skinner, *Genesis*, p. 15.

those which attach to the Carpenter of Nazareth.   As
the Christian may see the manifestation of the Eternal
Son of God within those limitations, so may be seen the
manifestation of the Eternal God Himself through the
limitations of ' Yahweh of Israel '.[1]

[1] Cf. the fine passage in Ruskin's *Frondes Agrestes* (p. 58), which draws a
parallel between the revelation of the Son, through ' the veil of our human
flesh ', with that of the Father, through ' the veil of our human *thoughts* '.

CHAPTER IV

THE IDEA OF MAN

DISCOVERIES that deserve to be called great are usually made in the realm of common things, for their greatness lies in the wide range of their application. The invention of printing from movable types, the use of the expansive force of steam, the principle of gravitation, owe their epoch-making importance to the uncounted multitude of their possible applications. It is not otherwise with the most far-reaching discovery ever made in the realm of religion—the discovery we owe to the prophets of Israel that the supreme worth of life is its morality.[1] They pointed to something that claimed its place in every life, something that found embodiment in the common round and daily task and instinctive personal relationships of men, and said in effect, 'This is man's life at its highest, and God demands the highest from man'. That simple truth was enough eventually to transform a Semitic cult into a universal religion. They brought their new sense of values into relation with the highest interpretative idea they knew—the idea of Yahweh as the God of Israel, and that idea was slowly expanded from the war-cry of militant tribes to a faith that does not dishonour the God and Father of our Lord Jesus Christ. We have now to see how this emphasis on moral experience could give to man himself a new place and dignity, transforming the

---

[1] This culminates in the eighth century, but, as already stated, the moral emphasis of the prophetic spirit may be traced back to a much earlier time, if not to Moses himself (see chap. ii. § 2).

crude material of Semitic animism until it expressed an idea of human personality second only in its lofty claims to that of the Christian faith for which it prepared.

The course of the development of the idea of man is less obvious and explicit than that of the idea of God, just because the literature of Israel is almost wholly religious. In the realm of religion, most of all in that of Israel's religion, the stress falls on God, not on man. Morality is central, but not morality for its own sake ; morality is what Yahweh wants from man, who exists to obey Him. Consequently the influence of the moral emphasis on the idea of man is indirect, rather than direct. The majesty and glory of morality are, as it were, first seen in the face of God, before they are flung back in light on the nature of man. Israel had no Socrates to turn men's thoughts from the outer world to the inner, and to compel them to know themselves. But Israel had an Isaiah to see the holy God in His temple, and seeing Him, to cry, ' I am a man of unclean lips '. In technical terms, the religion of Israel is theocentric, not anthropocentric. One result of this is that there is relatively a much larger survival of primitive ideas about man than about God in the Old Testament. In the case of the doctrine of God we are made aware of a distinct cleavage between the new and the old, a conscious antithesis between the Baalism of Canaan and the Yahwism of Israel's prophets. The writers of the Old Testament hardly permit us to hear of the defeated foe, save as an object of abhorrence and a stone of stumbling.[1] But there was no such explicit opposition between the old and new ideas of human nature. The new idea of man which sprang from the religious realisation of the worth of his morality was as the leaven hid in the ' three measures of meal ', till it was all leavened.

[1] *E.g.*, the very name ' Baal ' is altered into ' Bosheth ', meaning ' shame ', as in Jer. iii. 24. and in certain proper names (Ishbosheth, Jerubosheth) in which ' Baal ' originally stood (1 Chron. viii. 33 ; Jud. vi. 32).

There were, in fact, three features of Semitic animism
to be so leavened. They are more or less common to all
primitive culture—the ideas of the breath-soul (and blood-
soul), of the psychical function of physical organs, of the
ascription of all that is abnormal in conduct and character
to the action of invasive spirits. These were the chief
origins of the psychology involved in the common speech
and thought of the Hebrews. This the prophet of
Yahweh transformed, even whilst he shared in it. Yahweh,
he taught, framed those organs, and animated them with
living breath ; Yahweh claimed the blood of the sacrifices ; Yahweh sent His Spirit into man. It was the
exception, rather than the rule, for the prophetic religion
to challenge such popular conceptions ; it was done only
when, as by some of the death customs, the sole supremacy
of Yahweh seemed to be imperilled. For the most part,
the primitive ideas about human nature survived, though
the primitive high places of the gods perished. They survived to make their own contribution to religious experience. Crude as some of them were, they were capable
of being shaped into vivid and forcible expressions of
fundamental truths, and we owe to them much in the
Scriptural vocabulary of religion. There is no more
impressive illustration of this transformation than the
doctrine of the Spirit of God, which is ultimately rooted
in Semitic demonology. We shall trace this assimilation and transformation in regard to (1) the psychology
of the Hebrews ; (2) the dependence of man on God ;
(3) the relation of the individual to the society ; (4) the
future life.

1. *The Psychology of the Hebrews*

There is a logic in primitive thought which is often
obscured to modern eyes because it works from premises
so different from our own. We are apt to dismiss as
fanciful metaphor much that was simple realism ; in

fact, the science of the ancient world has often become the poetry of the modern. This is evident in regard to those speculations about human nature which the Hebrews, or their ancestors, shared with primitive peoples in general. The obvious explanation of the difference between a dead and a living man was the respective absence or presence of breath, and in consequence there is no more common theory of the soul than that which identifies it with the breath. To the Hebrew, the soul is not an esoteric and mystical abstraction; it *is* the breath, and the breath which is the principle of life naturally comes to be regarded as the centre of the consciousness of life, and of all its physical or psychical phenomena. The Hebrew word for this breath-soul is *nephesh*, and the best translation of it is often simply ' life'. When the prophet Elijah has prayed for the restoration to life of the child of the widow of Zarephath, ' the child's *nephesh* returned upon his inward parts, and he lived '.[1] The idea is clearly that of the breath as animating the physical organs of the body, almost as materialistically conceived as when we think of steam setting an engine in motion. Equally obvious and natural is the extension of the term *nephesh* to cover the inner consciousness of life. The early ' Book of the Covenant' says, ' a sojourner thou shalt not oppress, for *ye* know the *nephesh* of the sojourner, since ye were sojourners in the land of Egypt '.[2] The usage of *nephesh* could extend to

> ' All thoughts, all passions, all delights,
> Whatever stirs this mortal frame ',

but, in practice, for reasons to be given, it was chiefly used of the emotional life, and, in particular, of physical appetite, or psychical desire.[3] All this is perfectly straight-forward, and raises no problems. The complications that have arisen for the study of Hebrew psychology are due

---

[1] 1 Kings xvii. 22.   [2] Ex. xxiii. 9.   [3] 1 Sam. ii. 16; xx. 4.

to a feature common to much primitive thought. That thought does not start from one centre only in its explanation of phenomena, but from several independent ideas. These distinct explanations eventually converge on the fact to be explained, and are reconciled by some form of syncretism, which continues to puzzle the modern investigator until he ceases to expect a systematic arrangement, and looks simply for the different lines of approach. The second line of approach to the problem of life adopted by Hebrew thought is also shared with primitive peoples in general. It sets out from the different organs of the body, both central and peripheral. These are credited with different contributions to the conscious life, because ancient and primitive thought has not learnt to distinguish between the physical and the psychical. Thus the Hebrews spoke of the (physical) heart as the actual centre of the conscious life in general, and of both its emotional and intellectual aspects. The term is as general in its original scope as was *nephesh*. But, as a result of the syncretism of these two parallel ideas, 'heart' and *nephesh* come to denote predominantly the intellectual and the emotional aspects of consciousness respectively, without complete surrender of their more comprehensive usage. This is the explanation of such words as those of the Deuteronomic appeal: 'Thou shalt love Yahweh thy God with all thy heart and with all thy *nephesh*, and with all thy might' (vi. 5). This sentence covers the conscious life of the whole personality, in both its thought and its feeling.

There is also, however, in the Old Testament, a third line of approach to the mystery of human personality— viz. that afforded by the term *ruach*, or 'spirit'. This forms one of the most fascinating and important subjects of Biblical theology, and the ideas which cluster around it are the most characteristic of Old Testament ideas in regard to human nature. It is often said, by those who have not studied the history of the usage in its chrono-logical development, that *ruach* is simply another term for the breath-soul, a synonym of *nephesh*, though with a higher range of meaning. To say this is to neglect the important fact that *ruach* is not used of the breath-soul in man, or with psychical predicates, in any pre-exilic passage. The original meaning of the term, a meaning it retains throughout all periods of Hebrew literature, is 'wind'. From that usage it passed over to denote the mysterious wind-like influences, the demonic forces, which were supposed to account for what is abnormal and strange in human conduct. We have to remember that primitive thought, to a degree we find it hard to imagine, supposes man to be constantly accessible to such influences. The quarrel that arose between Abimelech and the men of Shechem is ascribed to an evil *ruach* sent by God ; the madness of Saul and the remarkable strength of Samson are similarly explained.[1] But that which was more or less abnormal before the Exile comes to be more or less normal after it ; by the time of Ezekiel, *ruach* is used of the breath-soul in man, as was *nephesh*. Yet it always retains—and this is a most important point to notice—the 'higher' associations of its origin. It stands for those more exceptional and unusual endowments of human nature which suggest God as their immediate source, the more normal *nephesh* being taken for granted. It links man to God, as though it were a door continually open to His approach. The function which Professor James [2] ascribed to the 'sub-consciousness' was fulfilled by the idea of *ruach* to the spiritually-minded Israelite. Through his own *ruach*, that is, through his conscious life viewed in its highest possibilities, he was in touch with the *ruach* of God, the source of man's greatest achieve-ments. The nature of man, regarded as in contrast with

---

[1] Jud. ix. 23 ; 1 Sam. xviii. 10 ; Jud. xv. 14.
[2] *The Varieties of Religious Experience*, pp. 512 f.

the nature of God, might be called 'flesh', as the divine
nature was called 'spirit'; yet man could pray, 'with
my *ruach* within me, I seek longingly for Thee'.[1]

If we bring together these three chief terms—*nephesh*,
'heart', and *ruach*—in the working syncretism of their
ultimate usage, we shall see that there is before us a
striking theory of human nature, which may be taken as
characteristic of the Old Testament. The idea of human
nature implies a unity, not a dualism. There is no contrast between the body and the soul, such as the terms
instinctively suggest to us. The shades of the dead in
Sheol, as we shall see, are not called 'souls' or 'spirits'
in the Old Testament; nor does the Old Testament contain
any distinct word for 'body', as it surely would have done,
had this idea been sharply differentiated from that of
soul. Man's nature is a product of the two factors
—the breath-soul which is his principle of life, and
the complex of physical organs which this animates.
Separate them, and the man ceases to be, in any real sense
of personality; nothing but a 'shade' remains, which
is neither body nor soul. If this seems but a poor idea
of human nature, we must set over against it the great
redeeming feature, that there is an aspect of this nature
which relates man to God, and makes man accessible to
God. Man had only to find along this line the fulfilment
of the deepest moral and religious demands of his life,
to be lifted into a realm where personality is victorious
over death.

2. *Man's Dependence on God*

The foundation for the conception of human nature just
outlined was already in existence when the prophetic theology first began to transform the religion of Israel. The
prophets shared in the psychology of their time; their

---

[1] Is. xxvi. 9; cf. xxxi. 3.

own message, as will be seen further on, in large measure owes its form to that psychology.   But the old anthropology, tacitly accepted, could not escape gradual transformation by the new doctrine of God.   Human nature gained a new significance as the creation of Yahweh, whose hands had shaped its prototype, and whose breath had given the body its vitality.   The moral consciousness of man, which was in process of evolution through his social relationships in the family, the local group, and the nation, attained a new value and a characteristic interpretation as the moral law of Yahweh.   The very effort to obey this law, and to promote obedience to it on the part of others, threw men back on the thought of the *ruach* of Yahweh, the potent influence from without which could create new conditions within human nature. The common feature in these diverse applications of the new doctrine of God is insistence on man's dependence on Him.

It is matter of general knowledge that the Book of Genesis offers us two distinct narratives of the creation of man.   That of the first chapter (P) is the later, being post-exilic ; that of the second chapter (J) was written approximately in the ninth century B.C.   In the naïve and frankly anthropomorphic narrative of J the interest centres in man and his life, just as in the more restrained description of a later age the theme is rather God and His glory.   ' Yahweh Elohim ', runs the earlier story, ' shaped man, earth from the ground ', as a potter would shape his clay on the wheel,[1] ' and blew into his nostrils life-breath ; so man became a living being (*nephesh*) '.   Here we have the two elements which make the unity of human nature —the physical organism, and the breath-soul which animates it ; both are due to God, and there is no hint,

---

[1] ii. 7.   Cf. the picture of the Egyptian god Chnum shaping men on the potter's wheel, reproduced by Jeremias (*Das Alte Testament im Lichte des alten Orients*,[2] p. 146).

in this pre-exilic narrative, of any third element in the nature of man, viz. *ruach*, nor any suggestion of dualism. There is nothing here to distinguish the life-principle in man from that of the animal world in general, the same phrases being used of them,[1] though the way in which it is imparted to man naturally singles him out from other creatures. This distinction is emphasised in the later narrative, in which all details of the creative process disappear. ' Elohim created man in His image, in the image of Elohim created He him ; male and female created He them ' (i. 27). Here man is no longer the central figure in a garden, where Yahweh walks to enjoy the evening breeze ; man falls into his proper place in an ordered world, though he has dominion over all other creatures. Whatever the doubtful phrase, ' the image of God ', may mean, it is certainly intended to recognise man's unique relation to God, and his supremacy over the animal world (cf. p. 72). This is the thought which fills the writer of the eighth Psalm with wonder and gratitude ; a glory has been given to man little lower than that of the Elohim, the whole class of supernatural beings in the over-world.[2] In the 104th Psalm the stress falls on the continuous dependence of all living creatures, including man, on divine support :

' All of them wait upon Thee
    For Thy giving their food in its season ;
  Thou givest unto them, they gather (it),
    Thou openest Thine hand, they are satisfied with good.
  Thou hidest Thy face, they are dismayed,
    Thou withdrawest their *ruach*, they expire,
    And unto their dust they return.
  Thou sendest Thy *ruach*, they are created '.[3]

---

[1] vii. 22 (J), i. 20 (P).

[2] On the other hand, the contrast between nature and man is used in the Book of Job to teach humility (cf. Bertholet, *Bib. Theologie des A.T.*, ii. p. 133).

[3] Ps. civ. 27-30. Cf. the phrase used by P, 'the God of the spirits of all flesh' (Num. xvi. 22, xxvii. 16 ; in both cases expressive of man's dependence on God).

Again, in the 139th Psalm, this dependence of man on
God is carried to its fullest extent.   God knows that
inner life, the organs of which He has fashioned ; He is
present from end to end of the earth, in the heights above,
and in the depths below :

> 'Behind and before hast Thou enclosed me,
>   And hast put upon me Thine hand' (verse 5).

That Psalm fitly ends with the prayer that God may
search the heart, because the true outcome of man's dependence, and of God's purpose, is the obedient life of
righteousness.

The moral demands of Yahweh were too great to be
satisfied without help from Yahweh Himself. The prophets
who attempted great things for God in the eighth century
were followed by prophets who expected great things
from Him.   Accordingly, Ezekiel lays a characteristic
emphasis on the supernatural help that is to create a new
Israel, able to accomplish that in which the old Israel
had failed. ' I will put a new spirit within you : and I
will take the stony heart out of their flesh, and will give
them a heart of flesh : that they may walk in my statutes,
and keep mine ordinances and do them : and they shall
be my people, and I will be their God. . . . I have poured
out my spirit upon the house of Israel '.[1] It will be seen
that the prophet is working with a conception drawn from
the old anthropology, the conception of invasive influences, affecting human lives, and imparting new powers
to them.   These influences were once thought to come
from many quarters, for man's life was encircled with
demons and spirits.   But now Yahweh is supreme, and
it is His *ruach* alone that will change human character,
and make the impossible to be possible.   It is in this
faith that the Psalmist prays, ' Take not Thy holy *ruach*

---

[1] xi. 19 f. ; cf. xxxvi. 26, xxxix. 29. Cf. the 'new covenant' of Jer. xxxi.
33 f.

from me ', and that the bearer of the Old Testament evangel
cries, ' The *ruach* of the Lord Yahweh is upon me '.[1]
The universal outpouring of the Spirit of God upon man,
awaited by Old Testament prophets and experienced by
New Testament believers,[2] is thus linked to primitive
ideas of man, and Paul is a debtor to the barbarians for
his spiritual Gospel in a sense other than he recognised.

3. *The Relation of the Individual to the Society*

Many people are apt to think that the increasing ' social
consciousness ' of the present time is something entirely
new in the history of civilisation. The impression is true
only so far as the immediate economic and civic applications are concerned. At other periods of human development a similar sense of social solidarity has been prominent, and has led to results which, from the modern
standpoint, are often startling, and even immoral. Much
that is strange to us in ancient thought is due to what we
may best call the sense of ' corporate personality '. The
unit for morality and religion is not so much the individual
as the group to which he belongs, whether this be, for
particular purposes, the family, the local community, or
the nation. There are many evidences that this was the
case in pre-exilic Israel. Yahweh was the God of Israel,
and only secondarily the God of the individual Israelite.
Individual religion of course existed, but it was construed
through the society to which the individual belonged.
In other words, the relation of man to God, like the relation of God to man, was mediated through the corporate
personality of the nation.

The general principle of corporate personality may be
illustrated, in the case of Israel, by the practice of blood-
revenge, which receives religious sanction in the earlier
part of the Old Testament. David consulted the oracle

[1] Ps. li. 11 ; Is. lxi. 1.   [2] Joel ii. 28 f. ; Acts ii. 16 f.

of Yahweh as to the cause of a protracted famine, and
was informed that it was due to the slaughter of the
Gibeonites by Saul.[1] The survivors of the Gibeonites
were asked to name their terms of compensation, and
they demanded seven lives from the descendants of Saul,
according to the ordinary principle of blood-revenge,
which treated the whole family of the slayer as the guilty
unit. David therefore handed over to them two of Saul's
sons by Rizpah, and five of his grandsons. These men
were killed by the Gibeonites, and their bodies exposed
'before Yahweh', the wrath of whom, as the guardian
of social morality, was thereby removed. There was
no thought of any injustice to the individual men who
were killed. They perished as an act of social justice,
which was demanded by the contemporary religion of
Israel. Another instructive example is supplied by the
story of Achan.[2] Achan offended Yahweh by secreting
some of the spoil of Jericho, which had been 'devoted'
to Him. This act of one man put the whole nation
in the wrong with Yahweh, and He visited His wrath
upon them as a nation by allowing them to be defeated.
Inquisition revealed Achan as the offender, and he was
accordingly executed. But that same sense of corporate
personality which recognised that the whole nation was put
in the wrong by the act of one man is further shown in
the fact that not Achan only, but his whole family, were
stoned to death and burnt. This was no isolated instance
of vindictive spite, but the deliberate application of a
principle which nobody at that time thought of challeng-
ing, a principle represented as having the full approval
of Yahweh. It is seen again in the familiar words of the
Decalogue, which represent Yahweh as 'visiting the
iniquity of the fathers upon the children, upon the third

[1] 2 Sam. xxi. 1 f.
[2] Josh. vii. 24-26. Cf. Dan. vi. 24: Daniel's accusers, *with their wives
and children*, are cast into the lions' den.

and upon the fourth generation of them that hate me '.[1]
We must not soften such words into a statement of the
consequences of heredity and social law, which, indeed,
do often make the innocent child suffer for the parent's
fault. They simply mean that the principle of corporate
personality is involved, which regards not the mere
individual, but his whole family-group, as the unit of
condemnation.

A fuller recognition of the claims of individuality
was implied in the moral appeals of the eighth-century
prophets, but it does not become explicit until the publi-
cation of the Deuteronomic Law, a century later. The
general principle is there asserted that ' the fathers shall
not be put to death for the children, neither shall the
children be put to death for the fathers : every man shall
be put to death for his own sin '.[2] It is, however, the
contemporary prophet Jeremiah who makes the most
notable contribution to the principle of individuality.
He does this, in the first place, by the intensity of his
own individual relation to Yahweh, at a time when the
national relation seems in imminent peril of dissolution.
But his personal attitude becomes explicit in the prophecy
of the ' New Covenant ', which Yahweh will make with
individual Israelites.[3] This prophecy seems to be set in
intentional antithesis to the Deuteronomic Covenant with
the nation as a whole, which had failed of its purpose,[4]
though perhaps supported by Jeremiah himself in the
first instance.[5] A little later, the principle of individual
responsibility was argued in detail by Ezekiel. He rejects,
as Jeremiah had done,[6] the current proverb by which
people were explaining the troubles of their age : ' The
fathers have eaten sour grapes, and the children's teeth

[1] Ex. xx. 5. Cf. 2 Kings v. 27, where Elisha says to Gehazi : ' The
leprosy of Naaman shall cleave unto thee, *and unto thy seed*, for ever '.
[2] Deut. xxiv. 16.   [3] Jer. xxxi. 33, 34.
[4] Jer. vi. 16-21, xxxiv. 8 f.   [5] Jer. xi. 1-14.
[6] Ezek. xviii. 2 ; Jer. xxxi. 29, 30.

are set on edge '. ' All souls ', he declares in Yahweh's
name,[1] ' are mine ; as the soul of the father, so also the
soul of the son is mine : the soul that sinneth, *it* shall die '.
But the older principle of the solidarity of the family
still flourished, as is plain from the protest against it in
the Book of Job :

> ' God layeth up his iniquity for his children ?
>   Let Him recompense it unto himself, that he may
>   know it '.[2]

The recognition of the rights of the individual life was
certain to be reached by any real progress in morality
and religion, and when it was reached it had important
consequences. It raised the whole problem of suffering,
for the experience of life did not confirm Ezekiel's declaration of an exact individual retribution and reward. The
problem of suffering, as will be shown, raised the related
problem of the future life. The corporate future of the
family or the nation on earth could no longer satisfy those
who had come to feel their individual relation to God,
and to consider what death meant. The effects of the
new demands are visible in the literature of the period
between the Old Testament and the New, with its marked
accentuation of individualism, and its complex eschatological developments. It is, however, only in the New
Testament that we find ' a synthesis of the eschatologies
of the race and the individual '.[3] The individualism of
the New Testament owes its peculiar qualities to that
social emphasis from which, in the Old Testament period,
it had been developed. For, just as the older emphasis
in morality and religion on the sense of corporate personality did not exclude the growth of individual experience,
so the newer emphasis on the individual did not imply the
rejection of a very real and vital social solidarity. What
we regard as the old error contributed, and contributed

---

[1] Ezek. xviii. 4.   [2] Job xxi. 19.   [3] Charles, *E. Bi.*, col. 1372.

richly, to the new truth. Whether we think of the remarkable patriotic solidarity of the Jewish people, maintained at such cost, and for so long, or of the finest and highest religious conception of the Old Testament, that of the mission and work of the corporate Israel as the Servant of Yahweh, or of the foundation laid by the Old Testament religion for the social individualism of the New—we may see, once more, that without the shadowed valleys of the religion of Israel we should not have had its mountain peaks.

4. *The Future Life*

Just because the sense of corporate personality was so strongly developed in early Israel, the idea of a future life for the individual was hardly reached within the Old Testament. The Israelite felt that he went on living in his children to a degree that really made their life his own. We have seen, as in the case of Saul's descendants, that he could be punished through his children, according to contemporary thought. When the prophet pictures Rachel at her grave in Ramah weeping for her children,[1] it is much more than metaphor. The woman of Tekoa appeals to David to spare the life of her surviving son, who has slain his brother, because, as she says, ' thus shall they quench my coal which is left, and shall leave to my husband neither name nor remainder upon the face of the earth '.[2] Hence the importance attached by the Hebrew to a numerous posterity ; it is not said to the good man that he shall be rewarded in some future life, but

> ' Thou shalt know also that thy seed shall be great,
> And thine offspring as the grass of the earth '.[3]

When men die they are gathered unto their fathers, and

---

[1] Jer. xxxi. 15.   [2] Sam. xiv. 7.   [3] Job v. 25.

desire to be buried in the family grave.[1] Israelite customs
in regard to the burial of the dead seem to point to some
form of ancestor-worship as surviving from previous
times into the earlier centuries of Yahwism.[2] This would
explain the opposition of the prophets to some of these
customs, as well as to the practice of consulting the dead
for information unattainable by natural means. ' Ye
shall not cut yourselves, nor make any baldness between
your eyes, for the dead ', says the Book of Deuteronomy
(xiv. 1), whilst Isaiah speaks contemptuously of those
who resort ' unto them that have familiar spirits and unto
the wizards, that chirp and that mutter ' (viii. 19). An
instructive example of such necromancy is afforded by
the well-known visit of Saul to the witch of Endor, when
' Yahweh answered him not, neither by dreams, nor by
Urim, nor by prophets '.[3] The shade of Samuel, attired
as of old, is represented as asking, ' Why hast thou dis-
quieted me, to bring me up ? '

The dead are thus supposed to go on existing in some
sense or other, even by the early thought of Israel. But it
is an existence that has no attraction for the Israelite, and
falls outside the sphere of his proper religion. It is not
his soul that survives at all ; the dead are called ' shades '
(*rephaim*), not ' souls ', in the Old Testament. The (sub-
terranean) place of their abiding is called Sheol, and in
many particulars it is like the Greek Hades. Sheol seems
to be an outgrowth of the family grave, probably under
the influence of Babylonian ideas. It is ' the house of
meeting for all living ', ' the land of darkness, and of the
shadow of death ',[4] where the distinctions of earth, even
its moral distinctions, cease to operate :

> ' There the wicked cease from raging,
> And there the weary be at rest.

---

[1] Jud. ii. 10 ; 2 Sam. xix. 37.
[2] In support of this view, see Charles, *E. Bi.*, col. 1335 f. ; against it,
Kautzsch, *D. B.*, v. pp. 614 f. Samuel's shade is called ' Elohim '.
[3] 1 Sam. xxviii. 6.   [4] Job xxx. 23, x. 21.

> There the prisoners are at ease together ;
>> They hear not the voice of the taskmaster.
> The small and the great are there ;
>> And the servant is free from his master '.[1]

The most vivid description of Sheol, however, is that
which is found in the Book of Isaiah, describing the fall
of a tyrant :

> 'Sheol beneath is thrilled at thee,
>> Meeting thine advent ;
> Arousing for thee the shades,
>> All the bell-wethers of Earth,
> Making rise up from their thrones
>> All the kings of the nations.
> They shall all of them answer
>> And say to thee,
> " *Thou*, too, art made weak as we,
>> Unto us art made like".
> Brought down unto Sheol is thy pomp,
>> The music of thy lutes ;
> Beneath thee maggots are spread,
>> And (of) worms is thy coverlet '.[2]

This gives the characteristic feature of Sheol for Hebrew
thought—'made weak as we'. The same note echoes
through the literature of the Old Testament, as in the
Song of Hezekiah,[3] and in many of the Psalms. To pass
into Sheol is to pass from life into death, for ' in Sheol
who shall give Thee thanks ? '[4] Sheol is a survival of
the pre-Yahwistic beliefs of Israel, and is not usually
conceived as lying within the jurisdiction of Yahweh.

It will be apparent that so cheerless an outlook as this
could provide no doctrine of a future life worthy of the
name. Israel remained content with it so long because,
as we have seen, the hope of Israel lay with the future of

---

[1] Job iii. 17-19.
[2] xiv. 9-11. Trans. by G. B. Gray, in the *International Critical
Commentary*, p. 248. For another account of Sheol, see Ezek. xxxii. 13 f.
[3] Is. xxxviii. 10 f.　　　　[4] Ps. vi. 5.

the family or of the nation, a future to be realised on earth. But, with the failure of the national hope, involved in the destruction of the Judæan kingdom, and with the rise of the new individualism, the outlook on the individual future beyond death was necessarily affected. The same monotheistic influences which extended the sway of Yahweh beyond the land of Israel over the whole earth tended, sooner or later, to carry it into the dark land of Sheol. Already we find Amos saying in Yahweh's name, ' Though they dig into Sheol, thence shall my hand take them ', whilst a Psalmist confesses the omnipresence of God in the words, ' If I make my bed in Sheol, behold, Thou art there '.[1] Sooner or later, men found that the hard and fast doctrine of individual retribution enunciated by Ezekiel broke down, so far as the visible lives of individual men were concerned. It lay in the nature of things, therefore, that the book which especially handles the problem of suffering, the Book of Job, should make the first tentative demand for a life beyond death.[2] The problem would not have existed in the form it did for Job, if he had been able to maintain, with the support of established belief, that in some future life the injustice of his sufferings would be rectified. He does, in fact, for a moment imagine that there might be some such future in his own case, but the transient imagination cannot bear the weight of his cares :

' Oh, that Thou wouldest hide me in Sheol,
    That Thou wouldest keep me in secret, until Thy wrath be
        past,
    That Thou wouldest appoint me a set time, and remember
        me !

---

[1] Amos ix. 2 ; Ps. cxxxix. 8.   The *character* of Sheol remains unaltered by this inclusion in Yahweh's dominion.

[2] The suggestion that the tree of life in Eden might have conferred immortality on Adam (Gen. iii. 22), and the translations of Enoch (v. 24), and Elijah (2 Kings ii. 11), are exceptional cases, and simply prove the rule for the common man, that no real life beyond death awaited him.

If a man die, shall he live again?
All the days of my warfare would I wait
Till my release should come.
Thou shouldest call, and I would answer Thee:
Thou wouldest have a desire to the work of Thy hands'.

(xiv. 13-15.)

This desire for some exceptional vindication of the speaker's innocence finds yet stronger expression in famous and frequently misunderstood words :

'But I—I know that my Vindicator liveth,
And in after time shall take His stand upon the dust;
And after my skin, which has been thus struck off,
Even without my flesh shall I see God.
Whom I shall see for myself,
And my eyes shall behold, and not a stranger;
My reins are consumed within me!'[1]

Here, again, the hope is not so much of a future life, as of a future vindication, for the sake of which life shall be exceptionally restored. Even from this hope Job falls back in the following chapters, showing clearly that it is a personal venture of faith which is in question, and not an established doctrine.

We may find similar ventures of faith in certain of the Psalms, prompted by the same problem of human fortunes, and characterised by the indefiniteness which we should expect to find in such gropings after a dimly conceived truth. The most important of these is the great passage in the 73rd Psalm :

'Nevertheless, I am continually with Thee;
Thou holdest my right hand.
Thou wilt guide me with Thy counsel,
And afterward receive me with glory.

---

[1] Job xix. 25-27. The translation is Burney's, in *Israel's Hope of Immortality* (p. 52), which gives a fuller (popular) discussion of the whole topic.

Whom have I in heaven but Thee ?
   And there is none upon earth that I desire beside Thee.
My flesh and my heart faileth,
   God is the rock of my heart, and my portion for ever '.[1]

The important point to notice in this, and in other possible references, is the particular quality of the hope
resulting from the way in which it was reached. The
hope of a future is made to depend on the relation of the
soul to God. That relation is felt to have a mystical value,
transcending the fact of death. We have here, as has
been truly said, ' a strength of conviction of the reality
of personal union with God, under which the thought of
death as it were fades into the background and is ignored.
. . . This conviction of a personal relation to God independent of time and change, and not any particular theory
as to the character of the life after death, is the lasting
contribution of the Old Testament to the doctrine of a
Future Life '.[2] The fact that this belief appeared so late
gave it the opportunity, when it did come, to absorb
the noblest moral and spiritual elements in Israel's religion,
and to transcend all the ideas of the future held by
contemporary nations.[3]

But such a faith in the future as this perhaps demanded
too high a degree of spiritual development for it ever to
become the faith of the average man. To translate it into
his vernacular, moreover, would have required the philosophical outlook of the Greek world, with its characteristic doctrine of the immortality of the soul. This Greek
doctrine is, in fact, borrowed by the author of the Apocryphal book known as the Wisdom of Solomon.[4] But

---

[1] The reference to a future life found by some in Pss. xvi. 10, 11 and
xvii. 15 is improbable ; that alleged in Ps. xlix. 15 is more likely. The
subject is discussed in detail by Cheyne, *Origin of the Psalter*, pp. 381-425.
[2] Burney, *op. cit.*, pp. 46, 104.
[3] Cf. Sellin, *Die ältest. Religion*, p. 55. On the other hand, a ' natural '
immortality (on Greek lines) would have made man too independent of God
for Hebrew-Jewish thought.
[4] iii. 1-9.

Hebrew psychology pointed along another line, that leading to the idea of the resurrection of the body. We have seen that human nature was conceived by the Hebrew as a unity requiring both elements, body and soul, to constitute it. Existence in Sheol lacked vitality, because it lacked both body and soul. If the Hebrew was to acquire any idea of life after death which possessed a real vitality, according to his native conceptions of life, there would have to be a resurrection of the dead body for the recovered soul to animate it. This is the line along which the thought of Palestinian Judaism, as distinct from the Alexandrian or Græcised Judaism, actually developed in the period between the two Testaments. The beginning of this idea of a resurrection of the body is already found in two passages of the Old Testament, both of them connected with the Messianic hope of Judaism.[1] The earlier of these, belonging possibly to the fourth century B.C., is obscure in detail, but clear as to the point in question, the faith that Yahweh will raise to life the bodies of His martyrs : 'Thy dead shall live ; my dead bodies shall arise. Awake and ring out your joy, ye that dwell in the dust ; for a dew of lights is thy dew, and the earth shall give birth to shades '.[2] It should be carefully noticed that this resurrection-life is to be realised in Palestine, with the earthly Jerusalem as its centre ; there is no reference to a future life in some other world, nor is it believed that any but faithful Israelites will be raised.[3] The later passage, found in the Book of Daniel, belongs definitely to the second century B.C., that book having been written in the period of persecution suffered by the Jews from 168 to 165 B.C. We there read, 'Many of them that sleep in the dust of the earth shall awake, some to everlasting life, and some to reproaches and everlasting

[1] Ezekiel's vision of the Valley of Dry Bones (xxxvii.) is a metaphor, describing the restoration of the Jewish people, and not a promise of actual individual resurrection.
[2] Is. xxvi. 19.   [3] Contrast verse 14.

abhorrence' (xii. 2). Here there is a notable advance on the previous conception of the resurrection. It is not yet universal, for apparently it is confined to those only who have been prominent for good or for evil in contemporary events. But there is a resurrection of the wicked, as well as of the good, and punishment and reward are respectively assigned to them. Here, also, it is in the future life of the Messianic kingdom to be established *on earth* that the saints of God will share. The faith of the writer of the Book of Daniel was continued in the Pharisees of the New Testament, just as the Sadducees continued the entire scepticism as to any future life displayed in Ecclesiastes.[1] The elaborate development of eschatology in the Apocalyptic literature, *e.g.* the Book of Enoch (part of which belongs to the same age as the Book of Daniel), necessarily falls beyond our subject. All that we have to note is that the Old Testament lays the foundation for the doctrine of future life given in the New, both on the cruder side of a Messianic resurrection, and on the finer, more spiritual side, which is represented in the ultimate outlook of the Apostle Paul.[2]

As we look back on the Old Testament idea of human nature and destiny, we see that man stands out in clear distinction from both Nature and God.[3] Man is no mere item in the natural world, but is separately created by God, who controls Nature in the interests of His purposes for man. Man is linked to God by the moral law which God has made known to him ; in the companionship for which this law is the condition, man and God stand together far above Nature's level. In fact, there is no 'Nature', written with a capital letter, as a unity apart from God, but simply a world of natural phenomena entirely in God's hand, and made the arena for human history. But, in

[1] iii. 19-22 ; ix. 3-6 ; cf. p. 174.
[2] Cf. H. W. Robinson, *The Christian Doctrine of Man*, pp. 129-31.
[3] Cf. the excellent presentation of this in Koeberle's *Natur und Geist*, chap. xxii. ('Die Stellung des Menschen in der Natur').

contrast with God, man is characterised by his utter
dependence on Him, both for his existence and for his
destiny. If that destiny is to be achieved, it will be only
by the help of God. Whilst it is seen that that destiny
is the realisation of righteousness, the plane on which it
is to be realised is held to be the present world. The
intensity with which the Israelite clings to the present
life corresponds to his belief that personality is a unity,
demanding both soul and body, and that there is no life,
worthy of the name, beyond death. When his faith does
begin to assail the iron gate of death, it is with a demand
for future life all the richer and fuller because of his long
concentration on the life that now is. The immortality
he craves is essentially the society of God, already opened
to him in moral and spiritual experience. The resurrection of the body for which he ultimately asks, as necessary to the restoration of personality, is the prelude to
the establishment of a society of the servants of God.
For, however much the Old Testament comes to realise
the individuality of salvation, that individuality always
carries with it the wealth of social relationship which is
the legacy of centuries of closely-knit corporate life.

We have but to contrast this idea of man with others
widely current in the ancient or modern world to recognise
that the conception held by Israel most of all deserves
the title 'religious',—*i.e.* human nature is interpreted
through its relation to a personal God. The thought of
India is ultimately metaphysical; the human soul in its
successive transmigrations is always dominated by its background of Pantheistic absorption. The thought of Greece
banishes its gods, and enters the scientific realms of biology
and psychology, though numerous cults and mysteries testify
to the irrepressible religious needs of the soul. It is less
easy to analyse the subtle combinations of modern thought,
which borrows from so much of the past professedly left
behind. But a clear contrast with the Hebrew idea of

man is supplied by those who philosophise from the stand-point of natural science. Man is 'Nature's Insurgent Son',[1] 'a part of Nature, a product of the definite and orderly evolution which is universal; a being resulting from and driven by the one great nexus of mechanism which we call Nature'; 'Man forms a new departure in the gradual unfolding of Nature's predestined scheme'; 'Man is Nature's rebel'; 'the knowledge and control of Nature is Man's destiny and his greatest need'.[2] Here Nature as creator takes the place of Israel's God, and man is left to work out his own salvation without religious fear or trembling. By the side of this current idea of man we may set the Pantheistic optimism to which Emerson has given striking and memorable expression. Take, for example, his essay on 'The Over-Soul', any page of which would supply illustrative examples. 'Within man is the soul of the whole; the wise silence; the universal beauty, to which every part and particle is equally related; the eternal ONE. . . . The simplest person, who in his integrity worships God, becomes God. . . . I am somehow recep-tive of the great soul, and thereby I do overlook the sun and the stars, and feel them to be the fair accidents and effects which change and pass'. Here Nature, in the narrower scientific sense, has become as subservient to Spirit as it is for Hebrew thought, but the mystical relation of man to the 'Over-soul' is entirely different from that Hebrew 'mysticism' which brought the human and the divine spiritually face to face, without losing their distinction.

The Psalmist whom the night-sky stirred to ask the great question, 'What is man?' found a double echo to his words.[3] One was a bitter parody of them, wrung from a sufferer's lips; the other an *Ecce Homo*, applying

[1] The title of Ray Lankester's Romanes Lecture in 1905; given in his book, *The Kingdom of Man*, pp. 1-61, and forming a good statement of the evolutionary' point of view.

[2] *Op. cit.*, pp. 7, 25, 26, 60.   [3] See Job vii. 17, 18; Heb. ii. 6-9.

them to 'Him who hath been made a little lower than the angels, even Jesus, because of the suffering of death crowned with glory and honour'. Around the explanation of these three passages, so closely linked, might be gathered no small part of the Biblical doctrine of man. They respectively teach that the fundamental fact of human life is man's dependence on God, that much in the course of man's life appears to be tragic defeat, that through the discipline and sacrifice of suffering man can achieve a victory worthy of his God-given nature and place in the universe.

CHAPTER V

THE APPROACH OF GOD TO MAN

ANCIENT religion does not, in the first instance, spring from pious meditation on the universe, or from the aspirations of moral and spiritual life after fellowship with the gods. It usually begins in some definite occurrence, some surprise on the path of familiar custom, some unexplained experience. In religion, as in science, the exception does not so much ' prove the rule ' as form the point of departure for the discovery of new rules. Just as the slight deviation of one planet from its path in the skies has, before now, served to discover the presence of another, so any interruption of a man's normal life may open his eyes to a 'supernatural' world. 'Looking upon the religious tradition of Beny Israel, from the soil of the desert ', says Doughty, speaking with his unrivalled knowledge of the modern Beduin, ' we might muse of its rising in Jacob's family, out of the nomad Semites' vision of the *melûk* ', *i.e.* the ' angels of the air ', perhaps originally suggested by mirage.[1] ' Jacob's ladder ' may be but the stairway of a dream ; yet, given certain conditions of thought, it may be transformed into the greatest of spiritual realities, ' the great world's altar-stairs that slope through darkness up to God '.

The attitude of ancient religion towards both psychical and external events is different from our own. Primitive thought is wanting in any sharp distinction between subjective and objective experiences ; a dream, for example,

---

[1] *Arabia Deserta*, ii. p. 379 ; cf. i. pp. 449, 548.

is regarded as a vision of something externally existent. Similarly, there is nothing like that clear-cut line which is often drawn to-day between the natural and the supernatural ; there is no conception of ' Nature ' as an entity, with laws of its own in contrast with ' supernatural ' interferences with those laws ; the whole environment consists partly of the visible and partly of the invisible, and the practical distinction is that between the usual and the unusual. The result of these conditions is that something *we* might explain as a purely natural phenomenon may be taken as the revelation or manifestation of some power of the mysterious world, and may become the starting-point of religious belief or practice.

The beliefs of Semitic nomads, in ancient and in modern times, suggest four principal ways in which the ' spiritual ' powers of their environment were conceived to approach men, and to influence their lives. (1) A man's attention might be drawn to something peculiar or unusual in his immediate surroundings, *e.g.* a desert mirage, or a rustling tree.[1] (2) Good or bad fortune, especially as concentrated in some particular event, might be ascribed to spirit interference.[2] (3) An ancient worshipper was generally very definite in his petitions ; he wanted practical guidance and help, and expected some sign or token as the response of the spirit-world to his questions.[3] (4) Any

---

[1] Thus an Arab of the Moabite country was frightened at sight of a group of horsemen ; when he saw the mirage effect vanish, he ascribed the vision to a demon (Jaussen, *Coutumes des Arabes*, p. 322). A holy man at Nebk claimed to have seen a sacred walnut-tree in flames near a shrine (Curtiss, *Primitive Semitic Religion*, p. 93)—probably like the burning bush of Moses, an appearance due to some electrical phenomenon (Robertson Smith, *Rel. Sem.*, p. 194). Doughty slept once in a ruin supposed to be haunted by jinns, or spirits, and traced the belief to the waving branches of a palm in the orchard near (*Ar. Des.*, ii. p. 3).

[2] An absent-minded rider passed a sacred tomb near Ter'in without saluting it, and within half an hour was thrown from his horse and broke his leg ; he rapidly recovered, however, when a she-goat was sacrificed at the tomb (Jaussen, *op. cit.*, p. 299).

[3] A favourite form amongst the ancient Arabs was the casting of lots by blunt arrows ; these signified ' yes ' and ' no ', in connection with sacrifice before an idol (Wellhausen, *Reste*, p. 133). Holy wells gave oracles, as at

peculiar physical or psychical state of personal life could be ascribed to an invasive spirit or demon. In ancient Arabia the ' jinns ' were made responsible for everything abnormal, but especially for madness, passion, the inspiration of seer, poet, or musician.[1]

The general influence of Semitic animism upon the religion of Israel has already been noticed.[2] These four ways of conceiving the contact of the spirit-world with human life are all represented in the Old Testament, but they are appropriated for Yahweh alone, who draws near to man ' by dream, by oracle, or seer ', and by His control of the fortunes of a nation or an individual. The entrance of Yahweh into human life, as conceived by the earlier religion of Israel, is made through (a) theophanies, *i.e.* appearances of Yahweh ; (b) miracles ; (c) various forms of oracle ; (d) the abnormal physical and psychical states explained by reference to the Spirit of Yahweh. These, it will be seen, correspond to the four ways indicated for the Semites in general. In connection with the last of them, when transformed by a growing sense of morality, there appears that peculiar and distinctive feature of Israel's religion, the prophetic consciousness. Finally, the message of Yahweh through the living voice is replaced by that through the written word, which is itself, in large measure, a secondary product of the prophetic consciousness and of the priestly oracle.

1. *Early Manifestations of Yahweh*

(a) The theophanies recorded in the Old Testament are of two principal types, according as the media of mani-

Aphaca, by the sinking or casting forth of the gift (*Rel. Sem.*, p. 178). After sacrifice at a sacred tree, a modern Arab who is sick will sleep beneath it, in faith that the spirit will come to him and, in a dream, tell him how to get well (*Ar. Des.*, i. p. 449).

[1] Wellhausen. *op. cit.*, p. 156. Doughty was often expected to show his skill as a physician by binding and casting out ehe jinns causing sickness (*Ar. Des.*, i. p. 548).

[2] Chap. ii. § 3.

festation are supplied by natural phenomena or by the human form.[1] In the former class, the dominating idea is that which brings Yahweh into special relation with storm-phenomena. This has led to the belief that Yahweh was originally, in pre-Mosaic times, a storm-god. There is no question that Hebrew thought interpreted the thunder-storm as an avenue of approach peculiarly appropriate to Yahweh. The Law was given on Sinai to the accompaniment of ' thunders and lightnings and a thick cloud upon the mount ', and it was in the calm after a thunder-storm that Elijah heard God there.[2] When Yahweh came from the south to help His people on the Great Plain, ' the earth trembled, the heavens also dropped, yea, the clouds dropped water '.[3] The thunder is the ' voice ' of Yahweh ; the lightnings are His arrows and glittering spear ; the original suggestion of the rainbow was that Yahweh had laid aside His battle-bow.[4] Samuel offers and obtains thunder and rain in harvest-time as a token from Yahweh.[5] Prophets describe the judgment of Yahweh against His enemies as accomplished through the storm : ' Yahweh shall cause His glorious voice to be heard, and shall show the lighting down of His arm, with the indignation of His anger, and the flame of a devouring fire, with a blast, and tempest, and hailstones '.[6] The cherubim and seraphim are mythological figures apparently derived from the thunder-cloud chariot of Yahweh, and from His serpent-like lightning. Yahweh is also manifested by the phenomena of fire in general, as by the stove vomiting smoke and flame that passed between the pieces of Abram's sacrifice, the burning bush seen by Moses, the pillar of cloud-shrouded fire that led the Israelites, the cloud that filled the temple of Solomon.[7] Similarly, in the later

[1] See Additional Notes. [2] Ex. xix. 16 ; 1 Kings xix. 11, 12.
[3] Jud. v. 4 ; cf. the storm-theophany of Ps. xviii.
[4] Ps. xxix.; Hab. iii. 11 ; Gen. ix. 13 (P). See J. Skinner, *Genesis* (I.C.C.), p. 173. [5] 1 Sam. xii. 17, 18 ; cf. 1 Kings xviii. 44. [6] Is. xxx. 30.
[7] Gen. xv. 17 ; Ex. iii. 2, xiii. 21, 22 ; 1 Kings viii. 10.

literature, the 'glory' of Yahweh is often a fiery appearance ; [1] beyond the limits of the Old Testament it becomes the 'Shechinah', the Light of God's presence.[2]

The second type of Old Testament theophany is afforded by 'the angel of Yahweh'. This remarkable figure, who appears in the earlier narratives, is not to be confused with any of the later 'angels'. They are clearly distinguished from Yahweh, and subordinated to Him, but this theophanic figure is frequently identified with Yahweh, as when 'the angel of God' says to Jacob, 'I am the God of Bethel'.[3]   At other times, probably representing a somewhat later stage of thought, there is a measure of distinction from Yahweh, as in the case of the 'angel' sent from Sinai to be Israel's guide to Canaan, and Yahweh's representative.   Yet, even in this case, Yahweh is present in His 'messenger', for it is said, 'My name is in him'.[4] Thus, the 'angel of Yahweh' may be described as 'an occasional manifestation of Yahwè in human form, possessing no distinct and permanent personality but speaking and spoken of, at times as Yahwè Himself . . . at times as distinct from Him '.[5] The figure of this 'angel' marks the growing recognition of the truth that the vision of God Himself is too terrible for human eyes : 'man shall not see me and live'.[6]   But we must not fall into the error of tracing this to any metaphysical ground. It is not actually impossible to see God in realistic fashion, for, as an exceptional case, it is recorded that Moses and others saw the God of Israel, without His hand being laid upon them.[7]   Such a story as that of Jacob's struggle

---

[1] Ezek. i. 4, x. 4, etc. ; Ex. xxiv. 17 (P).

[2] See G. F. Moore, *Judaism*, I. pp. 434 ff., and compare Dante's symbolism in *Par.* xxxiii. 115 f.

[3] Gen. xxxi. 11, 13. 'In all the old accounts of such appearances the *mal'ak* is, first or last, identified with the deity' (Moore, *Judges*, p. 183).

[4] Ex. xxiii. 21 ; cf. Is. xxx. 27. The conception of the 'name' as a partial manifestation of the personality is frequent in primitive thought ; the goddess Astarte is called the 'Name of Baal'. See Additional Notes.

[5] Gray, *E. Bi.*, col. 5035.

[6] Ex. xxxiii. 20.

[7] Ex. xxiv. 9 f.

with God at Peniel is full of the deepest moral and spiritual
suggestiveness for the modern mind.   But we can hardly
exaggerate the crude realism of its original meaning, and
of the words, ' I have seen God face to face, and my life
is preserved '.[1]

(b) A miracle for the Hebrew mind is what its etymology
ought to imply to us ; it is simply ' something wonderful '
from the standpoint of the observer, not by comparison
with any established natural order existing in quasi-
independence of God.   ' Every event in Nature is looked
at merely as a single act of God's free will, rain and sun-
shine as well as earthquake and prodigy '.[2]   Accordingly,
what the Hebrew mind regards as a miracle [3]—a wonderful manifestation of the divine presence—may or may not
be a miracle according to the popular meaning of the
word to-day.   The Hebrew could regard the drowning
of the Egyptians in the Red Sea and the speaking of
Balaam's ass as both miracles ; whereas the first would
ordinarily be explained to-day as a ' natural ' event due
to meteorological causes, and the second as a piece of un-
natural folk-lore.   The fact is, that we apply to all events
a standard which did not exist for the Hebrew—the
standard of an established natural order, which by no
means excludes what is ordinarily called the miraculous,
when this is understood to be the manifestation of a not
less established spiritual order.   It should be noted that
' miracles ', in the Old Testament, are not confined to
Yahweh and Yahweh's servants,[4] and that the mere
ability to work a miracle is not held to prove prophetic

---

[1] Gen. xxxii. 30. See Additional Notes.

[2] Schultz, *Old Testament Theology*, E.T., ii. p. 192.

[3] The word ' miracle' is not used in the R.V., but in the A.V. it trans-
lates three Hebrew terms, viz. *niphlā'ōth* (wonderful acts, Jud. vi. 13),
mōphēth (a portent or extraordinary event, Ex. vii. 9), and *'ōth*, 'a *sign*, *i.e.*
something, ordinary (Ex. xii. 13, xxxi. 13 ; Is. xx. 3, etc.) or extraordinary,
as the case may be, regarded as significant of a truth beyond itself, or
impressed with a Divine purpose' (Driver, *Deuteronomy*, on iv. 34).

[4] Cf. those of the Egyptian magicians (Ex. vii. 11, 12) ; note, also, those of
the opponents of Jesus (Luke xi. 19

inspiration and veracity.[1]   On the other hand, even so
spiritual a prophet as Isaiah is so confident of the immediate support of Yahweh as to offer to Ahaz any sign the
king may choose in confirmation of the prophet's word.[2]
To the prophets, indeed, the whole history of Israel is a
continuous miracle, though particular events stand out
from the rest because of their striking nature, or peculiar
significance.

(c) The simplest form of oracular guidance is illustrated
by the sign asked by Eliezer as an indication of the divinely
appointed wife for Isaac ; she is to be the maiden who offers
drink for his camels as well as for himself.[3]   Or the sign
may be something abnormal, such as the condition of
Gideon's fleece.[4]   Peculiar means of divination were
employed in early times, such as the divining-cup of
Joseph,[5] the resort of Saul to the spirit of Samuel,[6] the
sound of the wind in trees,[7] etc.   In the Deuteronomic
reformation, however, the official use by the priests of
the sacred lot, known as the Urim and Thummim, survived to the exclusion of all other methods of obtaining
guidance from the spiritual world.[8]   The nature of this
practice is best illustrated by the Greek version of 1 Samuel
xiv. 41, which here preserves the original of the now
mutilated Hebrew text : ' And Saul said, Yahweh, God
of Israel, why hast Thou not answered Thy servant to-day ?
is the wrong in me or in Jonathan my son ?   Yahweh,
God of Israel, give Urim ; and if thus Thou say, give to
Thy people Israel, give Thummim '.   This shows that the
oracle simply settled the alternatives which were put
before it.   The Urim and Thummin are employed in
connection with the ephod, which is usually understood

---

[1] Deut. xiii. 1 f.   [2] Is. vii. 11.
[3] Gen. xxiv. 12 f. ; cf. 1 Sam. xiv. 10 f.   Even a chance word might yield
an omen (1 Kings xx. 33, R.V. mar.).
[4] Jud. vi. 36-40.   [5] Gen. xliv. 5, 15.
[6] 1 Sam. xxviii. 7 f.   [7] 2 Sam. v. 24.
[8] Deut. xviii. 10, 11.

to be some form of image of Yahweh ;[1] appeal to this
kind of oracle is frequent in the early period, but was not
available at the Return,[2] and cannot be proved for the
post-exilic period. To this or some similar method of
casting lots, either at a sanctuary or in some solemn ritual,
are to be referred various other instances of resort to an
oracle of Yahweh in connection with the guidance of
military movements, the selection of a king, discovery of
the cause of a famine.[3] Parallel with this official use of
the sacred lot, we have also to remember the frequent
cases in which dreams are made the channel of some
divine communication, especially in connection with a
sanctuary.[4] It was a widespread ancient practice to sleep
in some holy place or temple, and to regard any dream
that came as a divine revelation. On many occasions
Yahweh is said to have revealed Himself or His purposes
in dreams, as when He warns Laban and Abimelech, or
foretells the future to Pharaoh and to Joseph, or calls
Samuel, or encourages Gideon through the dream of the
Midianite.[5] The psychological conditions of dreaming—
the passivity of the sleeper, the disregard of temporal
and spatial limitations, the unconscious reproduction of
the dreamer's own thoughts as though spoken by another,
and in some cases the actual intensification of psychical
activity in dream-states—have made dreams a favourite
channel of revelation amongst many peoples. The most
vivid account of the dream-state as revelation is that
given by Eliphaz in the Book of Job (iv. 13 f.) :

> ' In thoughts from the visions of the night,
>   When deep sleep falleth on men,

---

[1] See Additional Notes.
[2] Ezra, ii. 63. A keen sense of loss in post-exilic days is reflected in the
Rabbinic tradition that five things were missing from the second Temple—
Ark, Urim and Thummim, the Fire from heaven, the Shechinah and the
Holy Spirit.   [3] Jud. i., cf. xviii. 5, 6 ; 1 Sam. x. 22 ; 2 Sam. xxi.
[4] 1 Kings iii. 5, ix. 2 ; cf. Gen. xxviii. 12.
[5] Gen. xxxi. 24, xx. 3 f., xli. 1 f., xxxvii. 5-10 ; 1 Sam. iii. 3 f. ; Jud. vii.
13 f.

Fear came upon me and trembling,
Which made all my bones to shake.
Then a breath passed over my face;
The hair of my flesh stood up.
It stood still, but I could not discern the appearance thereof;
A form was before mine eyes:
There was silence, and I heard a voice'.

(d) In regard to the early ideas of the Spirit of God, the Christian suggestions of moral and spiritual meaning must not be read into a phenomenon which was more or less physically conceived. The ancient Hebrew, like the nomadic Arab of ancient and modern times, ascribed to an invasive spirit those phenomena of human personality which he could not otherwise explain. But, in the Old Testament, all these influences from without which act on man are more or less subordinated to Yahweh, the ultimately supreme power in Hebrew experience. Just as the mysterious 'wind' is one of His instruments, so the 'spirit' is another. Both are denoted by the same word in Hebrew, for both are energies much akin in their effects, especially to those who have not learnt to distinguish clearly between the physical and the psychical worlds. A man who is influenced by angry excitement, by mad impulses, by ecstatic tendencies, usually shows his psychical condition by his physical state, as by panting, gasping, etc. The Hebrew seems in this way to have connected the 'blowing' of the wind without, and the 'blowing' of the wind-like spirit within. Consequently, the Hebrew referred to the direct action of the Spirit of God the passionate indignation through which Saul roused Israel against the Ammonites, the superhuman strength by which Samson tore a young lion to pieces with his hands, the trumpet-note of Gideon against the Midianites and Amalekites.[1]   The transitory madness of Saul is ascribed to 'an evil spirit from Yahweh'.[2]   Similarly,

[1] 1 Sam. xi. 6; Jud. xiv. 6, vi. 34.   [2] 1 Sam. xvi. 14.

the ecstatic conditions of early 'prophecy', the abnormal state in which the early prophet chanted his message, is traced to the Spirit of Yahweh, as we see in the narrative of Saul's meeting with the wandering band of these prophets;[1] he caught the contagion of their influence, and displayed the same physical and psychical excitement. In process of time, anything remarkable in a man's conduct or ability, quite apart from the exhibition of passionate excitement, comes to be traced to the Spirit of God. Joseph is described as 'a man in whom the Spirit of God is', apparently with reference to his skill in the interpretation of dreams; the spirit of wisdom in Joshua is mediated through the laying on of the hands of Moses; whilst, in post-exilic writings, even the remarkable skill of an artificer is thought to be the result of inspiration.[2] Thus, by the time of Ezekiel, we find the idea of the Spirit of God applied to ethical and spiritual characteristics, in accordance with the new idea of the divine character. Not only does Ezekiel think of the nation as brought to life again from its valley of dry bones, but he looks for supernatural aid in the creation of a new character within those who shall live as Yahweh requires; this character he ascribes to the Spirit of God.[3] But such ideas were not attained in the earlier period, during which the Spirit of God is a quasi-material energy producing results in human lives that have nothing essentially ethical or religious in their content. How materialistic this conception is may be seen from the narrative which describes the transference to the seventy elders of a portion of the Spirit given to Moses, or from the prayer of Elisha for an eldest son's portion of Elijah's spirit.[4]

In this review of the four principal ways in which Yahweh is conceived to approach man in the pre-prophetic religion

[1] 1 Sam. x. 5 f.; cf. xix. 20 f.
[2] Gen. xli. 38 ; Deut. xxxiv. 9 ; Ex. xxviii. 3.
[3] xi. 19, xxxvi. 26, xxxix. 29.   [4] Num. xi. 25 ; 2 Kings ii. 9, 15.

of Israel, their distinct limitations, as media of revelation, have been made apparent. Theophanies in the human form belong to the more naïve anthropomorphism which was eventually left behind; in the form of natural phenomena they were inadequate to the advancing needs of the religion. A 'miracle' would reveal much or little according to its interpretation; however wonderful its circumstances, a prophet was needed to point its moral. Oracles might give practical guidance, but their scope was obviously limited, and they easily became, in their chief forms, mere weapons of the hierarchy. The idea of the Spirit of Yahweh does not, in its earlier history, rise essentially above the level of Semitic animism. So far, there is nothing commensurate with the unique power of Israel's religion, and with the wealth of the content of its revelation of God. On the other hand, there were possibilities even in these ways of conceiving His approach which were destined to become actualities when employed in the service of higher ideas, and especially when supplemented by a new and incomparably greater channel of communication. That new channel is the prophetic consciousness, in the higher meaning of the term—rising above the ecstatic frenzy and ravings of abnormal psychical states, into the sane, steady, moral consciousness of God, and the confidence that through moral fellowship with Him He gives His divine message. The material medium is largely replaced by a spiritual; the indirect relationship by one that is direct, and independent of artificial stimulus.[1] A vast new range of possibility was thrown open, and the older means fell into a subordinate place. Theophany and occasional miracle were replaced by a vision of history as the revelation of God; oracles and ecstasies became inadequate to hold the message God might send by the whole mental, moral, religious consciousness of a prophet. The greatness of the change is

[1] Contrast Elisha's dependence on the minstrel in 2 Kings iii. 15.

shown by the passage in Deuteronomy [1] which contrasts the augury and divination of other nations (to which the earlier ideas of Israel are so closely related) with revelation through a line of prophets, following in the footsteps of Moses, and giving reality to the ideals ascribed to his traditional personality.

2. *The Prophetic Consciousness*

The cardinal fact of the prophetic consciousness, as it is displayed in Amos and his great successors, is the absolute conviction of a divine call, mission, and message. This conviction is expressed in the reiterated formula of introduction to what is said, *i.e.* 'Thus saith Yahweh', or the equivalent 'Utterance of Yahweh'. The prophet is convinced that he stands in the council of Yahweh, and that Yahweh will do nothing, but He revealeth His secret unto His servants the prophets.[2] By fidelity to the highest truths, the prophet becomes the mouth of Yahweh,[3] and this conception is well illustrated in the account of the relation in which Aaron stands to Moses : ' he shall be thy spokesman unto the people ; and it shall come to pass, that he shall be to thee a mouth, and thou shalt be to him as God. . . . I have made thee a god to Pharaoh : and Aaron thy brother shall be thy prophet '.[4] Such language gives no warrant for a mechanical theory of inspiration. Just as, for Hebrew psychology, independent qualities, psychical and moral, belonged to the different physical organs, such as the mouth, so there was a real contribution to the divine message made by the prophet himself as the 'mouth' of God.[5] This, indeed, needs no demonstration to any one who approaches the prophetic writings without a preconceived theory. The message of

---

[1] xviii. 14, 15.   [2] Jer. xxiii. 18 ; Amos iii. 7.
[3] Jer. xv. 19 : ' if thou take forth the precious from the vile, thou shalt be as my mouth '.
[4] Ex. iv. 16, vii. 1.   [5] See Additional Notes.

each is as distinct and as characteristic as are the circumstances of his call. Both in the language and in the thought the human agent is visible. In what way, then, are we to conceive that approach of God to the prophet which constituted him what he claimed to be, the spokesman of God ?

Three contributory elements may be traced in the working of the prophetic consciousness. (1) Fellowship with God and sympathy with man, such as belong to the prophets of Israel, imply a remarkable development of moral and spiritual character. (2) The origin and literary records of Hebrew prophecy point to more or less abnormal psychical experience as its frequent, if not universal, accompaniment. (3) The prophet's own explanation of his experience was necessarily drawn from a psychology differing from our own in certain important features. Of these three factors, the first would be admitted by all. The contents of the great prophetic books have passed into current coin in the realm of morality and religion ; it is obvious that the men through whom these classical conceptions were created must have been men under the influence of the ideals they present, and of the demands they make. It is not less clear, especially in the case of those prophets in whom the emotional life finds fullest expression, such as Hosea and Jeremiah, that they felt the profoundest sympathy with the nation to which they belonged, even in the midst of their denunciation of its conduct. Thus the prophet became an effective link between God and Israel ; the current of divine revelation flowed because there was contact at both ends, and that contact was provided by a personal character conspicuous for obedience to God and for sympathy with man. The first and most important feature, therefore, in the prophetic consciousness consisted in the possession to an eminent degree of the same qualities and characteristics as, in all ages, underlie communion with God and service to men.

The presence of the second element, abnormal psychical characteristics, is much more open to controversy, and can easily be misrepresented. The prophets who so profoundly transformed the religion of Israel and of the world were assuredly not men of unbalanced mind. But certain features of the prophetic writings do seem to point to an intensity of psychical experience, and therefore of temperament, which distinguishes the prophets generally from other men. There is the remarkable sense of an *external* compulsion, felt from the ' call ' onwards, often urging the prophet to that from which he naturally shrinks —a compulsion psychologically due, no doubt, to the vivid imagination by which ideas in the prophet's mind acquired objective reality, independent of the prophet's own personality. ' The Lord Yahweh hath spoken ', says Amos, 'who can but prophesy ? ' [1] Isaiah writes, ' Yahweh spake thus to me *with strength of hand* '.[2] Jeremiah describes the divine message as ' a burning fire ' within him, which is irresistible.[3] On the other hand, the message sought is sometimes withheld.[4] Further, in the case of Isaiah, Jeremiah, and Ezekiel,[5] their call to ministry takes the form of a vision, their account of which seems to be more than a device of exposition. Some of the prophets, *e.g.* Amos and Zechariah,[6] give part of their message in the form of sights actually presented to the eye : ' Thus the Lord Yahweh showed me ', or ' I saw in the night '. It is less easy to show that the prophets believed they heard external voices. But when we remember such experiences as are described by Augustine and Bunyan,[7] experiences even occurring to-day, in moments of intense feeling, we can well believe that the prophets mean much more by such a phrase as ' The voice of one saying, Cry ',[8] than a dramatic figure of speech, and that

---

[1] iii. 8.   [2] viii. 11.   [3] xx. 9.
[4] Hab. ii. 1 ; Jer. xlii. 7.   [5] Is. vi. ; Jer. i. ; Ez. i.-iii.
[6] Amos vii.-ix.; Zech. i. 7 f.
[7] *Confessions*, viii. 12; *Grace Abounding*, §§ 22, 174, etc.   [8] Is. xl. 3.

the passionate dialogues between Jeremiah and Yahweh are not simply a literary fiction. The act of Isaiah in 'walking naked and barefoot three years for a sign and a portent'[1] suggests a close parallel in the case of George Fox, who put off his shoes outside Lichfield at the Lord's command, and saw channels of blood in the streets through which he went to cry 'Woe to the bloody city of Lichfield!'[2] The abnormal psychosis is surely present in both cases. Further, in the case of Ezekiel, physical phenomena are described that bear some resemblance, at least, to catalepsy: he remains dumb for seven days after his call; he is to lie in one position for a lengthy period; he is conscious of being transported from Babylon to Jerusalem, that he might describe to the elders what he has seen in the temple, apparently during a trance-state.[3] Such phenomena as these, of course, no more discredit the inner worth of the prophetic ideas than the eccentricities of genius in other realms discredit its own high achievements. But they do suggest that the prophet was usually distinguished from other men by a peculiar psychical development. These abnormal features must not be exaggerated. In the historical result, they are, of course, a quite negligible feature. But they help to explain the status of the prophet for the common people, and the prophet's own conviction that he was set apart from other men. This conclusion finds some measure of confirmation in the links that connect the prophecy of the eighth century with that earlier ecstatic prophesying ascribed to the Spirit of Yahweh. Psychopathic features in the earlier prophets are unmistakable, as when the madness of Saul is described by the same word as that

[1] Is. xx. 2, 3.   [2] *Journal*,[8] i. p. 78.
[3] Ez. iii. 14, 15; iv. 4; viii.-xi.   Cf. Is. xxi. 1-10 (Gray's translation, *Comm.*, pp. 348 f.) for an example of dual personality (verse 6) in the prophetic consciousness.   The Arabic *kahin*, or 'seer', was believed to have an indwelling demon, who addressed the seer as 'thou' (Wellhausen, *Reste*, p. 135).   See also Additional Notes.

used for prophesying,[1] or as when he is said to have been infected by the contagious influence of the prophets at Ramah : ' And *he* also stripped off his clothes, and *he* also prophesied before Samuel, and lay down naked all that day and all that night '.[2] The difference between the earlier and later phases of prophecy in Israel is that the abnormal was driven from the centre to the circumference,[3] and subordinated to that moral and spiritual message which became the prophet's dominating interest.

The third contribution to the prophetic consciousness results from the characteristics of Hebrew psychology, in particular from its idea of the Spirit of God. It is clear that a prophet's conception of his own personality, and of its relation to God, must have profoundly affected his interpretation of religious experience. A modern believer in telepathy is ready to explain a given fact of consciousness, especially if it is of a striking nature, as due to the action of mind other than his own. But this accessibility to influences other than those acting through the ordinary sense-organs was universally recognised by the Hebrews.[4] The Hebrew doctrine of the Spirit of God, in fact, springs from the attribution of all such external influences to Yahweh as their source. Anything abnormal in the psychical life would instinctively be referred to Him, and dissociated from the prophet's own personality. Indeed, one natural consequence of the prophet's ' call ' would be that even quite normal elements of his subsequent consciousness could be regarded as messages of Yahweh.[5] Some of the details of Hebrew psychology must have contributed to this conviction. We have already seen that the Hebrew did not think of himself

---

[1] 1 Sam. xviii. 10.   [2] 1 Sam. xix. 24.
[3] Cf. Sellin, *Die alttest. Religion*, p. 75.   [4] See chap. iv. § 1.
[5] It may be the earlier ' ecstatic ' prophesying of ' men of the Spirit ' which prevents the eighth-century prophets from directly ascribing their inspiration to the 'Spirit' of God. But the idea is really implicit in their claim to prophesy, and it reappears explicitly in later prophets, *e.g.* Ezekiel.

as a soul within a body, still less as a personality with different levels of consciousness. The unity of his personality lay for him in the harmonious working of a number of organs, each with its own powers[1]; his life ended when the co-operation ceased, as it did at death. But not less did his own psychical life seem temporarily to end, whenever one of his organs functioned in quasi-independence of his volition; for the time being, some external power had taken possession of it, some external influence was acting upon it. Thus, experiences which a modern mind would ascribe to illusions of the senses, or dual personality, or some other subjective phenomenon, would naturally be interpreted as direct and unmistakable communications from Yahweh.[2] Given, then, the two features of the prophetic consciousness already indicated —the moral and spiritual character, and the sign and seal of some abnormal psychical experience—the general psychological atmosphere of the age enables us to understand the prophet's 'Thus saith Yahweh', so far as it can be understood on a purely scientific and historical level of inquiry. But such an analysis of the prophetic consciousness relates only to the subjective origin, not to the objective value, of revelation. It professes to do no more than to show how the prophet of Israel could believe in all sincerity that the convictions of his own heart were really a message of God to His people. The fact that a modern mind would explain the origin of such convictions, and their psychical accompaniments, in a different way, by no means serves to invalidate the truth of this belief. Psychological analysis of the prophetic consciousness, however successful, simply brings us to the threshold of the great philosophical problem—the relation of human personality to the divine. Religious experience rests

[1] See Additional Notes.
[2] A good example of it is seen in the supernatural character assigned to dreams (Deut. xiii. 1 f.; 1 Sam. xxvii. 6, 15; Joel ii. 28; Num. xii, 6 f.). The general tendency is common to ancient psychology in general.

on the assurance that the relation is of such a kind that man can enjoy the fellowship of God, and that God draws near to man, in order to make that fellowship possible. The prophetic consciousness is ultimately a peculiar variety of religious experience, dedicated to great ends, and having great historic results. But the crowning mystery of personality, human and divine, always remains at the centre of this experience, and evades our analysis.

The immediate work of the great prophets was the interpretation of Israel's history. Under the guidance of Israel's God, the prophet found himself brought to a vision of Israel's history, past, present, or future, which dominated his thought and shaped his message. The course of events visible to all was the handwriting of Yahweh, which it was the prophet's task to explain to his fellow-countrymen. The ultimate test of prophecy was its conformity with actual history. To this confirmation one of the later prophets appeals, when he says, ' My words and my statutes, which I commanded my servants the prophets, did they not overtake your fathers ? ' [1] The confident assertions of the prophets in regard to current events would be inexplicable, had they not felt that they possessed the divine secret of history, the knowledge of the principles on which Yahweh administered the government of the world. They would all of them have been prepared to stand or fall by the ultimate agreement of their utterances with Yahweh's judgments. But mere agreement between a prophetic utterance and external happenings was not accepted as proof in itself that the speaker of the prophecy was a genuine man of God. Already in the Book of Deuteronomy there is reference to a further test, which springs from the intrinsic character of true prophecy, as being always consistent with the revelation given in the past. ' If there arise in the midst of thee a prophet, or a dreamer

[1] Zech. i. 6.

I

of dreams, and he give thee a sign or a wonder, and the sign or wonder come to pass, whereof he spake unto thee, saying, Let us go after other gods, which thou hast not known, and let us serve them; thou shalt not hearken unto the words of that prophet, or unto that dreamer of dreams: for Yahweh your God proveth you '.[1] This is a logical deduction from faith in God, for the revelation He gives will necessarily be self-consistent. The difference between the recognised prophets of the Old Testament and those who are called 'false' is due to something more than a mere 'survival of the fittest', judged by the successful anticipation of events. There exists in the minds of those prophets we call true the conviction of an intrinsic difference between their own testimony and that which they condemn, a difference which events will confirm, not create. When the 'false' prophets foretell a prosperous campaign for Ahab and Jehoshaphat, Micaiah at first mockingly echoes them. But, adjured to speak in the name of Yahweh, he declares his vision of a kingless army, and explains the prophecies of success as due to the inspiration of a lying spirit commissioned by Yahweh to entice Ahab.[2] Micaiah is ready to stand or fall by the result of the campaign: 'If thou return at all in peace, Yahweh hath not spoken by me'. But it is not less clear that his declared conviction, 'Yahweh hath spoken evil concerning thee', springs from his personal judgment of Ahab's character and policy, not, as does theirs, from the mere desire to please the king. The presence of more than a merely external criterion of prophetic truth is equally apparent in the story of Jeremiah's encounter with the prophet Hananiah. Jeremiah meets with suspicion this man's prophecy of the breaking of the Babylonian yoke within two years.

[1] Deut. xiii. 1-3. But disagreement with the event is held to disprove the alleged prophecy (Deut. xviii. 21, 22).
[2] 1 Kings xxii. 1-28. The objectivity of their inspiration, it should be noted, is allowed by Micaiah.

His suspicion is based on the continuity of warning in the prophets who have preceded him. Time must show, he says, whether a prophecy of peace will be confirmed. But, after this interview, Jeremiah receives a divine revelation which enables him to encounter Hananiah with a definite denial of the truth of his words. ' Yahweh hath not sent thee ; but thou makest this people to trust in a lie '.[1] This narrative not only illustrates the idea indicated in the Book of Deuteronomy, that there is a certain self-consistency in genuine revelation, but also the presence of a common moral judgment in the prophets as a whole, prior to Jeremiah, by which they condemned the spirit of their times, and declared its penalty. In this sense the pre-exilic prophets were pessimists, but moral pessimism is preferable to immoral optimism. The time was not yet ripe for a true prophet to say that Israel had received of Yahweh's hand double for all her sins. When that time did come, Deutero-Isaiah was not less convinced, whilst saying it, that ' he stood in organic relationship with earlier prediction '.[2] The claim is justified, if the predictive element in Hebrew prophecy is a product of the moral and spiritual insight of the prophets, which draws different consequences for different generations. They could foretell the future with general, if not with detailed accuracy, because they were admitted to the council of Yahweh; their ears were trained to catch, in the music of the universe, the moral harmonies, the discords, and the resolutions into triumphant chords. They had surrendered their hearts to the moral principles according to which God governs the world. To their passionate confidence in the victory of right and the overthrow of wrong, the Day of Yahweh seemed always at the gates, and the final consummation already begin-

[1] Jer. xxviii. 15. Cf. Gressmann, *Der Ursprung der isr.-jüd. Eschatologie*, p. 154.
[2] Duhm, *Jeremia*, p. 225. Cf., *e.g.*, Is. xliv. 7, 8 : ' who, as I, shall call, and shall declare it ? . . . have I not declared unto thee of old, and showed it ?

ning. The problems of divine government were sometimes more complex than their simple principle of retribution allowed, as the spiritual agony of Job was to demonstrate. But, like him, they built their faith on inner conviction, rather than on outward event. The true prophet looks for confirmation and final justification on the arena of history, as the true artist may look for the world's ultimate approval of his work. But both prophet and artist have learnt to look beyond the changing processes of time into the unchanging realms of truth and beauty, which time exists to serve.

The religion of the prophetic consciousness must always have been the exception rather than the rule. The prophetic literature is itself evidence of the prophets' failure to raise their nation to their own high level. The change from oral to written prophecy, which practically begins in the eighth century, seems to have been due to the failure of the prophets to shape national thought and conscience to their high ideals. This is indicated clearly enough by the prophets themselves. Isaiah is bidden take a great tablet and write upon it with the pen of a man the symbolical name of his son as a testimony to the future ; one of his prophecies he is ordered to inscribe in a book, that it may be a perpetual witness to a later age.[1] Only after twenty-two years of oral prophecy is Jeremiah bidden to write on a roll the messages he has delivered throughout the whole time to his fellow-countrymen, ' that they may return every man from his evil way'.[2] It is in harmony with Israel's spiritual mission, and with the Cross which was its supreme achievement, that its greatest literary product was the offspring of defeat. Nations, like individuals, have great creative epochs. Thought and feeling are usually sublimated to their

---

[1] Is. viii. 1, xxx. 8 (R.V. *mar.*); cf. also viii. 16, though the terms in this case may be figurative.
[2] Jer. xxxvi. 1 f.

highest possibilities through national victories, expanding horizons, the exalted vision of great destinies. The golden age of a literature is thus the age of Pericles, Augustus, Elizabeth. But the golden age of Israel's literature, the period to which we owe the great prophetic records, did not fall during the national ascendancy under David and Solomon. It was thrown into relief by the dark background of Assyrian and Babylonian empire, and the prophets who occupy its foreground were men who carried the cross of lonely obedience to a Calvary of apparent failure.

3. *The Written Word*

The Scriptures of the Old Testament have gained a unique authority over both Jew and Christian as being the Word of God, the disclosure of the divine nature and will through self-revealing grace. This canonical authority, whether recognised or rejected, must be clearly distinguished from the intrinsic character of the literature. The history of Old Testament literature begins in the twelfth century, but that of the Canon in the seventh.[1] It was in the year 621 B.C. that, for the first time, a portion of the literature of the Old Testament acquired a recognised public place as a divine revelation. This was the central part of the present Book of Deuteronomy. The second step in the formation of the Canon was taken in 444 B.C.,[2] when the Law-book brought by the scribe Ezra from Babylon was solemnly accepted by the new community as its divinely ordained basis. This seems to have been what is known as the Priestly Code, of which the Book of Leviticus may be taken as representative. Within a century of their acceptance, *i.e.* by about

[1] For an account of the literature prior to the beginnings of the Canon (songs, laws, histories, prophecies), see A. Bentzen, *Introduction to the Old Testament*, Vol. 1, pp. 102 ff.

[2] Or nearly half a century later, see p. 5, n. 1.

350 B.C.,[1] this Law-book was combined with the already canonised Book of Deuteronomy, and with other not yet canonised literature of still earlier date, dealing with Israel's origins, to form the Pentateuch, or, to use the Jewish name, the Law.[2] This is the basis of Judaism. No other part of the Old Testament ever equalled the Law in authority, though prophetic writings (with certain histories) were collected by about 200 B.C., to form a second part of the Canon, and the remainder of the present Old Testament shortly before the rise of the New, to form a third part, known as the ' Writings '.

From this outline of the history of the Canon, it is apparent that the priest, rather than the prophet, was the actual centre around which the *authoritative* Scriptures gathered. This is partly explained by the fact that the priestly oracle was a source of divine revelation from the earliest days, and that the established ceremonial of religion aroused continuous reverence cumulatively greater than that inspired by any single prophet. Yet the prophet contributed very materially to the creation of the Law. In the Book of Deuteronomy, the old priestly law and the new prophetic teaching have mingled their strongly contrasted influences to work together for the reformation of Israel's religion. This seventh-century work could not have been so shaped but for the prophetic teaching of the century before it ; but neither would there have been material to shape, nor the motive to ascribe it to Moses, but for the immemorial law and ritual which

[1] The Samaritan and Hebrew Pentateuchs practically agree, and the final separation of the two peoples is usually supposed to have taken place towards the middle of the fourth century. Josephus places it about 330, and the Elephantine Papyri suggest that in 408 there was no Samaritan high priest. On the Samaritan Pentateuch see B. J. Roberts, *The Old Testament Texts and Versions*, 1951 and R. H. Pfeiffer *op. cit.*, pp 101-104.

[2] The successive Codes which constitute it were originally meant to *replace* each other, so that the inconsistencies apparent to us were hardly felt, especially as few could have access to the written documents. When the combination of the Codes was ultimately made, each possessed authority, and editorial revision sufficiently disguised the differences.

centred round Solomon's Temple. Priest and prophet
met again in the person of Ezekiel. We have only to
compare the sacerdotal ideals he records in the last section
of his book with the Levitical 'Law of Holiness' (Lev.
xvii.-xxvi.) to see how much a prophet could contribute
to the making of the Law. Even the interminable description of the sanctuary in the Book of Exodus is but the
application in detail of Isaiah's words : ' Great is the Holy
One of Israel in the midst of thee '.[1]

The constituents of the Law are very varied. It contains song and story as well as sermon, myth and legend
as well as law, and this variety of its contents must be
remembered in order to account for the wonderful fascina-
tion and influence which the Law has been able to exert
over so many generations. But the priestly editors to
whom its final form is due have given it a certain systematic unity, springing from their theory of divine revelation. They conceive that revelation to be made and
confirmed by a series of covenants, the last and greatest
being that of Sinai, when God gave to Israel through
Moses, in the ordinances of the sanctuary, knowledge
of His requirements. It is in these ordinances that the
priestly interest lies. Such connective history as they
supply, whilst incorporating the more naïve and human
stories of the past, dwells lovingly on the institutions of
Israel and their supposed origin. They think of God
as brought near to man through the institutions of the
sanctuary of the desert, which is idealised into the pattern
of the existent temple. 'There I will meet with the
children of Israel ; and it shall be sanctified by my Glory.[2]
And I will sanctify the tent of meeting and the altar :

---

[1] Is. xii. 6. ' Ezra's Law did not materialise the worship except in relation
to us, so to speak, and not in comparison with what had existed previously
. . . there never was any prophetical religion, but only a criticism by the
prophets of a worship thoroughly engrained with idolatry and superstition '
(Loisy, *The Religion of Israel*, E.T., p. 211).

[2] *I.e.* the luminous Presence of God, as noticed in § 1 (*a*) of this chapter.

Aaron also and his sons will I sanctify, to minister to me in the priest's office. And I will dwell among the children of Israel, and will be their God '.[1]

The sanctuary alone would simply have continued and developed those ideas of holy places, seasons, and persons which will be considered (from the standpoint of man's approach to God) in the following chapter. The new feature due to the Written Word was that the worship of the temple was now conceived to rest on a closely-knit series of divine commands, a full and explicit statement given by God to His servant Moses of the conditions to be satisfied, in order that Israel might become a holy people. Revelation was no longer the spoken word of the prophet; it was the written word of the Law. With the introduction of that Law, prophecy disappears except in the form of anonymous literature.[2] That immediate fellowship with God through moral and spiritual character, which is the glory of the great prophets, is replaced by a prescribed knowledge of His will, a formulated statement of His requirements for all time. Revelation is a great fact still, but it is thrown out of the living present into the dead past. In that past God speaks with Moses ' mouth to mouth, plainly and not in riddles, and the form of Yahweh he beholds '.[3] But now He speaks through the words He gave to Moses, and His will must be ascertained by diligent study of the Law. The inevitable adjustment of that revelation of the past to the ever-changing needs of the present ultimately brought in the artificial and casuistical labours of the scribes. The very conception that God had spoken once for all in the Law removed Him further off from the ordinary worshipper, and in combination with other influences, yielded the post-

---

[1] Ex. xxix. 43 f. ; described by Driver (*Literature of the Old Testament*, p. 129) as ' the culminating promise ' of the Priestly Narrative.

[2] Cf. Neh. vi. 14, Zech. xiii. 1-6, for significant side-lights on the decline and fall of prophecy.

[3] Num. xii. 8.

exilic idea of the transcendent God, who deals with His world only through the agency of innumerable intermediate beings.

The angelology which arose to satisfy this new need largely belongs to post-canonical Judaism, which believes that God deals with men and nations through a vast hierarchy of angels. But the Old Testament sufficiently illustrates the general character of this conception. Angels already begin to appear in the later prophets, viz. Ezekiel and Zechariah ; [1] in fact, Zechariah's visions are controlled by angels. In the Book of Daniel, the heathen gods have been transformed into angelic chiefs or princes who superintend their respective nations. Israel falls to the share of Michael.[2] The office of revealer to Daniel is discharged by Gabriel.[3] The Law itself is ultimately believed to have been given through the agency of angels, as is shown by various passages in the New Testament and in Apocryphal literature.[4] In contrast with such elaborate mediation, the New Testament proclaims a *direct* communion with God through Christ. This contrast must be remembered if we are to realise the impression made on the Judaism of New Testament times by such words as ' Our fellowship is with the Father, and with His Son Jesus Christ '.[5]

On the other hand, it must be recognised that the earlier Judaism, at least, was not conscious that any barrier between man and God had been created by the Revelation of the Law. Some of the Psalms describe the Law in terms of the warmest devotion and the most sincere enthusiasm. The Law is a life-giving stream to those who meditate on it day and night. It is more desirable than gold, sweeter

[1] Ezek. ix. ; Zech. i. 9, etc.
[2] Dan. xii. 1 ; cf. x. 13, and the Greek version of Deut. xxxii 8, 9.
[3] viii. 16, ix. 21.
[4] Acts vii. 53 ; Gal. iii. 19 ; Heb. ii. 2 ; see also Charles's note on *Jubilees*, i. 27.
[5] 1 John i. 3 ; cf. Heb. iv. 14 f., x. 19 f., for the corresponding directness of man's approach to God.

than honey. It is a lamp to men's feet, a song for their pilgrimage.[1] In the Maccabæan Revolt, Judas and his followers lay before God a copy of His holy Law which the heathen have desecrated, that they may move Him to action; to possess a copy meant death at the hands of the persecutors.[2] The Law was the charter of Judaism, the real source of its strength through the many centuries. The institutions which it enjoined were, in large measure, brought to an end in A.D. 70; but the Law showed its power by the creation of a new Judaism, able to endure without land, city, or temple. Through the reading of the Law, supplemented by that of the prophets, in the scattered synagogues of the Dispersion, the knowledge of the one holy God and of His covenant with Israel was kept fresh in the hearts of all. In spite of all that may be said, with perfect justice, of the limitations on God's approach which revelation by the written word imposes, and especially of the equalisation of ceremonial with moral law, history has shown that the Law contained a latent life awaiting its opportunity for new and yet more vigorous growth. The Priestly Code became the shell in which the kernel of Deuteronomic, that is prophetic, teaching was safely kept, until such time as it could grow into the Gospel.

As we glance at the whole course of Israel's idea of the approach of God to man, from the primitive beliefs of Semitic nomads, through the characteristic and unique prophetic consciousness, to the final fixity of the Written Word, two important features are noticeable. In the first place, Israel has grasped the essential truth for all religion, that in the fellowship of God and man God must be active as well as man. Yahweh of Israel, in definite and unmistakable ways, comes out to meet man, and does not simply wait for man's approach. In the second place, Israel has

---

[1] Pss. i. 2, 3, xix. 10, cxix. 54, 105.
[2] 1 Macc. iii. 48 (see note in *Cambridge Bible* edition), i. 57.

reached the far-reaching principle that the highest revelation of God must be made through human personality. This is the philosophic statement, at least, of that for which the prophetic consciousness stands. But the demand on personal religion, which is made by the direct relation to God of the prophetic consciousness, was too high for the people generally. The Law was a compromise between the personal and sacramental sides of religion— that compromise which, in some form or other, is inevitable, when individual piety is given corporate and social expression.

CHAPTER VI

THE APPROACH OF MAN TO GOD

IT is characteristic of Christian faith, whenever it seeks conformity with its New Testament type, to claim for every believer the right of direct approach to God through Christ. The one condition Christ laid down is moral; those who do the will of God are already spiritually related to Him, and through Christ Himself they find the Father He revealed. This profound conception is so simple in its statement as to seem obvious. Yet it is really the goal of a long development. This direct moral access to God, available wherever there is harmony of purpose between the human will and the divine, begins with the prophetic consciousness of Israel. Two permanent contributions to it were made by the prophets, as a result of their experience of the approach of God to their own hearts. They showed the possibility of direct spiritual communion between human and divine personality, apart from all sacramental religion, and they taught that the holiness of God is primarily constituted by His moral character. But, as already indicated, this was not the idea of the divine 'holiness' with which the religion of the Old Testament began. The holiness of the gods, in the Semitic religions, is a negative rather than a positive conception. Its original meaning seems to be *unapproachableness*, an element which 'is never absent from the notion'.[1] In Robertson Smith's words, 'it is not so much a thing that characterises the gods and divine things in

[1] Skinner in *D. B.*, ii. p. 397.

themselves, as the most general notion that governs
their relations with humanity '.[1] The mysterious and
perilous powers which the gods possess check every rash
and ill-advised attempt to approach them. The same
halo of holiness attaches to all that is connected with
their worship. This is precisely the same kind of idea
as comparative religion designates by the term ' taboo '.
Sacred objects can be touched only under the strictest
precautions ; they are as dangerous to the uninitiated as
the switchboard of an electrical power-house might be
to a child. The various abstinences, ablutions, wearing
of ornaments or special dress, found amongst the Hebrews
as amongst other peoples in their approach to the deity,
spring from the assumption that the divine holiness
makes approach unsafe, without the insulation they afford.
The whole conduct of war in early times is regulated by
taboos, because of the presence of Yahweh of Hosts in
the camp ; the warrior must observe certain forms of
abstinence, and the spoil is frequently ' devoted ' to
Yahweh, *i.e.* put under a taboo so deadly that the smallest
portion withheld for private advantage can infect the
whole camp, as we see in the well-known story of Achan.[2]
All this is capable of throwing much light on early conceptions of worship. Whether the holy Yahweh be
approached in the consecrated battle-array, or on the
sacred mountain, similar rules must be observed.[3]

This non-moral conception of the holiness of Yahweh
finds frequent illustration in the early literature. One
of the clearest examples is afforded by the Ark. Later
on, the Ark came to be represented as simply a convenient
receptacle for the tables of stone on which the Decalogue
was inscribed.[4] But, at an earlier period, the Ark is a

---

[1] *Religion of the Semites*, p. 142.
[2] Deut. xxiii. 13, 14 ; 1 Sam. xxi. 5 ; 2 Sam. xi. 11 ; Josh. vii.
[3] Is. xiii. 3 ; Jer. vi. 4, R.V. *mar.* ; Ex. xix. 14, 15.
[4] Deut. x. 1-5. The origin of the Ark remains obscure. It is thought by
some scholars that its earliest form was that of a portable throne, possibly

nomadic shrine, identified with the presence of Yahweh in the midst of Israel. Its movements are accompanied by solemn adjurations; when the Ark goes forward, Moses says :

> ' Arise, Yahweh, and let Thine enemies be scattered,
> And let those that hate Thee flee from Thy presence ! '

When the Ark halts, he says :

> ' Return, Yahweh, to the ten thousands of the families of Israel ! ' [1]

The fall of Jericho is secured by carrying the Ark round and round the city like any fetish.[2] In the war with the Philistines, the Ark is taken into battle from its resting-place at Shiloh, that its presence may secure victory; when it is captured, ' the glory is departed from Israel '.[3] The rest of the narrative shows how perilous it is for man to approach Yahweh. The Philistines learn this, through the fall of their idols, and through the pestilence that breaks out among them, until they are glad to get rid of their prize. The men of Beth-shemesh learn it, through the slaughter of a multitude of them, ' because they had looked into the Ark of Yahweh'. They are glad to pass on their perilous visitor to the men of another city, saying significantly, ' Who is able to stand before Yahweh, this holy God ? ' [4] Even when, after twenty years, David is bringing it up with all reverence to his city, Uzzah dies, because he tries to save it from a fall when the oxen stumble; there is a physical contagion that operates through contact, and has nothing moral in it.[5]

Even when, through the prophetic teaching, the holi-

---

box-shaped. If the throne was without an enthroned image, it may well have contributed to the spirituality of Israel's religion. See W. Eichrodt, *Theologie des Alten Testaments*, I, p. 47.

[1] Num. x. 35, 36.
[2] Josh. vi. 4 f.
[3] 1 Sam. iv.
[4] 1 Sam. v. l-vii. 1.
[5] 2 Sam. vi. 6, 7.

ness of God was filled with moral content, the ritual of worship, with its holy places, seasons, persons, and sacrifices, retained many practices and some ideas from the earlier non-moral stage. There is much in the Priestly Code which is explicable only as a survival from the past.[1] But the institutions of the temple worship, the external conditions by which Israel's holiness was to be realised, were now charged with new meaning. The God who said to His people, ' Be ye holy, for I am holy', was the God who had revealed Himself in the prophets, even though approach to Him was limited by a network of conditions woven from an entirely different set of ideas. The task of this chapter is, therefore, both to survey the external means of approach to God, in their development to the final form they assumed in the Law of Judaism, and to recognise the contrasted prophetic idea of moral holiness which is their accompaniment in the later worship of Israel, especially as illustrated by the Book of Psalms. In the moral holiness of clean hands and a pure heart, regarded as essential in the sight of Yahweh, we have the characteristic idea of worship in the Old Testament. The essential fact to be remembered in the study of man's approach to God is this gradual transformation of the idea of holiness.

1. *Holy Places and Seasons*

The holy places of Israel's religion are the natural starting-point for the study of Israel's approach to God. Because Yahweh is conceived to be in some sense there,

---

[1] *E.g.*, the holiness of the Nazirite (Num. vi. 5). The rules of ceremonial cleanness and uncleanness which figure so largely in the Priestly Code belong to the same circle of ideas as those of ' holiness '. Both are a development of the taboo. But the holy thing, place, or person is now fenced off because of its relation to Yahweh, whilst the ' unclean ' is separately classed because the associated ideas have not been incorporated in the religion of Israel ; *e.g.* the corpse, because of the ' heathen ' death customs (Num. v. 2 ; cf. 1 Sam. xx. 26).

they become points of possible contact between God and man. They are constituted holy by the divine initiative. Here Yahweh has chosen to reveal Himself ; here, therefore, His presence may still be sought, and is likely to be again found. In the earliest conception, and even to the latest phase in the case of Zion, they are His dwelling-places. Horeb is in this sense ' the mountain of God '. Here He reveals Himself in the flaming bush to Moses, saying, ' Put off thy shoes from off thy feet, for the place whereon thou standest is holy ground '.[1] Even as late as the time of Elijah, Horeb continues to be the dwelling-place of Yahweh, to which the disconsolate prophet resorts to find Him.[2] But Israel's gradual appropriation of the Canaanite sanctuaries, combined with the distance of Horeb, led to the belief that Yahweh might be found at these holy places also. This appears in the patriarchal stories. Jacob is represented as discovering the sanctity of Bethel by the vision of angels. To the writer of the story Bethel is actually and topographically the gate of heaven, the way of access into the heavenly dwelling of Yahweh.[3] He comes this way to the earth, as He came down (from heaven) on Sinai.[4] The ' heaven ' of such an age must not be confused with our own ideas ; it is very locally conceived, and not far off. The need of early religion is to find some spot of earth where He whose heavenly abode is inaccessible may be approached and

[1] Ex. iii. 5. Cf. the similar command to Joshua at Gilgal (Josh. v. 13-15), another sanctuary, from which the angel of Yahweh comes to Israel (Jud. ii. 1). The command is illustrated by the practice of modern Samaritans and Muhammedans, when entering the sanctuary : the shoes would be rendered unsuitable for common wear when infected with ' holiness ' (Robertson Smith, *Religion of the Semites*, p. 453).

[2] 1 Kings xix. 8. Cf., also, the representation in the Song of Deborah. ' Throughout antiquity, the sanctuary represents, first and foremost, the dwelling of a god ' [rather than, as in our modern idea, a place of worship] (Jastrow, *Religious Belief in Babylonia and Assyria*, p. 265).

[3] Gen. xxviii. 10 f.

[4] Ex. xix. 11, etc. On the whole subject, see Westphal, *Jahwes Wohnstätten*. The idea of heaven as Yahweh's dwelling-place is thus an early one, not unrelated to that of Yahweh as a ' storm ' god.

found. This need was met by the different holy places
of Canaan.

It must be remembered that, prior to the Deuteronomic
Reformation, the worship of Yahweh at these ' high
places ' was perfectly legitimate. In the early Book of
the Covenant, Yahweh is represented as saying : ' In
every place where I cause my name to be remembered,
I will come unto thee ',[1] *i.e.* wherever a theophany has
marked out a sanctuary, Yahweh may be worshipped,
and will approach those who approach Him. Before the
seventh century there is no indication whatsoever that
any law exists against worshipping Yahweh elsewhere
than at Jerusalem. Samuel grows up at the local sanctuary
of Shiloh, and there receives the revelation of Yahweh ;
later on, according to a most instructive narrative, he is
found officiating at the sacrifice at a local high place.[2] There
is a vivid picture of the thirty guests waiting for Samuel
to bless the sacrifice, before they eat the holy meal in the
special guest-chamber attached to the sanctuary. Besides
the altar on which the sacrificed animal was slain, the
constant accompaniments of these high places were the
Asherah, a sacred wooden post which was apparently a
survival from earlier tree-worship, and the Mazzebah,
the sacred stone pillar, like that erected by Jacob at
Bethel, or by Joshua at Shechem.[3]

The Deuteronomic Reformation of the seventh century
centralised all worship in Jerusalem. The high places,
with their sacred stones and posts, their altars and their
images, were to be destroyed.[4] Henceforth, there was
to be but one sanctuary of Yahweh, where His worship
could be kept free from those alien associations which
were corrupting it at the local sanctuaries. The prophets
of the eighth century had attacked such practices, but
their failure had been shown by the long reign of Manasseh,
in which various cults flourished. How real the danger of

[1] Ex. xx. 24.   [2] 1 Sam. ix.   [3] See Additional Notes.   [4] Deut. xii. 2, 3.

corruption was may be seen from the term which denotes those who abandoned themselves professionally to sexual immorality at local sanctuaries. They are called 'holy ones'.[1] The law of the single sanctuary, supported by the influence of the Exile (which began a generation afterwards), succeeded where the prophets had failed, and was practicable, because of the small extent of the territory to which the sanctuary ministered.[2]

The temple at Jerusalem was already singled out from the local sanctuaries for various reasons. It was probably erected on a site indicated by a peculiar theophany.[3] It was the official temple of the chief city, and stood in special relation to the royal house. It alone possessed the sacred Ark, after the recovery of this from the Philistines, and its brief sojourn in the house of Obed-edom. Consequently, the temple at Jerusalem occupied a unique position even prior to Deuteronomy. But the importance of the Deuteronomic centralisation of worship can hardly be over-estimated. Henceforth this temple alone expressed the idea of the approach of man to God. 'The symbolism of the second temple', it has been said, . . . 'with its graduated series of sacred spaces culminating in the inmost shrine or most holy place, its different classes of ministers, and its minutely regulated ceremonial, was so designed as to form an impressive exhibition to the Israelites of the ruling idea of holiness'.[4] Here dwelt Yahweh,[5] and here the approach of man to Him found its great opportunity and its unique privileges. We must realise the intensity of this conception of His local presence at Jerusalem, even when (in post-exilic

[1] Hos. iv. 14 ; Deut. xxiii. 17 ; 2 Kings xxiii. 7 ; cf. Amos ii. 7. Another practice condemned (Deut. xviii. 10) was the sacrifice of children, which recent excavations show to have been so frequent (Vincent, *op. cit.*, pp. 189 f.).

[2] 'The whole land of Israel is small : Jerusalem is distant from the sea only thirty-three miles, from Jordan about eighteen, from Hebron nineteen, and from Samaria thirty-four or thirty-five' (G. A. Smith, *E. Bi.*, col. 2417).

[3] 2 Sam. xxiv. 16, 17.

[4] Skinner, *D. B.*, ii. p. 396.

[5] Ps. cxxxii. 14.

religion) the ideas of worship had been spiritualised, if we are to do justice to the passion with which the Jew regarded the temple, the passion which throbs through the Psalter.[1]

The necessary and genuine service rendered to man's approach to God by holy places has for its parallel that rendered by holy seasons. Just as there are local centres at which men feel themselves nearer than anywhere else to the mysterious powers that influence human life—the oasis in the desert, the awe-inspiring mountain, the scene of a divine theophany—so there are particular times at which they feel drawn to approach the deity with peculiar earnestness of supplication or thanksgiving. The three annual festivals of Israel, the Feast of Unleavened Bread, the Feast of Weeks, and the Feast of Ingathering, all spring from the manifestations of divine power in the operations of the agricultural year. In consequence of the historical character of the religion, they eventually became anniversaries of the great events of history in which Yahweh's power had been manifested.

The three annual festivals are already enjoined in the Book of the Covenant,[2] at a time when they were naturally celebrated at the local sanctuaries. They are occasions

---

[1] The temple founded by Onias IV. at Leontopolis in Egypt about 160 B.C. (which existed until A.D. 73) was intentionally a rival to that at Jerusalem, which had been desecrated by Antiochus Epiphanes, and was in the hands of usurpers. Recently discovered Aramaic papyri have shown that a Jewish community, with a temple for the worship of Yahweh, existed at Elephantine (near the First Cataract of Egypt) at least as early as 525 B.C., and quite possibly at a considerably earlier date. The ritual included the meal-offering (*minchah*), the incense-offering (*lebōnah*), and the burnt-offering (*'ōlah*), but not the post-exilic sin-offering and guilt-offering. Possibly the Deuteronomic Law of the single sanctuary, though known to the original founders of this temple, was considered not to apply to the Jews of the Dispersion. But it seems probable that this was a pre-Deuteronomic foundation in the interests of Jewish troops sent into the service of Egypt in the seventh century (cf. Deut. xvii. 16). The Aramaic texts with English translations and notes may be found in the editions of Cowley and Kraeling (for details see Bibliography).
[2] Ex. xxiii. 14-17.

of *agricultural* rejoicing, and it is natural to suppose that they were adopted from the Canaanites after the transition of Israel from nomadic to agricultural life.[1]   The first was a spring festival, celebrated when the barley-harvest ripened.   Cakes of unleavened bread were hurriedly made from it, and formed the food for seven days.   The second fell seven weeks later, when the corn-harvest was completed, and the first-fruits of the wheat were offered. The third fell in the autumn, and marked the ingathering of the grapes and other fruit.   The common note in these festivals is the joyous recognition of Yahweh's gifts in the produce of the land, and the dedication of the first-fruits to Him.   But from a very early period the first of these agricultural feasts was connected with sacrifices of another kind (familiar to us under the name of the Passover), which probably go back to Israel's nomadic period.[2]   Here the associations are with the nomad's cattle ; the firstlings are sacrificed in the spring season.[3]

The earliest reference to the Passover which we possess,[4] already gives it historical meaning by connecting it with the Exodus from Egypt.   This connection becomes a primary reason for the celebration of the Passover in the month Abib, according to the Deuteronomic Code : ' In the month of Abib Yahweh thy God brought thee forth out of Egypt by night '.[5]   A striking liturgy of thanksgiving for some one of the three feasts is also given, in which the Israelite looks back across his basket of offered fruit to the far-off days of Jacob's wanderings.[6]   In the

---

[1] The Canaanites at Shechem, for example, celebrated a vintage festival in connection with their Baal, when the grape-harvest had been gathered in (Jud. ix. 27 ; cf. xxi. 19).   The Hebrew festivals mark three such periods in the agricultural year.   See Additional Notes.

[2] Ex. xii. 21 f.

[3] Ex. xxxiv. 19, 20.   Combined with this, there are other rites, *e.g.* the sprinkling of the door-posts with blood, which connects with forms of a threshold covenant found amongst many peoples.   The fact that the celebration is held at night has suggested to some scholars a connection with the phases of the moon.

[4] Ex. xii. 21 f.   [5] Deut. xvi. 1.   [6] Deut. xxvi. 5 f.

later ' Law of Holiness ', the custom of living in booths
at the time of the autumn ingathering is interpreted as a
commemoration of Israel's life in the desert.[1] At a later
date still (beyond the limits of the Old Testament), the
Feast of Weeks, or Pentecost, was made an anniversary
of the giving of the Law on Sinai. This enlargement of
the meaning of the great festivals is very significant. It
shows that Israel recognised in Yahweh no mere nature-
god, the giver of the kindly fruits of the earth like the
Baalim of the Canaanites, but One who manifested Himself by His acts in the history of the nation. The memory
of those acts, handed on by father to son,[2] guaranteed
the redemptive relation in which Yahweh stood to Israel.
We may compare the influence of these festivals, thus
interpreted, with that exercised by the festivals of the
Christian year, similarly transformed from their earlier
meanings into anniversaries of redemptive history.

A similar process of religious or moral interpretation
may be observed in regard to the weekly Sabbath. The
custom of observing the seventh day of the week as ' holy '
is very ancient in Israel.[3] It is coupled with the observance of ' new moons ',[4] and seems to be derived originally
from ideas concerning the seven planets, though Babylonian origin is not yet clearly shown. But, in the Old
Testament, it is explained along two different lines, one
moral and the other religious. The Book of Deuteronomy
characteristically urges the weekly rest on grounds of
humanity to dependents.[5] The version of the Decalogue
which is found in the Book of Exodus makes the seventh
day a memorial of Yahweh's rest upon the completion
of the (actual) week of creation, in agreement with the

---

[1] Lev. xxiii. 43. [The Law of Holiness is found in Lev. xvii-xxvi.]
[2] Deut. vi. 20 f.
[3] 2 Kings iv. 23; cf. Amos viii. 5; Hos. ii. 11.
[4] Cf. 1 Sam. xx. 5.
[5] Deut. v. 14 (cf. Ex. xxiii. 12).   In Deut. v. 15 the Sabbath becomes a
memorial of the deliverance from Egypt.

opening chapter of Genesis.[1]   The important religious
influence of this recurrent day, especially in those later
centuries when synagogues formed the local centres of
Judaism, needs no comment.   Together with circumcision,
the Sabbath became a distinctive mark of Judaism.[2]

The centralisation of worship at Jerusalem naturally
involved considerable changes in the celebration of the
annual festivals ; for example, it was now possible to
fix the time for the nation as a whole, whereas, previously,
the different parts of the country followed their respective
local harvest-times.   But, in the various developments,
nothing is more remarkable or characteristic than the
rise of the Day of Atonement, observed on the tenth day
of the seventh month.[3]   The solemn ceremonies of that
great Day are well known, if only through the use made
of them by the author of the Epistle to the Hebrews.
The high priest laid aside his usual dress for simpler attire
that he might enter in all humility, on this day alone, into
the incense-filled Holy of Holies.   There he made sacrificial atonement for the sins of the people, having first
made an offering for his own sins.   The fact that this
became, for the later Judaism, the most important of all
holy seasons, marks the change of spirit which came over
the religion of Israel in post-exilic times.   In the shadow of
the national tragedy, the early spirit of rejoicing which
accompanied the three annual festivals gave place to
a deepening sense of sin and a self-abasing penitence.

---

[1] Ex. xx. 11—probably a later expansion in the spirit of P ; see the Oxford
Hexateuch, ii. p. 112.

[2] The observance of the seventh year as a 'Sabbath' (Lev. xxv. 1-7 ; cf. Ex.
xxiii. 10 f.) is historically attested (*e.g.* 1 Macc. vi. 49), but not that of the
fiftieth year as a 'Jubilee' (Lev. xxv. 8 f.), which is an impracticable
priestly ideal, further expressing the principle that the land is Yahweh's.

[3] Lev. xvi. 29.   This date for the national fast of humiliation was probably
chosen as being 'New Year's Day' (Lev. xxv. 9 ; *D. B.*, i. p. 199).   Earlier
instances of fasting will be found in 2 Sam. xii. 22 ; 1 Kings xxi. 27 ;
Jer. xxxvi. 6 ; Zech. vii. 3, 5, viii. 19.   Ezekiel desiderated ceremonies of
atonement on certain days (xlv. 18-20), but even in Nehemiah's time, though
there is a fast-day on the 24th of the seventh month (ix. 1), there is no
Levitical Day of Atonement on the 10th.

The ordinary ceremonies, also developed in the same direction, were felt to be inadequate to express this. The Day of Atonement is an attempt to regain the holiness lost in the year that has gone. Its ritual enables the people, through their representative, to approach the holy God. Thus, as has often been said, the religion of Judaism finds in the Day of Atonement its culminating point. ' The leading idea of the entire Priestly Law found here its best expression. . . . It is the key-stone of the whole system, the last consequence of the principle, " Ye shall be (ceremonially) holy, for I am holy " '.[1]

The salient facts in Israel's approach to God through holy places and seasons are, therefore, these two—the centralisation of worship at a single temple, where its purity could be successfully guarded, and the deepened moral meaning which special days of approach acquire, in the light of historical experience, whether redemptive or punitive. This will be illustrated more fully by the ritual of the temple.

2. *The Priesthood and the Sacrifices*

The Jewish priest may be defined as the (ceremonially) ' holy ' person through whom God is approached in the divinely prescribed way. As such, he forms the direct contrast to the prophet who is the (morally) holy person through whom God approaches man. In the regulations of the Priestly Code, the appointment of Aaron and his sons to be priests follows naturally upon the account of the altar ; the ministry of that altar can be discharged only through priests so appointed, so arrayed, so consecrated.[2] This holy priesthood is set apart as represent-

---

[1] Benzinger, *E. Bi.*, col. 385; but the moral element in this ' holiness ' must not be forgotten.

[2] Ex. xxviii., xxix. Cf. P's story of the revolt of the laity under Korah against Moses and Aaron (here representing the Levites). The (unholy) rebels presume to approach Yahweh with an offering of incense. They are destroyed

ing the people. The representation finds fullest expression in the person of the high priest. He bears the names of the twelve tribes on his shoulders and breast, ' when he goeth in to the holy place, for a memorial before Yahweh continually '.[1] If he sins, he brings guilt on the people.[2] This representation of man before God should be clearly distinguished from that very different type of priesthood, in which God is represented to man through the priest.[3] In the case of Israel, this latter representation belongs not to the priest but to the prophet, through whose moral consciousness God speaks.[4] Subordinated to the priestly Aaronites in the post-exilic religion are the Levites. They are selected, according to the Priestly Code, by a further divine command, that they may perform the humbler, non-priestly ministry.[5] They, also, have a representative character, since they are supposed to replace the first-born of all Israel, who, according to primitive ideas, belong to Yahweh. The fact that they belong to the same ' tribe ' as the priestly Aaronites, must not be allowed to hide the fact that they are a distinct institution for a special purpose, sharply distinguished from the priesthood proper. This distinction belongs, however, wholly to the Priestly Code. Ezekiel prepares for it by his separation of the Zadokites, or priests of Jerusalem, from the country priests who had ministered at the local sanctuaries, and were therefore to be excluded from the priestly office proper.[6] But in pre-exilic times there is no distinction between priests and Levites ; in the Book of Deuteronomy the terms are applied to the same persons.[7] At a still earlier date, the term ' Levite ' was used of a professional

by fire, from which their censers are rescued, 'for these are holy' (Num. xvi., where the story is combined with that of a civil revolt under Dathan and Abiram).

[1] Ex. xxviii. 12, 29. [2] Lev. iv. 3 ; cf. Zech. iii.
[3] *E.g.*, Roman Catholic sacerdotalism (Kautzsch, *D. B.*, v. p. 719).
[4] Thus the high-priesthood of Christ, as the New Testament conceives it, is he adequate representation of man ' within the veil '.
[5] Num. iii. 5 f. [6] Ezek. xliv. 13. [7] xviii. 1.

priest, with no tribal meaning at all.[1] In these earlier days, as need hardly be said, the office of the priest was very differently conceived from the form it assumes in the Law. Not sacrifice, but the interpretation of the sacred oracle, would be the chief priestly function. It was, indeed, open to any Israelite to sacrifice, and the priest is not even mentioned in the Book of the Covenant.

The advancing specialisation of a sacrificial priesthood is naturally accompanied by that of the sacrifices themselves, of which four chief types may be here noticed. The most primitive example of bloody sacrifice recorded in the Old Testament is that described after one of Saul's victories over the Philistines.[2] His hungry soldiers were slaughtering and eating the captured animals without, according to custom, offering the blood to Yahweh. Saul therefore converts a great stone into an altar, where all the animals are to be slain, and the blood is to be poured out. After this procedure, the soldiers are free to eat of the animals, now drained of their blood. This is in perfect harmony with what we know of the practice of Semitic nomads. The altar of the pre-Muhammedan Arabs was not an idealised hearth, like the Vestal flame that was central in the Roman religion ; it was a stone on, or at, which the blood of the slaughtered animal was poured out.[3] The flesh was consumed by those who offered the sacrifice, and by their guests, just as was the case at the gathering to which Samuel invited Saul.[4] The most natural interpretation of this custom is that which regards it as a communion feast, strengthening the bond between the deity and his worshippers. The blood is peculiarly the

---

[1] Jud. xvii. 7. The duties of this Levite, who belongs to the clan of Judah, are the oversight of the ephod, the teraphim, and the idol.
[2] 1 Sam. xiv. 32-35.   [3] Wellhausen, *Reste*, p. 116.
[4] *Ibid.*, p. 118 ; 1 Sam. ix. 22 f. We must remember that the eating of flesh is, and was, a rare occasion for Semitic nomads, so that every such meal might be a sacred festival (cf. 1 Kings i. 9), as well as a time of hospitable rejoicing. 'Seldom', says Doughty (*Arabia Deserta*, i. p. 452), 'the nomads eat other flesh than the meat of their sacrifices'.

portion of the deity because of its mysterious and perilous qualities; amongst primitive peoples in general the use of blood is a central feature in both religion and magic. In the account of the covenant sacrifice at Sinai, the blood is sprinkled partly on the altar, and partly on the people.[1]

In the type of early sacrifice which has been named (known in our version of the Old Testament as the *peace-offering*), nothing more than the blood and portions of the fat [2] were reserved for the deity. But, already in pre-exilic times, there was another distinct, though far less frequent, form of animal sacrifice, known as the *burnt-offering*, which was wholly offered to God.[3] Here the underlying idea would seem to be the conveyance of a gift to the deity by the convenient means of the fire, which turns it into rising smoke. As such a gift, wholly given to Yahweh, the burnt-offering formed a proper accompaniment of peace-offerings, with which it occurs more often than alone.[4]

When we turn from these simple types of pre-exilic sacrifice (the peace-offering and the burnt-offering) to the elaborate ritual of post-exilic worship, we find perhaps the most striking and convincing proof of development the Old Testament affords. To the peace-offering and the burnt-offering of pre-exilic times two more types of bloody sacrifice are added, viz. the sin-offering and the trespass-offering, and the *sin-offering* claims the principal place amongst the four main types. This change points to a new tone and emphasis in the post-exilic religion. The rejoicing of the festal meal has been displaced by

---

[1] Ex. xxiv. 6, 8.

[2] This was burnt; cf. 1 Sam. ii. 15.

[3] Burnt-offerings were offered daily at Jerusalem in the time of Ahaz (2 Kings xvi. 15); we hear of them also on special occasions, such as the arrival of the Ark from the Philistine country (1 Sam. vi. 14), or when Solomon approached Yahweh at Gibeon (1 Kings iii. 4).

[4] So David, having bought the threshing-floor of Araunah, 'built there an altar unto Yahweh, and offered burnt-offerings and peace-offerings' (2 Sam. xxiv. 25).

penitent humiliation before Yahweh, which reflected the
later sorrows of the nation. The flesh of the sin-offering,
if offered on behalf of the high priest or the community as
a whole, was burnt away from the altar ; in other cases,
it had to be consumed by the priests, because of its special
' holiness ', and under special conditions.[1] The priests eat
the flesh of the sin-offering because, as Robertson Smith
says, ' the flesh, like the sacramental cup in the Roman
Catholic Church, was too sacred to be touched by the
laity '.[2] Nor must it be thought that the sin-offering has
a purely moral reference. The sin-offering is made, in
the case of the leper, as part of his official cleansing,[3] as
well as in other purificatory rites of a wholly non-moral
character. We must remember, also, in any endeavour
to understand what sacrifice means for the Jewish religion,
that no definite provision at all is made for what we should
call sin in the full sense—*i.e.* deliberate and voluntary
rebellion against God's law. With this the sacrificial system
does not deal. The nearest approach to it is perhaps the
trespass-offering (R.V. *guilt-offering*), the fourth main type of
bloody sacrifice. This seems to have arisen from cases in
which it was possible to make a restitution of misappropri-
ated property, human or divine. It was to be done with
the addition of a fifth of the value ; the trespass-offering
itself was a ram.[4] But even here, the case of wrong done
to God intentionally is expressly excluded.[5] For sin in
the full sense, there is but one issue according to the
Levitical theory : ' The soul that doeth aught with an
high hand, whether he be home-born or a stranger, the
same blasphemeth Yahweh ; and that soul shall be cut
off from among his people '.[6]

In regard to the general significance of the sin-offering,

---

[1] Lev. vi. 26 f. This is a serious objection to the common idea that the
victim *penally* represents the sinner.
[2] *Religion of the Semites*, p. 350.   [3] Lev. xiv. 19.
[4] Lev. vi. 1 f., v. 14-16.   [5] Lev. v. 15.   [6] Num. xv. 30.

which is the central form of sacrifice in the post-exilic religion of Israel, there seems no sufficient evidence for the idea of a vicarious *penalty*. Those who appeal to the case of the scapegoat, sent away for Azazel into the wilderness on the Day of Atonement (Lev. xvi.), overlook the fact that this was not a sacrifice at all ; the companion goat that was retained formed the sacrifice, whilst it is the non-sacrificial goat that bears away the iniquities of Israel into a solitary land.[1] Nor does the fact that the offerer lays his hand upon the victim [2] prove any transference of guilt, for the same ceremony occurs also in the case of the burnt-offering and the peace-offering,[3] where no such transference can be supposed. Such laying on of hands is sufficiently explained as a ritual expression of the relation of the offerer to the animal he is offering to Yahweh. Finally, nothing can be made out for the idea of a substitutionary atonement from the manipulation of the victim's blood. In the case of the burnt-offering, the peace-offering, and the trespass-offering, the blood of the victim was dashed against the sides of the altar ; in the case of the sin-offering, some of it was smeared on the four horns of the altar, and the rest was poured out at its foot. The object of this special treatment is apparently to establish an even closer relation with the deity. The statement that ' it is the blood that maketh atonement by reason of the life ' [4] is in perfect agreement with the Hebrew idea of the blood-soul ; but the ' atonement ' made consists in the restoration of a quasi-physical relationship, rather than in the forensic conceptions of Protestant theology. The blood-rites are, indeed, central in sacrifice, and they may form its original

---

[1] This is really a survival of symbolic magic ; cf. the Babylonian incantation : ' As this onion is peeled and thrown into the fire ', etc. (Jastrow, *Religious Belief in Babylonia and Assyria*, p. 315).

[2] Lev. iv. 29.   [3] Lev. i. 4, iii. 8.

[4] Lev. xvii. 11.   A poor man's bloodless offering of flour also atones (Lev. v. 13).

nucleus;[1] but they are to be explained from the ideas of primitive animism, not from those of modern jurisprudence.

In view of these facts, we must dismiss from the mind, in regard to the sin-offering of the Old Testament, the idea that the animal victim receives the penalty which is really due to the offerer of the sacrifice. At the same time, it must be recognised that the general idea of substitution (the emphasis falling on the value of the gift rather than the suffering of the victim) does occur amongst the Hebrews, as amongst other peoples. It is illustrated by the ransoming of the first-born,[2] and by the related story of Abraham's proposed sacrifice of Isaac,[3] apparently written to account for the substitution of animal for human sacrifice. The most important expression of the substitutionary idea is that of the fifty-third chapter of Isaiah, in which other peoples approach God through Israel, the nation being conceived as a 'guilt-offering', a lamb that is led to the slaughter.[4] But nothing is said, even there, which makes the value of this substitutionary offering to lie in the penal transference to Israel of the guilt of the nations. Israel actually suffers as the nations should have suffered; yet the purpose of that suffering is not to satisfy divine justice, but to move the nations to penitence, and to provide the costliest of gifts with which they might approach God.

As for the interpretation of sacrifice in general, it may be said that, in the pre-exilic period, its dominating idea was doubtless that of a gift to the deity; as such, especially

[1] Cf. Moore's excellent article, 'Sacrifice', *E. Bi.*, cols. 4217, 4218.

[2] Ex. xxii. 29, xxxiv. 20; cf. Micah vi. 7: 'Shall I give my first-born for my transgression, the fruit of my body for the sin of my soul?'

[3] Gen. xxii. The beloved son is to be a burnt-offering, not a sin-offering. The object of the sacrifice is attained (verse 12) when Abraham shows himself willing to make it. 'Thus early was the truth taught that the essence of sacrifice is the moral disposition' (Skinner, *ad loc.*).

[4] See more fully on this subject chaps. vii. § 3 and viii. § 5. The term rendered 'guilt-offering' implies compensation, not the suffering of a penalty. The phrases suggesting *to us* the latter are clearly figurative.

in the form of the burnt-offering, it made atonement by propitiating Him, whilst the peace-offering helped the worshipper to realise his communion with his God.   Practically all the Old Testament offerings take the form of food,[1] and the usual accompaniments of meals—salt, wine, oil—are often combined with the sacrifices, reminding us that once these were meals.   Originally, the idea would be that the deity profits by the food like some superior to whom a tribute is brought ; thus the smell of Noah's sacrifice is agreeable to Yahweh.[2]   In the post-exilic period such primitive ideas would be left behind, together with the anthropomorphism which they imply, though the practices which they explain continued as features of the ritual.   We shall perhaps keep nearest to the attitude and thought of the worshipper in this later period, by remembering the emphasis which the Priestly Code places upon the precise performance of the ritual.   The whole conception of sacrifice falls under the category of revelation ;   this is the way God has commanded sacrifice to be offered, and when it is offered in this prescribed way the worshipper effectually draws near to God.   Probably the ordinary worshipper concerned himself no more with the precise meaning of his acts beyond this attitude of obedience, than does the ordinary worshipper at the present day.   It was sufficient that, through the due performance of the ritual, the Israelite was confident of a real approach, if not one made with boldness, to the throne of holy grace.

3. *Worship in the Psalter*

The worship of the temple centred in the daily morning and evening sacrifices.   In the post-exilic period it was

[1] Incense is first named in the times of Jeremiah (vi. 20) and Ezekiel (viii. 11).   It was used at the Elephantine Jewish temple. according to the letter sent to Jerusalem in 408 (Cowley, *op. cit.*, Letter No. 30).

[2] Gen. viii. 21.   Cf. also the term "sweet savour to Yahweh" used to denote the purpose of offerings made by fire.

the chief task of the priests ' to offer burnt-offerings unto Yahweh upon the altar of burnt-offering continually morning and evening, even according to all that is written in the law of Yahweh '.[1] Notwithstanding the great development of individual religion, it was primarily through this sacrifice for the whole community that the Israelite approached God. There were, of course, many private offerings in addition ; but Israel's daily worship centred in this great act, as the worship of the whole year eventually centred in the Day of Atonement.[2] We must remember that the temple had a unique place after the Exile. In it, and through it, the nation's whole worship was brought to a focus. The synagogue is named but once in the Old Testament,[3] and we know practically nothing of its rise and early development. But the primary object of this important feature of the later Judaism, which may date from the Exile itself, was not worship, but instruction. For worship, the temple claimed a unique and unchallenged place.[4]

If we would understand the spiritual significance and inner meaning of this temple-worship, we must turn to the Book of Psalms, which is frequently called the hymn-book of the second temple. This title expresses a real though partial truth. Some parts of the Book of Psalms are clearly intended for liturgical use, and the inference is corroborated by later Jewish tradition. On the other hand, we must not think of the Psalter as a hymn-book in the hands of the worshipping congregation ; certain parts of it are rather to be regarded as anthem-books in the hands of the Levitical choirs, to the rendering of which

---

[1] 1 Chron. xvi. 40 ; cf. 2 Kings xvi. 15.

[2] Notice the sense of a great calamity when a plague of locusts had made it impossible to provide for the daily sacrifices (Joel i. 9).

[3] Ps. lxxiv. 8. See Additional Notes.

[4] On the significance of the Jewish temple at Elephantine, and the later temple at Heliopolis, see note 1 to p. 137. Ecclesiasticus l. should be read, in order to gain a vivid conception of the enthusiasm which the worship of the temple inspired.

the ordinary worshipper would listen, and respond at intervals. Many Psalms, however, do not belong to this category; even if they were adapted, by suitable changes, for use in public worship, they seem to have originated in private devotion.[1] Like our own hymn-books of to-day, the Psalter has been enriched by contributions inspired in very different circumstances. To this catholicity of origin must be largely due its catholicity of devotion, for Jewish religion covered Jewish life. There are many Psalms in it which may certainly be regarded as pre-exilic. But as it lies before us, it is primarily the witness to that spirituality of worship which gathered around the temple sacrifices after the Exile. No just view of Jewish religion can be gained by any one who does not see the Psalter written, so to speak, in parallel columns with the Book of Leviticus.

In this way, the Book of Psalms raises implicitly, and, indeed, in some cases explicitly, one of the perennial problems of the Church—the relation between the sacrificial or sacramental approach to God, and that approach which makes all outward acts secondary to the personal attitude of the worshipper. The explicit contrast of these historic conceptions, which divide Christianity into two great camps, is made only in three or four places in the Psalter; but it does not seem possible to explain these away, so as to reconcile them with the fervent acceptance of sacrifice and ritual in the rest of the book. We hear the echo of the voices of the great prophets [2] in such words as these:

'Sacrifice and meal-offering Thou hast no delight in . . .
Burnt-offering and sin-offering Thou hast not required' (xl. 6).

---

[1] There was the less difficulty in making the transition from the 'I' of personal religion to the collective expression of worship, because the personification of the nation as a single person is frequent in Hebrew literature, as well as in such solemn forms as the Priestly Blessing (Num. vi. 23-26) and the Decalogue. See, further, chap. viii.

[2] Is. i. 11; Hos. vi. 6, etc.; cf. 1 Sam. xv. 22.

'Should I eat the flesh of bulls,
  Or drink the blood of he-goats?' (l. 13).
'Thou delightest not in sacrifice, else would I give it,
  Thou hast no pleasure in burnt-offering.
  The sacrifices of God are a broken spirit :
  A broken and a contrite heart, O God, Thou wilt not despise'
    (li. 16, 17).

But these plain avowals form the exception rather than
the rule in the Psalter. In general, and in spite of the
great variety of religious mood represented, there is a
common acceptance of the temple-worship as the necessary
and sufficient means of approach to Yahweh. The passion
that has found such noble expression for all time in the
84th Psalm has surely risen through the particular to
the universal. The worshipper who could so realise the
joy of standing on the threshold of the earthly house of
his God [1] has surely learnt to worship God in spirit and
in truth, though he has never faced the issue which is
presented in the Catholic and Protestant conceptions of
worship. We may say of the Book of Psalms, as a whole,
that it is, like the Book of Deuteronomy, a compromise
between the priestly and the prophetic ideals of religion,
with their different ideas of what holiness is. But whereas
the practical outcome of the Deuteronomic compromise
was to confirm and establish the most elaborate ritual of
antiquity, the religion of the Psalter has smitten the
temple rock that a fountain of living water for Christian
faith might flow for ever. The presence of the Psalter
in the Bible, and its close relation to the worship of the
temple in the post-exilic period, must at least preclude any
idea that the Jewish approach to God was unspiritual.[2]

The Book of Psalms may justly be regarded as a collec-
tion of prayers, even more than as a liturgy of praise.

[1] Ps. lxxxiv. 10.
[2] The modern reader of the Book of Psalms tends, in one direction, to
exaggerate its 'spirituality', since he usually does not give the full value to
the references to sacrifice, the house of God, the music of the worship, etc.

The conception of prayer in the earliest period of Israel's religion is perhaps not misrepresented by that of the Arab who finished his prayers, whilst on a robber-raid, by saying, ' O my Lord ! I say unto Thee, except Thou give me a camel to-day with a water-skin, I would as it were beat Thee with this camel-stick ! ' It was natural for the man to say in the evening, when he had gained his wish, ' Now ye may know, fellows, ye who blamed me when I prayed at dawn, how my Lord was adread of me to-day ! ' [1] However exceptional may be the outspoken utterance of such an attitude, there is something much akin to it in primitive conceptions of prayer. The invocation of the supernatural power is not what it so often becomes in modern prayers, a conventional form ; it is the utterance of a secret name which gives a constraining power over the person addressed. Prayer of this kind belongs to the circle of primitive ideas to which also belong blessings and curses and oaths. It involves a superstitious belief in the magical power of the spoken name, just as, when prayer is linked to vows, it may be no more than a bargain struck with an unseen dealer. It need hardly be said that the Book of Psalms rises far above such primitive conceptions. Yet it must owe something of its own peculiar intensity to the soil from which it has sprung. These unpromising elements have been transformed into a deep reverence for the very name of God, and a sense of such living intercourse with Him, that He can be approached as a Person, close at hand, ready to respond, faithful in His promises.

The spiritual outlook of prayer and praise in the Psalter is very wide. In the first place, there is the consciousness of an adequate self-revelation of God through His providence on the one hand, and His written law on the other. The providence of God is visible in the whole course of Israel's history, the things ' which we have heard and

---

[1] Doughty, *Arabia Deserta*, ii. p. 241.

known, and our fathers have told us' (Ps. lxxviii.). It
is also visible in the natural world, where His manifold
works display His wisdom and His glory (civ.). In one
Psalm (xix.), the revelation of the natural world is placed
side by side with the companion revelation of the written
law ; the heavens declare the glory of God, and His
perfect law restores the soul. The happy man is he who
delights in that law and meditates in it day and night
(i. 2), whilst the longest of all Psalms is devoted to the
joy that written law can minister :

> 'Thy statutes have been my songs
> In the house of my pilgrimage' (cxix. 54).

Through the natural world and the written law, then,
the worshipper feels that he has access to God ; in these,
God has come forth to meet him, and to hold communion
with him. But, in the second place, the Psalter is profoundly conscious of the great barriers—sin and death.
He who would be a guest in God's house, approaching Him in the worship of the sanctuary and finding Him
there, must have clean hands and a pure heart (xxiv. 4) ;
he must be one who walks uprightly and works righteousness (xv. 2). Evil cannot be a guest with Him (v. 4),
for His holiness is now recognised as predominantly a
moral quality, a truth which the prophets had urged.
But sin is not the only barrier ; the gates and bars of
Sheol, the land of the departed, are only too effectual
in robbing man of any approach to God :

> 'The dead praise not Yah,
> Neither any that go down into silence' (cxv. 17).
> 'In death there is no remembrance of Thee,
> In Sheol who shall give Thee thanks?' (vi. 5).
> 'Shall the shades arise and thank Thee?
> Shall Thy kindness be told in the grave,
> Thy faithfulness in Destruction?' (lxxxviii. 10, 11).

It is here that one of the greatest differences between
the religion of the Old Testament and that of the New is

apparent ; the approach to God is temporally as well
as morally limited. The limit set by death accentuates the
great problem in the post-exilic period—that of retribution,
which is the third great topic of the Psalter. How can the
moral government of the world be justified, when it is
apparent that the wicked prosper ? Does not a fatal
doubt arise as to the divine equity, and hinder man from
that perfect trust of communion with God which is the
finest product of Israel's religion ? It was in this realm
of thought that one of Israel's chief contributions to
religion was destined to be made—in that interpretation
of suffering which prepared the way for the Gospel of
the Cross of Christ. The peculiar qualities of Old Testament religion were here concentrated on a definite issue,
so important as to call for separate consideration.[1] This
was the arena on which the victory of faith had to be won,
not by Job alone, but by all those who were Israelites
indeed. For ' faith ', in the Old Testament, is always
' trust ', confidence in the everlasting arms of God as a
sure support. Abraham is its great exemplar in Hebrew
story,[2] and ' in the Psalms, " trust " is the characteristic attitude of the soul towards God '.[3] This innermost quality of the worship of the Psalter is closely related
to the conception of moral holiness in which the Old
Testament approach to God is seen to culminate.

4. Moral Holiness

It is characteristic of Hebrew morality that its principles should be presented as laws of God, not, in the manner
of Greek ethics, as ideals of man. Even that handbook
of Jewish morality which we call the Book of Proverbs,
in which conduct is more detached from religion than

[1] See the following chapter, especially § 3.
[2] Abraham's trust is made the basis of Yahweh's approval of him (Gen.
xv. 6 ; on the sense of ' righteousness ' here, see chap. vii. § 1). In Hab. ii. 4
' faith ' should be rendered ' faithfulness ' or ' fidelity '.
[3] Cheyne, in E. Bi., col. 1496.

anywhere else in the Old Testament, maintains that the
fear of Yahweh is the beginning of wisdom (ix. 10).   Israel's
prophets do not say simply that the *summum bonum* of
human life is justice and mercy ; they add the typical
religious virtue of humility, and present them all as the
requirements of Yahweh.[1]   'Thus saith the high and
lofty One that inhabiteth eternity, whose name is Holy :
I dwell in the high and holy place, with him also that is
of a contrite and humble spirit '.[2]   This humility before
God, issuing in practical obedience to Him, is man's true
life, the scope of which is not sufficiently indicated in the
'Ten Commandments'.   They do indeed identify morality
with religion, in the spirit of the eighth-century prophets ;
but the morality is negative, the sins are crimes, and there
is a want of that inwardness of obedience which is the
life-breath of the deepest righteousness.   As a summary
of Old Testament ethics, the thirty-first chapter of the
Book of Job is greatly preferable to the Decalogue, as a
fine interpreter of Hebrew thought has pointed out.[3]
These ' moral ideals ' of Job (as Greece has taught *us* to
say), which are for him the laws of God, begin with the
rejection of the inward motions of desire towards sexual
sin, in a way that makes us remember Christ's condemnation of even the look of lust.   They place in the forefront
the duty of justice to dependents and the helpless, enforced
with a most striking declaration of the brotherhood of
man.   They pass beyond the letter of justice into the spirit
of humanity towards the fatherless and the stranger.
They rise almost to the height of the New Testament
injunction to love our enemies, for Job invokes a curse
upon himself,

> ' If I rejoiced at the destruction of him that hated me,
>   Or lifted up myself when evil found him ' (verse 29).

---

[1] Micah vi. 8.   [2] Is. lvii. 15.
[3] Duhm, *Das Buch Hiob*, p. 145 ; cf. Gray, *The Divine Discipline of Israel*,
p. 102.

No one who reads this great chapter thoughtfully can fail to realise the fine conception of human life which lies behind it. But there is much more here than a moral conception of life. The very point of the chapter is that it describes a relation of man to God, conceived almost throughout in purely moral terms. The remark made by Josephus is essentially true in principle, though it antedates the results of a gradual development : ' Moses did not make religion a part of virtue, but he saw and ordained other virtues to be parts of religion '.[1]

Whilst, in this way, morality is conceived from the standpoint of religion, it is not less true of their inter-relation to say that religion is conceived from the stand-point of morality. The notable contribution of the prophets of Israel has not been considered in any detail in this chapter, simply because it has been so prominent elsewhere. It is enough to refer to that vision of Isaiah in the temple which constituted his call to service. This illustrates better, perhaps, than any other passage, except the ' guest ' Psalms (p. 153), the cardinal transformation of the idea of holiness through the prophetic consciousness. Isaiah sees Yahweh of Hosts enthroned in the outer court of the temple, amid the seraphim who proclaim His holi-ness. The first thought of the prophet is of his own unworthiness to behold this vision. But the purging of his sin leaves him finely responsive to Yahweh's pur-pose, thrilling in sympathy with Yahweh's voice. Thus he receives the call to such service as is itself an ever-advancing approach to God, and is brought to proclaim a religion that has morality at its very core.

The clearest and noblest example of spiritual approach to God, after this great pattern, is that of the prophet Jeremiah. His autobiography, marked by convincing sincerity and the finest spiritual piety, is the best thing

[1] *Contra Apionem*, chap. ii. § 17 (vol. iv., p. 344 of Whiston's translation, ed. 1822).

to which we could point when we would say, 'This is Israel's religion at its highest'. We see him shrinking in humility from the call to ministry (i. 6), overcome by the awful majesty of the divine power (iv. 23 f.), seeking in vain for like-minded men (v. 1 f.). We hear his passionate protests against a thankless task, and that divine encouragement that bids him take the precious from the vile, his best from his worst, in order to become the very mouth of God (xv. 18, 19). We feel the heat of that burning fire of conviction which was aflame within him, and would not let him be silent (xx. 9). We rise with him to the knowledge of a new covenant, a divine revelation that shall be spiritual in the deepest sense, because impressed on the innermost spirit of man (xxxi. 31 f.). Doubtless, such detachment as his from the external means of grace was very exceptional, though its existence must not be forgotten when we consider the range and possibilities of Old Testament faith. Few could stand apart from the temple and distinguish, as he did,[1] the essence of religion from that expression of it which the temple-worship afforded. The ideals of Ezekiel, his younger contemporary, were destined to prevail in Judaism —the priestly-prophetic vision of a city bearing the name 'Yahweh is there', and of a land fertilised by living streams that issued from under the threshold of the temple.[2]

In these two prophets there is presented, as clearly as was possible for Old Testament religion, the ever-recurrent problem in the approach of man to God. The history of the sacraments within the Christian Church continually raises the antithesis between sacramental religion and personal or 'spiritual' religion. Between the two extremes of an utter denial of the worth of the sacramental, and an absolute assertion of its objective value, there has been room for many varieties of individual emphasis. This must have been the case in Israel's approach to God along

[1] Jer. vii. 4.   [2] Ezek. xlviii. 35; xlvii. 1.

the twofold road of the inner and the outer world. The Epistle to the Hebrews stands in the New Testament to remind us that Israel's religion, even in its external forms, could become a not unworthy setting for the figure of Christ. But a greater than its author stands by the well of Sychar to place the emphasis where it must always eventually fall in the highest religion, the religion which worships God who is Spirit, in spirit and in truth. Incalculably great as can be the service rendered by the outer forms, yet for such a spiritual religion it is service, not sovereignty. The master-thought, to which the transformation of the idea of holiness in the Old Testament leads up, is the benediction on the pure *in heart*.

CHAPTER VII

THE PROBLEMS OF SIN AND SUFFERING

PAUL'S words at Athens—'What therefore ye worship in ignorance, this set I forth unto you '—might well stand as a motto for the proud confidence of early Christianity, as it faced the seeker after truth. The confidence was justified, if only because of the new light which the Christian Gospel had thrown on the significance of morality, and on the hidden glory of a Cross. The dawn of that light is already to be seen in the Old Testament, but before the sun rises on Israel there is the darkness of strife with an unknown God. Israel's persistent purpose, in presence of the problems of sin and suffering, won a blessing for the world, the greatness of which is realised only when some fragment of the past shows the paralysis of ancient religion, through its sense of an inexplicable mystery at the heart of things. Take, for example, one of the Babylonian Psalms :

'What, however, seems good to one, to a god may be displeasing.
What is spurned by oneself may find favour with a god.
Who is there that can grasp the will of the gods in heaven ?
The plan of a god is full of mystery,—who can understand it ?
How can mortals learn the ways of a god ?
He who is still alive at evening is dead the next morning.
In an instant he is cast into grief, of a sudden he is crushed '.[1]

Such a passage indicates very clearly the way in which the problems of sin and of suffering arose for Semitic

[1] The translation is Jastrow's in *Religious Belief in Babylonia and Assyria*, p. 333.

religion. Sin is that which is displeasing to the gods; suffering is the sign of their displeasure. As long as the divine nature, and therefore the divine will, remain unknown to man, uncertainty attaches both to the conduct and to the interpretation of life. What is sin? or, in the more concrete form of the problem for ancient religion, what acts or states are sinful? Here it is of course necessary to put aside our modern assimilation of morality and religion. The sinful act might or might not be also an immoral act; the essential feature of ‘sin’ was that it displeased the gods. Further, how can man win forgiveness for his sins? What can man do to change the divine displeasure into approval, and to cancel the acts, possibly done in ignorance, by which offence has been given? These are the elementary questions that arise in all forms of religion which are above a certain level of culture. But the religion of Israel advanced to further and deeper questions, which were raised through its emphasis on morality. How is it that the (morally) innocent are found to suffer, as though they are still displeasing to Him whose requirements are believed to be moral? How does moral evil begin to be, under a divine government antagonistic to it? These, then, are the four chief problems of sin and suffering encountered in the Old Testament. Its solutions will be reviewed in the four corresponding sections of this chapter, viz.: (1) Sin and Retributive Suffering; (2) Forgiveness and ‘Righteousness’; (3) The Suffering of the Innocent; (4) The Cosmic Problem of Evil. They may all be regarded as different applications of that clearer experiential knowledge of God which Israel acquired in the course of its history.

1. *Sin and Retributive Suffering*

The characteristic idea of sin in the Old Testament is that of rebellion against a superior, taking the specific

form of disobedience to the moral law which Yahweh
requires of man.   This, at least, is the prophetic doctrine
of sin, and two familiar passages from the prophets sufficiently illustrate it.   Through the lips of Isaiah, Yahweh
reproaches Israel in the words : ' Sons I have brought
up and reared, and *they* have rebelled against me '.[1]   A
prophet of the same period declares : ' He hath shown
thee, O man, what is good ; and what doth Yahweh
require of thee, but to do justice, and to love mercy, and
to walk humbly with thy God ? ' [2]   Other terms, besides
those which imply ' rebellion ', are used to describe sin ;
it is a deviation from the right way, it is an act which
places its doer in the position of one found guilty before
the judgment-seat of God, it is something intrinsically
evil.[3]   But, broadly speaking, the idea of sin in the Old
Testament is that of the prophets—disobedience to the
moral requirements of God.   The Son of God employs
their figure, and familiarises us with their teaching, when
He represents sin as essentially the ' lawlessness ' of the
disobedient son, the moral evil of the unbrotherly spirit.

Not less fundamental to the prophetic religion is the
idea of suffering as the just recompense and reward of
sin, its necessary accompaniment in the moral government
of the world by Yahweh.   Almost any chapter of the prophetic writings illustrates the application of this principle.
Amos, for example, refers to a series of contemporary
cases of suffering—famine, drought, the destruction
of the harvest, pestilence, defeat in battle, earthquake—as warning penalties preparatory to Yahweh's
final judgment on sin.[4]   Yahweh declares through Hosea,
' I will punish them for their ways, and will reward them
their doings ' ; ' Israel hath cast off that which is
good : the enemy shall pursue him '.[5]   ' Wherefore will

---

[1] Is. i. 2.   [2] Micah vi. 8.
[3] See H. W. Robinson, *The Christian Doctrine of Man*, pp. 43 f. ; more
fully, Schultz, *Old Testament Theology* (E.T.), ii. pp. 281-91.   [4] iv. 6-12.
[5] iv. 9 ; viii. 3.   Hosea also dwells on the disciplinary purpose of suffering.

ye yet be smitten ? ' asks Isaiah, ' (wherefore) continue in
your defection ? ' [1]   Micah says of Israel's rulers, ' They
build up Zion with blood, and Jerusalem with iniquity.
. . . Therefore shall Zion for your sake be ploughed as
a field, and Jerusalem shall become heaps '.[2]   The same
principle of retributive moral government underlies the
whole of Deuteronomy, based as this book is on the prophetic teaching of the previous century ; [3]   it is applied
to interpret the past history by those writers called
' Deuteronomistic ', who gave to that history its present
form.   We meet with the same direct and obvious appeal
to facts in the teaching of Haggai, who asserts that the
sufferings of the returned exiles are due to delay in rebuilding the temple.[4]   In truth, the place and influence
of the prophets are largely due to the power of this appeal,
which conscience admitted, and the history of the nation
confirmed.

This simple and straightforward doctrine of sin and suffering is clearly linked to the prophetic idea of God.   But
when the Old Testament as a whole is under review, two
important qualifications of this doctrine must be made,
relating respectively to the idea of sin in itself, and to
the range of responsibility for it.   There was a certain
externalism in the earlier morality which was destined
to reappear in much of the legalism of Judaism.   The
morality of primitive peoples is largely tribal custom,
due to the pressure of the whole group upon the individual, and enforced by means of ' taboos '.   The point
of view of such ' customary ' morality may be seen in the
words ' no such thing ought to be done in Israel ', through
which Tamar protests against Amnon's outrage, or in
Nabal's churlish refusal of the usual ' tribute '.[5]   Such
customs, moral and non-moral, naturally pass under the

---

[1] i. 5 (Gray's trans., *Comm.*, p. 6).   [2] iii. 10, 12.
[3] Cf., in particular, chap. xxviii.   [4] i. 5 f.
[5] 2 Sam. xiii. 12 ; 1 Sam. xxv. 39.

protection of the tribal god, who may exert himself to
uphold them. But this external relation is something
very different from the prophetic identification of morality
with the true worship of Yahweh. The way is left open
for any act to pass under the jurisdiction of the deity,
by some purely artificial taboo, or for positively immoral
acts to remain outside his range of action, because tribal
or national custom has not condemned them. Both these
kinds of limitation may be illustrated from the history
of the early monarchy. Jonathan's unwitting breach of
the taboo placed by his father on all food until the evening of the battle of Beth-aven, resulted in the silence of
the oracle of Yahweh, and is described as ' sin ' ; in fact,
Saul would religiously have slain his son, in fulfilment of his oath, had not the people intervened.[1]
Nathan's parable is represented as revealing David's
conduct towards Uriah in an entirely new light to the
king himself ; the private wrong to a subject, which was
a king's privilege, is shown by the prophet to be a ' sin ',
i.e. a wrong done to Yahweh. Such an example is the
more instructive, because it shows the wide gulf which
must usually have existed between prophetic and popular
religion. But there are limitations in regard to the idea
of sin, in the writings even of the prophets, as when
Ezekiel includes a purely physical reference in a list of
sins.[2] The same inclusion of much that is non-moral
in the idea of ' sin ' survives into not a few of the commands of the post-exilic Law, such as that which enjoins
a sin-offering after childbirth.[3] Such features should be
clearly distinguished from limitations of the morality
itself, when judged from the standpoint of a higher moral
culture.

The second important qualification of the general
prophetic doctrine of sin and suffering follows from the
idea of ' corporate personality ', which has already been

[1] 1 Sam. xiv.   [2] Ezek. xviii. 6.   [3] Lev. xii. 6.

noticed.[1] The modern mind is instinctively repelled by the treatment of a group of innocent persons as not only legally responsible for, but even actually contaminated by, the act of one of their number ; our sense of individualistic morality makes such a doctrine untenable. But that idea seems to have been accepted in Israel without question until the time of Jeremiah and Ezekiel, when the moral claims of the individual asserted themselves. The eventual consequence of this individualism was that the doctrine of retributive suffering as the penalty of sin broke down. It was one thing to proclaim that doctrine and see its sufficient verification when the corporate personality of the nation was primarily in view ; it was quite another to enforce it as true for every individual member of that nation, since experience so often contradicted the doctrine. So arose the special problem of innocent suffering (see § 3).

2. *Forgiveness and ' Righteousness '*

The forgiveness of sins, like so many other of the Old Testament ideas, can be understood only from the standpoint of the covenantal relation between Yahweh and Israel. This relation virtually existed from the time of Israel's deliverance from Egypt,[2] though its moral and spiritual content was not fully unfolded until the time of the great prophets. When they proclaimed the moral demands of Yahweh, they did not conceive Him as a cold and unimpassioned Judge, but as Israel's King, Father, Husband, actively concerned to maintain the covenantal relation, even when it had been broken by Israel's sin. What He seeks, above all else, is the restoration of that relation by Israel's penitence and renewed righteousness. Consequently, He is always ready to forgive the penitent, though men may put off repentance too long, and find

[1] Chap. iv. § 3.   [2] Chap. viii. § 1.

themselves overtaken by the day of Yahweh and His destruction of the sinners. The prophetic idea of the forgiveness of sin would be quite misunderstood if approached through any elaborate ' plan of salvation ', involving conditions which must be satisfied before Yahweh is free to forgive. The prophets did not think, with Augustine, of a ransom to be paid to the devil, or, with Anselm, of a debt to God's honour to be discharged, or, with the Protestant Reformers, of a penal satisfaction to be rendered, before grace was free to prevail. The prophets of the eighth century do not even insist on sacrifice as a condition or means of forgiveness, so that their attitude is very different from that implied in the later Levitical system of offerings necessary to the restoration of ceremonial holiness. They think of a direct personal relation between Yahweh and Israel not destroyed, though challenged, by Israel's sin. The sins of Israelites are thrown into more striking relief by contrast with this permanent background of Yahweh's gracious purpose concerning Israel. The vision of that purpose is itself a motive to penitence and obedience, not far removed in spirit and aim from that of the New Testament Gospel. Yahweh has taken the initiative by sending His prophets. Above a people that will not listen to them, engrossed as it is in the despatch of embassies across the desert, and confident as it is in its resources for the day of battle, He is waiting His opportunity to be gracious, and rising from His throne to show compassion.[1]

The direct simplicity of this prophetic appeal for penitence, with the stated or implied truth that forgiveness is ready for the asking, needs little illustration, because it is so central and familiar in the utterances of the prophets. ' Seek good, and not evil, that ye may live ', says Amos,

[1] Is. xxx. 18. This verse should probably begin the section that follows, rather than end that which precedes, to which reference is made above; but the collocation of such sections, even when they are by different writers, is not without meaning.

'and so Yahweh, the God of hosts, shall be with you as ye say '.[1] Hosea compares right conduct with the work of the farmer on his land, and the divine response with the rain that falls from heaven,[2]—so naturally and simply linked are penitence and forgiveness. Deutero-Isaiah gathers up his evangelical promises and exhortations to the exiles of Babylon in a concluding chapter of invitation (Is. lv.), which has properly become a classic for a yet fuller Gospel. He promises welcome into a renewed and everlasting covenant,[3] springing directly from the gracious purpose of Yahweh. It is to the loving-kindness of such a covenantal relation that the deepest penitence appeals for pardon, in the confidence that the sufficient sacrifice is a broken and a contrite heart.[4]

But Israel, as we have seen,[5] had other sacrifices. In the earlier period, the worshipper brought some gift to the deity as naïvely as he would have done to some earthly superior who might be offended with him. This may be illustrated by David's words when protesting against Saul's treatment of him : ' If Yahweh has instigated thee against me, let Him smell an offering '.[6] The deepened consciousness of sin in the post-exilic period was reflected in its sacrificial system. It has been shown that none of the sacrifices implies penal substitution, or makes any provision, at least in theory, for those who have sinned intentionally against God. Intentional sin is itself an act of self-exclusion from the covenant of God with Israel, and, ideally, deserves death. The sacrifices operate within the covenant; they were ' offered to a God already in relations of grace with His people. They were not offered in order to attain His grace, but to retain it '.[7] Within this circle of free grace the priest is said

---

[1] v. 14.   [2] x. 12.   [3] Is. lv. 3.
[4] Ps. li. 1, 17.   [5] Chap. vi. § 2.
[6] 1 Sam. xxvi. 19 ; cf. Ex. iv. 24-26.
[7] Davidson, *The Theology of the Old Testament*, pp. 316, 317.

to ' atone ' (Heb. *kipper*) the sin by means of the sacrifice.[1]
Yet the sacrifice is not ultimately essential to forgiveness,
for atonement can be made in other ways, as Moses pro-
poses to make it through personal intercession for Israel,
or as Phinehas made it by slaying the Israelite and the
Midianite woman, or as when God is asked to forgive
(*kipper*) sin for His name's sake.[2]   We must not argue
from the elaboration of sacrificial detail in the Old Testament to an equally elaborate theory of atonement.   Of
the post-exilic sacrificial system it is probably true to say
that ' The one really essentially point in the whole ceremony of sacrifice is the confession of sin, whether that is
done through an act or expressly in a solemn form of
words '.[3]   To recognise this is to understand how such
wealth of prophetic teaching as the Book of Psalms contains could gather around the temple-worship.   The
sacrificial system, in fact, popularly expressed much that
the prophets demanded.   The difference between prophet
and priest was less one of theory, and more one of practical emphasis, than is often represented.   For, whilst
the emphasis of the prophets usually fell on the moral
conditions of penitence and obedience, that of the priests
marked the promise of divine grace, when Yahweh was
approached in the duly prescribed manner.

The deficiencies of the Old Testament idea of the forgiveness of sins spring not so much from the excesses of an
unspiritual sacramentarianism, or from the lack of an
adequate sense of divine redemption, as from difficulties
in the individual appropriation of the covenant made with
the *nation*.   How could the individual Israelite be sure that
the covenant was vital and unbroken for *himself* ?   What
pledge did he possess that his own sin was forgiven, even

---

[1] For the usages of the important word rendered ' atone ', *i.e. kipper*, see
Driver's *Deuteronomy*, pp. 425, 426, Herrmann, *Die Idee der Sühne im Alten
Testament*, and Pedersen, *Israel* iii-iv.   (See also Additional Notes.)

[2] Ex. xxxii. 30 ; Num. xxv. 13 ; Ps. lxxix. 9.

[3] Schultz, *Old Testament Theology* (E.T.), ii, p. 100.

though he had never questioned the reality of the covenantal relation between Yahweh and Israel—a relation
signed and sealed by redemptive acts in history, and a
revealed ritual of worship ? Here we realise one of the
great limitations of the Old Testament over against the
New—the absence of that direct individual relation to
God, which is offered to the Christian without other
necessary mediation than that of the eternal High Priest.
It is in the person of Jeremiah that we see individual
religion in its fullest Old Testament development, and it is
in Jeremiah's writings that we read of a *new* covenant,
framed to meet this deficiency in the covenant with the
nation.   The new covenant is to be inward and individual,
giving to every heart the direct knowledge that its iniquity
is forgiven, and its sin remembered no more.[1]   In the
absence of such an inner covenant, the one ultimate
test of forgiveness was that of ' righteousness ', *i.e.* the
prosperity which showed divine approval. The idea of
' righteousness' is not to be confused with that of 'morality',
or that of ' holiness '. Morality is properly actual ' rightness ' of conduct, judged by the customs of the society.
Holiness is properly the unapproachableness of God.
But the primary conception in the idea of righteousness
is not actual rightness, nor Godlikeness ; it is forensic, a
product of the primitive court of justice.[2]   ' There is
always a standard, always a cause ; a man's conduct in
a particular matter, or his life as a whole, is in question ;
and there is always a judge, real or imaginary '.[3]   In the
realm of religion, therefore, the righteous man is not the
man morally perfect, but he who is acquitted at the bar
of God.   ' It shall be righteousness unto us ', proclaims
the Deuteronomic exhortation, ' if we observe to do all

---

[1] xxxi. 34.
[2] But this must not be taken to imply that righteousness is attained or
assigned by the forensic conceptions of Protestant theology, or that sacrifice
is interpreted as penal substitution. See pp. 147, 177.
[3] Davidson, *The Theology of the Old Testament*, p. 267.

this commandment before Yahweh our God'.[1]   The corresponding term to 'righteousness' is therefore 'guilt', the status of the man who is condemned before God. If the individual Israelite were really on right terms with Israel's God, he would know it by his well-being in material things.[2]   That Psalm which describes most fervently the happiness of the forgiven man (xxxii.) sees the evidence that the transgression is forgiven, the sin covered, in the fact that the illness under which the poet groaned was removed after his penitent confession ; this attitude is characteristic of Old Testament religion.   It is easy to see how such an external view of the relation between God and man might lead to the characteristic defects of the later Judaism.   'It is able to say much about law and sin, little that is certain about God's grace. . . . What is said of the compassion and the fatherly love of God is as good as not said, if it does not lead to the rejection of the juristic idea of the relation between God and man, and the recognition that it is false in principle'.[3]   The results of this false principle in Judaism are focused for ever in our Lord's picture of the Pharisee praying in the temple side by side with the publican, who had so much less in moral discipline to bring, yet with a spiritual instinct so much truer cast himself on the mercy of God for the forgiveness of his sin, and went down 'justified', *i.e.* as one acquitted at the judgment-seat of God.

3. *The Suffering of the Innocent*

It is characteristic of the Old Testament religion that its central problem was that which sprang from unde-

---

[1] vi. 25.

[2] Cf. Davidson, *E. Bi.*, col. 1158: 'the old view of the Hebrew mind, which looked on prosperity and the blessings of life as in a sense sacramental, as the seal of God's favour'.

[3] Köberle, *Sünde und Gnade*, pp. 669, **672.**

served suffering. This is the shadow flung by the bright light of the prophetic interpretation of life. The implicit or explicit monotheism of the prophets traced all human fortunes to one common centre—Yahweh. At the same time, their emphasis on morality led men to believe that He administered human affairs on moral principles. As a result, every experience of suffering was ascribed to the direct will of Yahweh, and interpreted by the simple and obvious principle of moral retribution. ' Shall evil befall a city, and Yahweh hath not done it ? ' asks Amos (iii. 6), in a way that implies this to be an unanswerable challenge, and an accepted truth. The result is, as we have already seen, that the presence of suffering implies that of moral evil ; Joel, for example, builds up his whole prophecy around the visitation of a plague of locusts, clearly point-ing to the need for such heart-felt repentance as may move Yahweh to mercy.[1] This penal view of suffering naturally admits of extension to the idea of discipline, in the sense of suffering intended to produce moral improvement in the sufferer. Such was the suffering of Hosea's wife, and the suffering of Israel with which he compares it (iii.) ; it was morally deserved, yet its purpose was more than retributive. In this sense, it is perfectly natural that Eliphaz, the friend of Job, whilst maintaining the orthodox view of suffering as retributive, should also suggest that in his case it may be disciplinary also :

' Behold, happy is the man whom God correcteth :
    Therefore despise not thou the chastening of the Almighty.
  For He maketh sore, and bindeth up ;
    He woundeth, and His hands make whole '.[2]

This interpretation of suffering as penal or disciplinary could be accepted by all serious minds without question,

---

[1] ii. 12-14 ; cf. Amos iv. 6-11.
[2] Job v. 17, 18. This is the central thought in the speeches of Elihu (Job xxxii.-xxxvii.), afterwards added to the poem chiefly to bring out this principle of discipline more clearly ; cf. also Prov. iii. 11, 12.

so long as the religious unit was, primarily, the nation. There would always be enough evil visible in the national life, past or present, to make suffering seem just to the more thoughtful minds; that it was shared by the righteous and the unrighteous was amply explained by the principle of the solidarity of the nation, its corporate personality before Yahweh. But, with the rise of the new individualism, this explanation of suffering was no longer adequate. In the case of individual men, glaring inconsistencies arose between the apparent deserts and the visible fortunes. Accordingly, the problem of undeserved suffering finds expression first of all in the prophet who is most individualistic in his thought and experience —Jeremiah. 'Wherefore doth the way of the wicked prosper?' he asks, without finding any answer (xii. 1), just as the other side of the problem, the suffering of innocence in his own person, is left unexplained—'Why is my pain perpetual, and my wound incurable, which refuseth to be healed?' (xv. 18). This is the problem more acutely realised than any other, from the time that individual life came into prominence as a religious unit, down to one of the last Old Testament books to be written —Ecclesiastes. To carry the burden of this mystery was the price men had to pay for the privilege of contributing to the ideas of the Old Testament; to the pain of this problem we owe the deepest conception of piety, the demand for a life beyond death, the development of the principle of vicarious atonement. No more striking instance could be given of the general truth that true ideas are not to be distilled from life by those who shrink from the heat of its flames.

If we exclude disciplinary suffering as being simply a natural extension of penal or retributive (an extension ultimately based on the gracious purpose of Yahweh), then we may say that the Old Testament offers five different attitudes to this problem of the suffering of the innocent (with the related fact of experience, the prosperity of the wicked). These five attitudes, in logical, though not chronological order, are (1) Wait ! (2) There may be life beyond death for the righteous; (3) Life is a dark mystery; (4) Life is the bright mystery of a divine purpose higher than our grasp ; (5) The suffering of the innocent may avail for the guilty. The variety of these suggestions shows how widely the problem was felt, as their fruitfulness shows its intensity. We might almost write a history of Old Testament religion around the simple account of its development.

The first answer declares the problem to be temporary only ; the apparent inconsistency between desert and fortune will speedily be removed, whether by what we should call the ordinary course of events, or by the sudden manifestation of a divine judgment. It was this problem which sent Habakkuk to his figurative watch-tower : ' Thou that art of purer eyes than to behold evil, and that canst not look on perverseness, wherefore lookest Thou upon them that deal treacherously ? ' The vision he sees, for the appointed time of which he must wait, is that of the overthrow of arrogance, and of the maintenance of the life of the upright through his fidelity.[1]   Similarly, the author of the book called ' Malachi ' is faced by those who say, ' Every one that doeth evil is good in the sight of Yahweh, and He delighteth in them . . . it is vain to serve God . . . yea, they that work wickedness are built up '.   The answer is that God's servants have their names recorded in a book of remembrance, against that day of judgment when men shall ' discern between the righteous and the wicked, between him that serveth God, and him that serveth Him not.'[2]   Here, as elsewhere, the judgment is an event close at hand, to take place on this earth, not in some distant realm.   So, also, in the 37th Psalm, where the man perplexed by this problem is bidden ' Fret not thyself

[1] i. 13; ii. 3, 4.   [2] ii. 17; iii. 14, 15, 18.

because of evil-doers', but to rest in Yahweh, and wait patiently until His delayed judgment shall appear, in the passing away of that wicked man who seemed to flourish, or in some dramatic vindication of righteousness. 'I have been young', says this writer, 'and now am old; yet have I not seen the righteous forsaken, nor his seed begging bread'. In other words, he denies the existence of the problem in its acutest form, the suffering of the innocent to the very end of life.

The admonition to wait for the vindication of Yahweh's moral government of the world had, however, to face the difficulty that man's time of waiting was limited by the inexorable line drawn by death. The Hebrew outlook on Sheol afforded no prospect of the adjustment of desert beyond the grave. Consequently, the pressure of the problem compelled some men to put the question, 'Can there be a life beyond death which will compensate for the inadequate retribution of this life?' The two principal anticipations of faith in personal immortality—those of Psalm lxxiii. and the Book of Job [1]—are the direct outcome of the problem of suffering. The two assertions of resurrection which we find in the Old Testament [2] are due to the same demand for adjustment; there must be another life, supernaturally restored, though still to be lived on this earth. Thus, the martyred sufferers for truth to whom an apocalyptic writer refers are to be brought back to life; the faithful in the Maccabæan persecution are similarly to be restored in order to receive their permanent reward, whilst the traitors awake to receive the due punishment escaped in their previous life. In the subsequent apocalyptic literature of Israel, lying outside the limits of the Old Testament, this solution of the problem

---

[1] See p. 96 for the characteristics of the Hebrew approach to immortality. The Greek idea of immortality rests on the philosophical belief that reality is ultimately spiritual. In the *Wisdom of Solomon* we may see the two conceptions, Hebrew and Greek, held in unstable solution.

[2] Is. xxvi. 19; Dan. xii. 2.

of suffering occupies a central place. 'The sufferings of the righteous are no longer viewed as the consequence of their sins, but purely as a necessary link in the chain of events. . . . No attempt is made to reconcile the misfortunes of the pious with the righteousness of God; the Gordian knot is cut by the simple assertion that this world is essentially bad, and that for the solution of all enigmas we must look to the world to come '.[1]

That this view did not commend itself to all may be seen from the Book of Ecclesiastes. The author of that book explicitly denies the doctrine of a future life.[2] He is left face to face with a world-order which admits of no moral explanation : ' All things come alike to all : there is one event to the righteous and to the wicked; to the good and to the evil; to the clean and to the unclean; to him that sacrificeth and to him that sacrificeth not; as is the good, so is the sinner; and he that sweareth as he that feareth an oath '.[3] The author does not deny the existence of God, or His moral character; he simply confesses that this wearisome world, in which all is vanity, presents an inexplicable mystery of non-moral happenings, a mystery without hope of solution by man, here or hereafter.

But it was also possible for other men, of a different temperament and outlook, to see in life a mystery, not of darkness, but of light. This is essentially the answer reached in the most important discussion of the problem of suffering which the Old Testament contains—the poem of Job. The personal fortunes of Job are intended to exemplify that fact of experience which constitutes one side of the problem before us—the possibility of the concurrence of practical innocence with terrible suffering. The explanation of this suffering as retributive, offered

---

[1] Fairweather, *The Background of the Gospels*,[2] p. 273.
[2] See p. 98.
[3] Ecc. ix. 2, with R.V. *mar.* ; cf. verse 11 : 'time and chance happeneth to them all '.

by the three friends, is dismissed as quite inadequate ; the extension of this view, that the suffering is disciplinary, offered by Eliphaz, and in particular by the additional speeches of Elihu, is also rejected by Job. The position reached by Job himself, after the tentative longing for the restoration of his life after imminent death, is that of a direct challenge of the providence of God—a challenge that is at the same time an appeal to the heart of God, to reveal His true self in the vindication of Job. The speeches of the Almighty, describing the wonders of the universe, seem at first sight away from the point of the challenge. Yet they must have been intended by the author of the poem to suggest that the ways of God are *necessarily* a mystery to the human mind, a mystery before which the only right attitude is trustful humility. This Job himself acknowledges in the final chapter of the poem (xlii. 1-6). But the contribution of the book as a whole to the problem of suffering certainly goes beyond this. The prose prologue (i., ii.) and epilogue (xlii. 7 f.) may possibly have been incorporated by the author from an independent and older source, but they are an integral part of the work as he left it. Now, in the epilogue, besides the naïve restoration to Job of twice as much as he had before, Yahweh repeatedly speaks of ' my servant Job ', and declares him right in what he has said. If we ask what was the service which the suffering Job had rendered, we are thrown back to the opening scenes of the book, the heavenly court in which Yahweh entrusts the cause of disinterested religion to the unconscious fidelity of Job. The very point of the book is the mystery of this service ; the suffering must be borne under the pressure of an ever-recurrent and finally unanswered ' Why ? ' Neither at the beginning nor at the end is Job admitted to the secret of that heavenly court, which would be an adequate explanation of his suffering. But the author of the book asks us to believe that there is innocent suffering which must be explained on these lines—suffering which is the necessary condition for the manifestation of the deepest piety. The service could not be rendered without the trial; its issues lie beyond the horizon of the man who is tried. Personal religion has intrinsic worth for God, whose treatment of men belongs to a higher level than that of a merely juristic scheme of moral government.

Finally, the Old Testament reaches its deepest solution of the problem in the conception that the suffering of the innocent, so often inflicted *through* others, may also be endured *for* others. This is the idea incarnated in the figure of the suffering Servant of Yahweh, the noblest creation of Old Testament religion.[1] The view here taken of that great figure is that it represents Israel the nation,[2] and that the fifty-third chapter of Isaiah is, for historical exegesis, a philosophy of the sufferings of the nation, in themselves so perplexing to national pride and religious faith. In previous related passages, the Servant is depicted as the prophet of Yahweh, patiently and quietly teaching true religion to the nations, wherever the beginnings of true desire for it are found (Is. xlii. 1-5). The Servant is a weapon in the hand of Yahweh; discouraged, he renews his strength in the thought of God. His mission extends beyond his own borders to the ends of the earth (xlix. 1-7). The Servant is trained by regular and conscious fellowship with Yahweh to speak for Him. In this service he suffers, but is not dismayed, since he knows God to be with him (l. 4-9). At last, the sufferings of the Servant are brought to an end, to the astonishment of other nations. They confess that they never thought that this suffering nation was what it is now seen to be. They thought the Servant punished for his own sin; they now see that these

---

[1] For the striking parallels between Job and the Servant, see Cheyne's *Isaiah*, ii., Appendix ix., pp. 259-68 (ed. 5), and H. W. Robinson, *The Cross of Job*, 1916.   [2] See further, on this point, chap. viii. § 5.

sufferings of Israel should have fallen upon themselves. He has become an offering for their sin, and through His apparent defeat He has attained to victory (lii. 13-liii. 12). As has well been said, 'The fact of vicarious atonement could hardly be more clearly and definitely expressed; but still the passage does not provide us with any theory; it does not say why God should forgive sinners because an innocent man had suffered'.[1] The life of the Servant is compared to a 'guilt-offering' (*āshām*, verse 10), *i.e.* a compensation for guilt, but this does not prove that the idea of *penal* substitution is present, since, as we have seen, that idea cannot be proved for the Hebrew sacrifices.[2] In any case, the sacrificial idea is combined with that of the moral, *i.e.* the *effect* of these sufferings upon the nations who witness them. The importance of this interpretation of suffering for the future history of religion, and especially for the Pauline doctrine of Atonement, can hardly be overrated.

As we look back over the five attitudes or solutions to the problem, it is clear that the second, fourth, and fifth mark a real advance for religion. Besides the fundamental conception of suffering as penal and disciplinary, which continues to hold its proper, if partial, place in any moral view of the world, there is (*a*) the reminder that the portion of life we see is incomplete, and affords no sufficient data for a final judgment, (*b*) the idea of suffering as the necessary test and manifestation of disinterested religion, and (*c*) the conviction of its atoning value for others.[3]

[1] Bennett, *The Post-Exilic Prophets*, p. 327.   Cheyne (*Isaiah*,⁵ ii. p. 45) points out that there are 'twelve distinct assertions in this one chapter of the vicarious character of the sufferings of the Servant'.

[2] Chap. vi. § 2; cf. also chap. viii. § 5.

[3] Cf. Peake, *The Problem of Suffering in the Old Testament*, p. 144 : 'The most valuable thing the Old Testament has to offer is not a speculative solution.   It is the inner certainty of God, which springs out of fellowship with Him, and defying all the crushing proofs that the government of the world is unrighteous, holds its faith in Him fast'.

4. *The Cosmic Problem of Evil*

At the outset of this chapter, it was said that the problems of suffering and sin within the religion of Israel were of a practical, not of a speculative, character. The arena of the discussion was the visible world, where man stands face to face, as it were, with Yahweh. The prophets taught men to believe that the control of this world by God was absolute and unlimited. The nation lay in His hand as the clay in the hand of the potter.[1] A man's thoughts are his own, yet their issue is God's, and even moral evil is made to serve His purpose.[2] God even, on occasion, moulds men's thoughts; He hardens Pharaoh's heart.[3] He sends a lying spirit into the mouth of those who prophesy in His name.[4] Clearly, therefore, there is nothing in the world of human thought or act which is beyond the sovereignty and control of God. Yet this doctrine of divine providence is accompanied by the unbroken recognition of man's freedom and responsibility. The moral aspect of sin springs from this freedom; the challenge of Elijah,[5] implying freedom to choose and responsibility for the choice made, is typical of the law and the prophets as a whole; the relation between God and man is that between distinct persons. To ourselves, who approach this great antithesis of religion in the light of many centuries of speculation about it, psychological and metaphysical problems are raised which a thinker cannot evade. But the Old Testament shows no consciousness of these; whilst it draws the full circle of divine control, it superadds a segment within which human freedom and human responsibility are very real.

This may be seen, for example, from the story of the first sin, which is given in the third chapter of Genesis.

---

[1] Jer. xviii. 1-12.   [2] Prov. xvi. 1, 4.   [3] Ex. iv. 21, ix. 12.
[4] 1 Kings xxii. 23.   [5] 1 Kings xviii. 21.

It requires a considerable effort to realise that this narrative does not necessarily mean all that later theology has read into it. The most natural interpretation of the story, as first written for Hebrew readers, seems to be that it is meant to explain the darker conditions of human life, the painful facts of daily experience.[1] Why does a man earn his bread and a woman bear her children in pain and sorrow? Above all, why do men die? The natural answer of a Hebrew thinker, in the light of what has already been said, is that this suffering necessarily points to sin; these are the consequences of man's sin, inherited from the time of the first man's sin. It is not said that Adam's acquired sinfulness is inherited by his descendants; later Jewish theology held that other men repeat Adam's sin because their nature contains a tendency to sin like his. The interest, in fact, does not lie where later speculation has often found it, in the origin of sin. Sin is assumed to spring from human freedom, exposed to temptation, just as it did in the experience of the writer of the narrative. His interest lies in the moral explanation of experience. At the same time, there are features in the story, especially the emphasis on the knowledge of good and evil, which suggest that the ultimate form of the myth is an explanation of the progress of civilisation, the discovery by man of the things that make his 'culture'. This would probably become plainer if we possessed the parallel Babylonian story, which may fairly be assumed to have existed. Some future fortunate discovery may perhaps serve to show, by the contrasted tone and spirit of the Babylonian myth, the characteristic moral emphasis of the Hebrew narrative. That moral emphasis is presented with special reference to what we should call the psychology of adolescence. The instinctive truth of the story to life is seen in the central place it gives to the

---

[1] Cf. Skinner, *Genesis*, pp. 94-7; S. H. Hooke, *In the Beginning*, Ch. v.

mystery of the sexual relationship, still the effective test of the best and worst in human life. Thus the naïve and primitive details clothe a philosophy of life in the concrete form which was natural to the early Semitic mind; and that philosophy shows its kinship with prophetic teaching by its central moral emphasis.

The practical recognition of human freedom in the story of Genesis iii. is not materially affected by the introduction of the serpent as the primary instigator of evil. This feature of the story, which goes back to primitive demonic beliefs, simply provides one of the conditions of the temptation. The serpent is not to be identified with the later Satan; it simply shows the wider 'supernatural' environment of human life, which finds such abundant illustration in demonology and magic. There is also the implication that there are unseen spectators of the drama, who are addressed by Yahweh when He says, 'Behold, the man is become as one of us'. These are doubtless the Elohim, the 'sons of God', or members of the heavenly court, whom we see gathered around Yahweh in the prologue to the Book of Job.[1] Amongst them is 'the Adversary' (*Hassātān*), who challenges the disinterested piety of Job, and is allowed to test it by his suffering. The office of 'public prosecutor' in such conditions may be an unpleasant one, but the person who discharges it is still one of the 'sons of God'. 'The Adversary' discharges a somewhat similar function in the scene portraying Joshua the high priest, clothed in filthy garments.[2] Here, also, though in more direct manner, his accusation is repelled. We come upon a decided development in the idea of this personage in the later passage, 1 Chron. xxi. 1, where 'Satan' has become practically a proper name (without the article). The interest of this passage for our subject lies in the fact

[1] i. 6, ii. 1; cf. xxxviii. 7. A parallel scene is described in 1 Kings xxii. 19 f.
[2] Zech. iii. 1 f.

that it is a parallel to 2 Sam. xxiv. 1, which says that
Yahweh moved David to number Israel (an act bringing
speedy punishment), because His anger was kindled
against them.   In the later version of this incident, given
in the Book of Chronicles, this instigation is transferred
from Yahweh to Satan.   This revision of the earlier
statement is significant of the development in the ideas
of both Yahweh and Satan.   The identification of Satan
with the serpent of Genesis iii. does not seem to be made
before the apocryphal Book of Wisdom, where we read :
' By the envy of the devil, death entered into the world '.[1]

The later apocalyptic literature, as is well known, is
characterised by remarkable developments in the constitution of this supernatural world.   Multitudes of
angels, good and evil, unfallen and fallen, throng to the
leadership of God and Satan, and form two opposing
kingdoms, a conception we may safely connect with Persian
influence.[2]   But, for the Old Testament at any rate,
this division is not a dualism, in the Zoroastrian form.
Other beings, demonic or angelic, may influence man's
life, but, like man, they are all creatures of Yahweh, and
subordinate to Him.   They simply extend the realm in
which the scene of man's life is cast.   The ' sons of God '
are free to obey or to disobey Yahweh ; one obscure
passage in the Old Testament tells that they fell through
love of ' the daughters of men ',[3] as Adam fell through Eve.
The demons and heathen gods of antiquity, when absorbed
by Yahwism, and made subordinate to Yahweh, vastly
extend the human outlook into cosmic possibilities, as is
illustrated by the Book of Daniel ; but they do not alter
the essential problems of sin and suffering, as Hebrew
thought encountered them.

[1] ii. 24. This book belongs to the first century B.C.
[2] The Miltonic Satan is a post-canonical development ; see Bertholet, *Bib.
Theologie des Alten Testaments*, ii. pp. 374-95.
[3] Gen. vi. 1-4.

John Stuart Mill spoke of 'the impossible problem of reconciling infinite benevolence and justice with infinite power in the Creator of such a world as this'.[1] There are moods and experiences in which many men will feel that the existence of suffering is a reflection on the goodness of God. On the other hand, God's benevolence may be saved, at the cost of His omnipotence, as it was by Mill himself, and suffering may be ascribed to causes lying outside the divine causality. This is an idea of suffering which underlies popular thought more often than is usually realised. Yet again, it might be argued that suffering is the outcome of a blind universe, guided by no teleological principle, grinding out its products with no regard to those who suffer in the process. Of these three distinct modern attitudes the Old Testament illustrates the first, as in Job's doubts as to the righteousness of God; it rises above the second by its strong theistic emphasis, making a dualism or quasi-dualism of Nature and God impossible; it was without the necessary pre-suppositions for the third, because 'second causes' had not come in to displace the 'first cause', and Nature without God would have been an impossible conception to the mind of Israel.

The same general tendencies of Israel's thought differentiate its consciousness of the problems of moral evil from that of to-day. Modern thinkers relate moral evil to the principle of divine immanence, through which it becomes a transient stage of development to the ideal; or to the social environment, as that which is opposed to 'the greatest good of the greatest number'; or to the animal past of mankind, from which we 'move upward, working out the beast'. All these ways of accounting for moral evil yield different conceptions of its nature. But Israel's thought did not turn on this question of origin. Moral evil in the Old Testament was sin; it is related to God as the transgression of a law. This way of conceiving

[1] Essay on *Theism*, Part ii. (p. 80 of ed. 1904).

sin, by preserving intact the personality of both man and God, maintained the reality of moral evil; the painful problem for Israel's thinkers was whether sin might escape its due punishment, and this fall instead upon the innocent. Instead of the elaborate array of 'principalities and powers, world-rulers of this darkness, spiritual hosts of wickedness in the heavenly places', which later Jewish thought bequeathed to the early Christians, we have woven around man a network of quite different scientific and philosophic ideas. The result is not wholly gain, if the later conceptions conceal what the earlier reveal—the essential truth of human freedom and responsibility.

N

CHAPTER VIII

THE HOPE OF THE NATION

MORNING by morning, from the steps of the temple, the ministering priests proclaimed the ancient benediction :

'May Yahweh bless thee, and guard thee,
May Yahweh make bright His face toward thee, and be gracious to thee,
May Yahweh lift up His face toward thee, and appoint for thee well-being '.[1]

The continuity in the use of the benediction may fitly represent the longer continuity of the national faith. Yahweh was the God of Israel, and Israel the people of Yahweh, from the day of the great deliverance from Egypt. Out of that national faith sprang the hope of the nation, its confidence in Yahweh's ultimate purpose to bless His people. One of the wonderful things in the religion of Israel is the vitality of this hope through changing fortunes, and amid overwhelming disasters, as displayed in its adaptability and recuperative powers, its re-interpretation of the methods of God without forfeiture of faith in His redemptive purpose. That which the New Testament declares of a single generation is not less true of the thousand years of Israel's varied history— 'This is the victory that hath overcome the world, even our faith '.[2]

[1] Num. vi. 24-26 ; cf. the Mishnah, *Tamid*, vii. 2.
[2] The Targum to the ' Song of Songs' enumerates nine of the 'ten' great songs of the world, and characteristically adds, ' The tenth song the exiles will sing on leaving their exile '. The exiles of Israel were always 'prisoners of

In our previous study of the religious ideas born in the course of that history, we have frequently noticed that it is the nation as a whole which is primarily linked to Yahweh in this reciprocal relation of human trust and divine help. Even when the dissolution of political unity at the Exile introduced a new individual relation to God, this individualism was still interpenetrated by the old social values, and indeed never lost them, as the individualism of the New Testament, its ultimate issue, amply proves. The nationalistic consciousness of religion in Israel is something very different from the individualistic outlook of Protestantism; we come nearer to it, perhaps, in some aspects of Catholicism, on the one hand, and of the twentieth century 'Brotherhood' movements on the other. In the priestly benediction which has just been quoted, although the second person singular is used, the nation as a whole, not the individual Israelite, is primarily addressed. The many passages in which Israel is treated as a single person consequently imply much more than a mere poetic personification. We must read into them those ideas of 'corporate personality' which have already been emphasised; we must think of Israel as being actually treated as a person by Yahweh, and as conscious of itself with a sort of personal self-consciousness, which goes far to explain such a striking conception as that of Israel being the 'Servant of Yahweh'. 'When Israel was a child, then I loved him, and called my son out of Egypt'. . . . 'Hear, O Israel; *thou* art to pass over Jordan this day. . . . Three times in the year all *thy* males shall appear before Yahweh. . . . Many a time have they afflicted me from my youth up, let Israel now say'.[1] This self-consciousness of Israel passed through

hope' (Zech. ix. 12). Contrast the spirit of their captors: 'The fear of divine anger runs, as an undercurrent, throughout the entire religious literature of Babylonia and Assyria' (Jastrow, *Religious Belief in Babylonia and Assyria*, p. 326).

[1] Hos. xi. 1; Deut. ix. 1; Ex. xxiii. 17; Ps. cxxix. 1.

various phases, to some of which the term 'national' is
not strictly applicable. It was called into being through
the military organisation of a group of tribes under the
leadership of Moses ; it became political under David and
Solomon ; after the Exile it became ecclesiastical and
religious under Ezra and Nehemiah. Yet there is a real
unity which binds together these successive developments, a 'projected efficiency', not less efficient because
it was of faith. Because Israel belongs to Yahweh, and
can depend on Him, it has a future. The hope in this
future, springing from the faith in Yahweh, again and
again brings renewed strength, and becomes the chief
instrument in the maintenance of the 'national' existence. It is true that the nationalism which made faith
and hope strong sometimes narrowed love to the circle
of Israel, or even of faithful Israel. Moreover, the forms
in which the hope of the future clothed itself are often
to us strangely inadequate to a spiritual religion. Yet
it is to Israel's hope that we owe the bringing in of the
Christian hope ; for that hope is the pulse of Israel's vital
strength, the inspiration of its continued life.

1. *The Covenant*

The basis of Israel's hope is the peculiar relation which
exists between itself and Yahweh, already expressed in
the statement that Yahweh is Israel's God, and Israel
is Yahweh's people. This relation is said to have been
made explicit, from the earliest days, in the form of a
'covenant' (*berith*) between Yahweh and Israel. In a
certain sense, 'all religious ceremonial and worship is the
expression of a covenant relationship between men and
gods '.[1] Whenever religion ceases to be a perilous quest
in the dark, an unconfirmed venture of faith, and becomes
a confident and established resort to God, a strong con-

[1] MacCulloch, *E.R.E.*, iv. p. 208.

viction that He is a present help, one great aspect of a covenantal relationship exists—the assurance that God is waiting to be gracious, and that He changes not. Israel's land, kingship and priesthood were traced to divine 'covenants' made with Abraham, David, and Levi.[1] 'In the mind of one standing far down in the history of Israel in the midst of these established institutions, and conceiving of them as due to covenants made in the distant past by J[ahweh], one main conception in covenant must have appeared its immutability'.[2] Complementary to this confidence there is the consciousness of certain conditions on which alone God may be approached. These were laid down in the 'covenant' of Sinai,[3] the accompaniment of the historic act of redemption by which Yahweh took Israel to be His people.

In regard to the meaning of the word rendered 'covenant', our natural instinct is to start from the idea of a mutual agreement or alliance, such as that made between Abraham and Abimelech at Beer-sheba, or that between David and Jonathan.[4] But such an agreement, made between those who stand on a footing more or less equal, cannot adequately represent the meaning of 'covenant', when this denotes a relation initiated by Yahweh. When the victorious Ahab makes a 'covenant' with the defeated Ben-hadad,[5] the term implies the conditions of peace granted by the victor to the vanquished. Much more when God makes a 'covenant' with Israel, its simplest form will be a statement of God's requirements from

[1] Gen. xv. 18 (J) ; 2 Sam. vii. 8 f. ; Jer. xxxiii. 21. For the covenant with Abraham in P, see Gen. xvii. 7-9.
[2] Davidson, *D. B.*, i. p. 511.
[3] Ex. xxiv. 7, 8 (E). The 'blood of the covenant' is sprinkled partly on the altar and partly on the people, and 'the book of the covenant' states the divine conditions. In the Deuteronomic Code, whilst reference is made both to a covenant with the fathers (iv. 31, vii. 12), and to a covenant at Horeb (*i.e.* Sinai) essentially linked to the Decalogue (iv. 13, v. 2 f., ix. 9 f.), a further covenant is made with Israel 'in the land of Moab, beside the covenant which Yahweh made with them in Horeb' (Deut. xxix. 1).
[4] Gen. xxi. 32 ; 1 Sam. xviii. 3.   [5] 1 Kings xx. 34.

Israel. This is the general nature of the covenant at Sinai, as represented in JE, the earliest document describing it. We find the term 'covenant' approximating to this sense of 'command' in a contemporary poem, where it is used in parallelism with the 'word' of Yahweh.[1] The primary meaning of the term '*berith*' in Hebrew may have been either 'agreement' or 'command', but, in any case, we must beware of some of the suggestions of the English word 'covenant', *e.g.* that Israel and Yahweh met on equal terms. That the covenant, however, implies conditions on both sides is explicitly brought out in the form it assumes in Deuteronomy : 'Thou hast acknowledged Yahweh this day to be thy God, and that thou shouldest walk in His ways. . . . And Yahweh hath acknowledged thee this day to be a peculiar people unto Himself, as He hath promised thee'.[2] 'Here the idea of a compact between Yahwè and Israel involving mutual rights and obligations is fully developed'.[3] The Priestly Code, owing to its more transcendent idea of God, regards the covenant as His gracious promise to dwell among His people, and to welcome their approach to Him. 'Hence the need of the tabernacle, God's dwelling-place, offerings, and ministrants. These are all divine institutions, creations and gifts of God, the fulfilment in detail of the covenant to be their God'.[4]

These are the covenantal ideas of Israel. They would not cease to be important if they were wholly due to the later religious consciousness of the nation, for they show what that consciousness was. But at what point in the history of Israel did the idea of such a covenant first arise ? In particular, can that idea be traced back to Sinai ?

---

[1] Deut. xxxiii. 9 ; cf. Josh. vii. 11 (JE): 'they have even transgressed my covenant which I commanded them', and see Schmidt, *E. Bi.*, col. 928 f., who connects the Hebrew word with the Assyrio-Babylonian cognate *biritu*, in its primary meaning of 'fetter'. See Additional Notes.

[2] Deut. xxvi. 17, 18.   [3] Schmidt, *op. cit.*, col. 933.

[4] Davidson, *D. B.*, i. p. 513. See Additional Notes.

The answer is fundamental for the whole subject. As
Davidson has said, 'The question of the covenant runs
up into what is the main question of Old Testament
religious history, viz. To what date is the conception of
J[ahweh] as an absolutely ethical Being to be assigned ?' [1]
The answer to that question implied throughout the
present book is that whilst we owe the highest and fullest
ideas of the moral personality of Yahweh to the eighth-
century prophets, their work was not without preparation
in the teaching of such men as Nathan and Elijah ; in
fact, from the earliest period at which we can begin to
trace the history of Israel, viz. the Exodus, we find a
relation existing between Yahweh and Israel which is
moral. The earliest literature we possess concerning the
covenant made at Sinai is at least three centuries later
than the events it professedly describes. Nor is any
explicit reference to such a covenantal relation made by
any of the prophets before Jeremiah.[2] On the other
hand, this silence is hardly sufficient disproof that some
form of covenant existed in the earliest days.[3] The
relation between Yahweh and Israel from the days of
Sinai is at least virtually 'covenantal', and the subsequent history becomes more intelligible if the national
faith was then formally ratified and ceremonially established.[4] Such a ceremony as is described in the narrative of the Exodus, in connection with the signal display
of Yahweh's power in the overthrow of the Egyptians,
is not essentially alien to the religion of that time, so long
as we do not read into the earlier story the later developments in the idea of a covenant. But, through all the
changing conceptions of its nature, the primary truth for

[1] *Op. cit.*, p. 512.
[2] Cf. Stade, *Bib. Theologie des A.T.*, p. 254; on the interpretation of Hosea
vi. 7, viii. 1, see Harper, *Amos and Hosea, ad loc.*
[3] Cf. Harper, *op. cit.*, pp. lxxvi., lxxvii.
[4] Cf. the well-balanced study by Giesebrecht, *Die Geschichtlichkeit des
Sinaibundes* (1900).

our present purpose is unmistakable—the assurance that
Yahweh was able and ready to bless and save. His
covenant with Israel was as steadfast as what we call
the laws of nature : ' If ye can break my covenant of
the day, and my covenant of the night, so that there
should not be day and night in their season ; then may
also my covenant be broken with David my servant '.[1]

2. *The Day of Yahweh*

The popular religion of Israel in the eighth century
assumed that Yahweh was necessarily on the side of His
people. It was this false confidence that the prophets
of the time specially attacked. Amos did not complain
that the worship of Yahweh at Bethel and Gilgal was
neglected, but that the zeal with which the ritual was
performed at these places was a zeal not according to knowledge, a zeal ignorant of the true character and demands
of Yahweh. Because those demands were unfulfilled, the
popular expectation that Yahweh was certain to intervene on behalf of Israel was doomed to grievous disap-
pointment, and national confidence in presence of foreign
peril was utterly ungrounded. 'Woe unto you that
desire the day of Yahweh ! wherefore would ye have the
day of Yahweh ? it is darkness, and not light'. Clearly,
the phrase used by the prophet, viz. ' the day of Yahweh ',
was already familiar to the people addressed,[2] and, from
the time of Amos, it became a central idea in the prophetic utterances.[3] It denotes the day in which Yahweh
will intervene in the course of human history, so as
supremely to reveal His power and His purpose. Then
will be made plain to all the truth of the great doctrine

[1] Jer. xxxiii. 20, 21.
[2] Gressmann (*Der Ursprung der israelitisch-jüdischen Eschatologie*,
pp. 142 f.) plausibly argues that the idea belongs to a common stock of popular
eschatological beliefs, which were employed by the prophets as the most
impressive vehicle of their moral and spiritual message.
[3] See Additional Notes.

by which the prophet interprets the history of his own times, the doctrine of a divine moral government of the world. Since the day of Yahweh will thus be the vindication of prophecy, it is almost inevitably conceived by the prophets, one after another, as close at hand. It will usher in the Messianic age, as the startling prelude to the establishment of the Kingdom of Yahweh on earth. This dramatic immediacy of the day of Yahweh offers a strong contrast to many of the ideals of our own age. If the vision of a golden age of ideal human life is cherished to-day, it is as the goal of a long and toilsome journey, progress being made step by step through social evolution, humanitarian effort, or moral reformation. It may fairly be claimed that such a vision is not necessarily less religious than that of the Old Testament prophets; the gradual betterment of social life may be held to reveal the presence and activity of God not less surely, if less dramatically, than any sudden and startling display of His power. But the Old Testament expectation is essentially of an intervention from without, not of an evolution from within. In this it resembles the New Testament expectation of the Second Advent. The prophetic hope differs from the apostolic in two characteristics. It is wholly concerned with life on this earth, though the conditions of this life are to be supernaturally inaugurated, whereas the New Testament hope of the future claims the heavens as well as the earth, and moves in a more cosmic arena. The second difference is that the hope in the Old Testament is nationalistic, not individualistic. But, allowing for the limitations introduced by these differences, we may say that the eschatological expectation, at least among men of prophetic religion, is not less intense in the Old Testament than the New, and that 'the day of Yahweh' is as vital to the earlier expectation as the Second Coming of Christ is to the later.

It is characteristic of the earlier pre-exilic prophets

that they employ the idea of 'the day of Yahweh' to enforce their condemnation of Israel's sin. That day is a day of judgment on Israel itself, as we may see from the words of Amos at Bethel (vii. 10 f.), or from Isaiah's denunciation of the pride and idolatry of 'the house of Jacob', which Yahweh will abandon : ' Yahweh of hosts hath a day against all that is proud and haughty, and against all that is lifted up . . . and the pride of man shall be bowed down, and the haughtiness of men shall be brought low, and Yahweh alone shall be exalted in that day' (ii. 12, 17). The same thought meets us, a century later, in Zephaniah, where 'the day of Yahweh' takes the form of a sacrificial feast, at which Judah herself is the victim (i. 7). But the day of Yahweh's anger is extended by this prophet to the whole earth ; Philistia and Moab, Egypt and Assyria, are also to suffer from the Scythian invaders, whom Zephaniah has doubtless in view (ii.). In the contemporary prophecy of Nahum, the wrath of Yahweh is directed, not against Israel, but against Nineveh.[1] Similarly, in the sixth century, 'the day of Yahweh' is proclaimed against Babylon as to be realised through the instrumentality of the Medes.[2] In such prophecies the limitations of patriotism are more prominent than the morality, transcending them, which had distinguished the greater teachers of Israel. But a new tone enters with the Exile into even the highest prophecy. 'The day of Yahweh', which earlier prophets had expected, was the Exile itself ; but now Deutero-Isaiah awaits a day in which Yahweh will reveal Himself in gracious deliverance of His people from Babylon, as He had formerly revealed Himself in the deliverance from Egypt.[3] A

---

[1] It is uncertain what power is denounced in Hab. ii. 5 f. ; in i. 5 f. the Chaldeans appear as an instrument of divine punishment. The difficulties of this book are indicated in Pfeiffer's *Introduction to the Old Testament*, pp. 597 ff.

[2] Is. xiii.

[3] Is. lii. 3-6.

century after the return, ' the day of Yahweh ' is conceived chiefly as the purging of Judah from evil, a day of wrath against all wickedness ; Elijah, the great reformer of ancient time, who escaped the touch of death, will renew his labours on the earth in preparation for ' the great and terrible day of Yahweh '.[1] The Book of Joel, probably a little later, asserts the coming of that day in the form of a universal judgment upon the nations, of which the immediate signs will be a general outbreak of prophesying among Yahweh's people, and strange wonders in the heavens and on the earth.[2] Another late vision of ' the day of Yahweh ' sees the nations gathered in attack on Jerusalem, and Yahweh making a way of escape for His people through the cleft Mount of Olives, whilst a plague smites the besiegers ; Jerusalem subsequently becomes the exalted centre of the world's religion.[3] It will be apparent, even from the few illustrations here selected, how varied were the forms in which ' the day of Yahweh ' was presented. It is quite possible that much that is strange in the phenomena ascribed to it may be traced to earlier popular ideas of a mythical nature which the prophets adapted to their purpose. But the permanent and cardinal interest of the conception springs from their use of it to express the eternal principles of divine righteousness.

3. The Kingdom of God

' The day of Yahweh ' inaugurates the new conditions of life which are included in the idea of ' the kingdom of God ' (a phrase not actually found in the Old Testament). The relation of the two ideas may be illustrated from the prophecy of Obadiah, who first declares that ' the day of Yahweh is near upon all the nations ' (verse 15), and then

[1] Mal. iii. 2 f., iv. 5.
[2] Joel iii. 12, ii. 28-31.   [3] Zech. xiv.

goes on to say, ' the kingship shall be Yahweh's ' (verse 21).
The kingdom, or rather the kingly rule, of Yahweh will not
be fully displayed in human affairs until His intervention
—'the day of Yahweh'—has overthrown all opposition
to it. Thus the idea of the Kingdom of God, in the Old
Testament as in the New, is properly eschatological, *i.e.*
it denotes a consummation devoutly to be wished, rather
than a fact of present experience.[1] In one respect, however, the New Testament idea of the Kingdom of God
strikingly differs from that of the Old Testament, which
is its foundation. According to the general outlook of
the New Testament, this consummation of life on earth is
itself the prelude to life within a wider 'heavenly' horizon,
made credible by the doctrines of resurrection and immortality.[2] But the new order of life contemplated in the
Old Testament is to be realised wholly on the earth and
in the immediate future. It is itself the final stage, and
there is no sense of contrast with some heavenly life which
will follow it.

The title ' King ', as applied to the divine being, was in
general use amongst Semitic peoples, though we must
not read into the title all that it suggests to us in the way
of an elaborate and fully organised state.[3] The evidence
of Hebrew proper names makes it probable that the
Hebrews at times employed the title ' King ' as a substi-
tute for the proper name Yahweh, though this title was
falling into disuse before the Exile.[4] The growing differen-
tiation of the religion of Yahweh from that of the heathen

[1] Duhm (on Ps. xxii. 29) illustrates this combination of a present right with
its future realisation from the Lord's Prayer, where the doxological addition,
' Thine is the kingdom ', follows the petition, 'Thy kingdom come '.
[2] See chap. iv. § 4 ; it was along the present line of thought that the idea of
a partial resurrection first arose, though still simply with a view to the
Kingdom of God on earth.
[3] Cf. Robertson Smith, *The Religion of the Semites*, p. 63 : ' the ideas which
underlay the conception of divine sovereignty date from an age when the
human kingship was still in a rudimentary state '. He gives the evidence for
the use of this title amongst the Assyrians, Phœnicians, and Ammonites.
[4] Cf. Gray, *Hebrew Proper Names*, pp. 147, 253.

deities may have led to this disuse, especially in view of the fact that the Ammonites called their god 'King', employing the term as a proper name. We first meet with direct Hebrew use of the title (apart from its survival in proper names) in a poem of the eighth century,[1] and in the account of Isaiah's temple-vision (vi. 5). It was the human kingship over Israel (begun about 1030 B.C.) which eventually led to the revival of the old Semitic title of the deity, though the conception became current only when the human kingship had ceased.[2] The introduction of that human kingship was a perfectly natural development, forced on Israel by Philistine pressure, and the earlier of the two distinct narratives, now incorporated in the First Book of Samuel, shows that the appointment of a king had the full approval of the prophet Samuel.[3] But the later narrative regards the people's demand for a king as an implicit rejection of the kingship of Yahweh (viii. 7). This is the point of view found in the eighth century, and expressed by the prophet Hosea : 'I give thee kings in my anger, and I take them away in my wrath '.[4] It is in the later books of the Old Testament, notably in some of the Psalms,[5] that the emphasis falls particularly on the kingdom of Yahweh, in the eschatological sense already indicated. The most notable example is the Book of Daniel, devoted to the approaching establishment of the permanent and universal kingdom of the Most High, to be administered through the Jews.

[1] Deut. xxxiii. 5 ; the grounds for dating the ' Blessing of Moses ' in this period are indicated in the *Century Bible, ad loc.*, by the present writer.

[2] Cf. C. R. North, *The Old Testament Interpretation of History*, pp. 121 ff.

[3] 1 Sam. ix. 1-x. 16, xi. 1-11, 15 ; the later narrative is found in viii., x. 17-27, xii.

[4] xiii. 11. To the same date probably belongs Jud. viii. 22, 23, on which Moore says, 'The condemnation of the kingdom as in principle irreconcilable with the sovereignty of Yahweh, the divine king, appears to date from the last age of the kingdom of Israel, those terrible years of despotism, revolution, and anarchy which intervened between the death of Jeroboam II. and the fall of Samaria ' (*Comm.*, p. 230).

[5] *E.g.*, xxii. 28, xcvi.-xcix. The name *Malchiah* (my king is Yah) was a favourite after the Exile. See Additional Notes.

This kingdom has usually been called 'Messianic' by Christian theologians, but the name is misleading, because the 'Messiah', or personal representative of Yahweh in the government of His kingdom, is neither essential to the prophetic conception of it, nor so important a figure in its inauguration as Christian thought has imagined. This may be seen by taking such a typical prophecy of the future Kingdom of God as is found in Zephaniah iii. 8-13. There is here no reference to a personal Messiah, but we have what may be called the three leading features of 'Messianic' prophecy in the wider sense, viz. (1) the proclamation of a day of universal judgment against the nations, followed by their conversion ; (2) the purging of Israel from its proud and unworthy members ; (3) the righteousness and well-being of the humble remnant. There are, of course, many varieties of detail and sometimes of principle in the prophetic visions of this golden age, and the particular emphasis differs in different prophets, and at different periods. But it would be difficult to find any short passage more typical than this of the general character of the nation's hope concerning the Kingdom of God. The principles involved are simple but far-reaching. There is, first, the conviction that Israel is in the right, as over against the world. The divine purpose is identified with one group of men, rather than another, as it always will be where there is moral earnestness. The enmity of the world against God is incorporated in the successive enemies of Israel.[1] At its lowest level, this conviction may be no more than a narrow and intolerant patriotism ; at its highest, it is the condition of all progress in morality and religion. Its basis is, on the one hand, the intrinsic worth of the truth which Israel is conscious of possessing, and, on the other, the confidence

[1] 'Almost all the nations that ever came into historical contact with Israel are at some time or other so represented' (Schultz, *Old Testament Theology* (E.T.), ii. p. 373).

that Yahweh will not let that word of truth return to Him void. If we owe to this conviction the splendid but terrible vision of Yahweh as a blood-stained warrior, returning from the destruction of Israel's enemies, we are not less indebted to it for the anticipation of the time when Yahweh's mountain shall be exalted by becoming the centre of the world's faith and worship, and the clash of weapons shall be heard no more.[1] Secondly, there is the consciousness that Israel, though as compared with other nations it may be in the right, is not justified before Yahweh. Through the nation, as the prophets know it, He cannot accomplish His purpose ; that will be accomplished through the 'righteous remnant', the pure gold of those loyal to Him, when the dross consisting of unworthy Israelites has been removed. This is an important feature, for example, in the teaching of Isaiah :

> 'I will turn my hand against thee,
>   And I will smelt out thy dross in the furnace,
>   And remove all thine alloy.
> And I will restore thy judges as at the first,
>   And thy counsellors as at the beginning;
> Afterwards thou shalt be called City of Justice,
>   Faithful City'.[2]

This consciousness of Israel's unworthiness, combined with the conviction of the continuity of its mission,[3] may be compared with the similar combination of both penitence and assurance in the individual heart which characterises some notable forms of the Christian consciousness. Thirdly, in continuation of this doctrine of the 'righteous remnant', the Kingdom of God is to be characterised by moral and physical perfection, relatively, at least, to the present order. Many familiar passages will recur to the reader's

---

[1] Is. lxiii. 1-6 ; ii. 2-4=Micah iv. 1-3 (the date and authorship of this 'floating' oracle are uncertain).
[2] i. 25, 26. See Additional Notes.
[3] Mal. iii. 16, 17 ; Is. iv. 2-6. See Additional Notes.

mind in illustration of this faith, such as the promises that Israel shall be wholly righteous, that the earth shall be full of the knowledge of Yahweh, as the waters cover the sea, and that the light of the moon shall be as the light of the sun, the light of the sun sevenfold.[1] In one place it is said that there shall be no more death, in another that patriarchal longevity shall return.[2] The description of the streets of this earthly 'Jerusalem the golden', where the aged sit in peace and the children play joyfully,[3] is one of the most touching scenes in this kaleidoscopic panorama of the future.

The ideal of this Kingdom of God is a great one, and from Israel it has passed into the possession of the world. When the early Christian hope of its speedy realisation faded away, there gradually rose that vision of ' the city of God' to which Augustine has given classic expression, the eternal Kingdom represented by the Church. When the one Catholic Church lost her unique prerogative before the tribunal of advancing civilisation, a new individualism arose, which is even yet slowly feeling its way to the Kingdom of God on earth. But in the social and humanitarian emphasis of the present day there is an unmistakable tendency to disregard that which was the cardinal feature in the hope of Israel, the saving fellowship of Yahweh. The 'brotherhood of man' is hardly an Old Testament idea ; but the contribution made to that idea (within the limits of nationalism) is certainly dependent on the Fatherhood of God for its deepest motive and for its full realisation.

4. The Messiah

The figure of the Messiah, the kingly ruler who represents Yahweh, constitutes one element in the future

---

[1] Is. lx. 21, xi. 9, xxx. 26 ; cf. lxvi. 22, 23, and p. 72, note 1.
[2] Is. xxv. 8, lxv. 20.   [3] Zech. viii. 4, 5.

Kingdom of God, rather than the agent by whom it is to be introduced, or the centre around which it will revolve. That kingdom centres in Yahweh Himself, and will be inaugurated by His intervention in human affairs. The Messiah does not appear in all the pictures of the ideal future ; where He does, it is as Yahweh's administrator, vested with powers from Him, and wholly subordinate to Him. Consequently, it may be said that the figure of the Messiah is not of primary significance in the Old Testament, however important it subsequently became.

The term ' Messiah ' reproduces a Hebrew word meaning ' anointed ', and this is the meaning of the corresponding Greek title ' Christos '. The original idea in the practice of anointing was doubtless the actual communication of ' supernatural ' qualities through contact with the unguent used.[1] In Old Testament usage kings, priests, and prophets were actually anointed with oil, the underlying idea being that they were thus qualified for their office.[2] Thus the term ' anointed ' came to denote metaphorically those who were set apart for some particular work, such as Cyrus, the deliverer of Israel, the Jewish patriarchs, and Israel as a nation.[3] The Old Testament does not, indeed, employ the technical term, ' the Messiah ', which has become so familiar to us, to denote the princely ruler of the future Kingdom of God.[4] But the figure of the Messiah is clearly a development from the idea of the Hebrew king as ' Yahweh's anointed ', and more particularly from the idealised kingship of David, to whom the promise of perpetuity was thought to have been given : ' I will set up thy seed after thee . . . and I will establish the throne of his kingdom for ever . . . and thine house

---

[1] Animal fat is widely regarded by primitive thought as having a life within itself which is communicated with the substance ; cf. Crawley, *E.R.E.*, i. p. 550 ; Pedersen, *Israel* III-IV. p. 343.

[2] *E.g.*, Saul (1 Sam. x. 1); Aaron (Ex. xxix. 7) ; Elisha (1 Kings xix. 16).

[3] Is. xlv. 1 ; Ps. cv. 15 ; Hab. iii. 13.

[4] Dan. ix. 25 should be referred to Cyrus or the high priest Joshua.

and thy kingdom shall be made sure for ever before thee ; thy throne shall be established for ever '.[1] This points to a succession of 'kings and princes sitting upon the throne of David', so that 'David shall never want a man to sit upon the throne of the house of Israel '.[2] The 'righteous branch', or rather 'shoot', to be raised unto David is conceived as the beginning of a new line of Davidic kings : 'He shall reign as king and deal wisely, and shall execute judgment and justice in the land '.[3] It will be seen how naturally and imperceptibly this hope of a Davidic restoration becomes Messianic in the stricter sense of the term ; the future Davidic ruler is simply idealised, and becomes the prince of the Kingdom of God. We may learn how concrete and definite, how close to current life, these hopes were, by the fact that Zerubbabel, the governor of Judah in 520 B.C., is acclaimed by both Haggai and Zechariah as the Messianic prince.[4]

The relation to an actual historical environment is much less apparent when we turn to the three chief passages in the prophets which describe the personality of the Messianic prince.[5] In the first of these (Is. ix. 6 f.) the Davidic ruler of the righteous kingdom which Yahweh will establish is called 'Wonderful Counsellor, Mighty God, A Father for ever, Prince of Peace'. We must not

[1] 2 Sam. vii. 12 f. ; not earlier than seventh century. Cf. Ps. lxxxix. 19 f.
[2] Jer. xvii. 25, xxxiii. 17 ; cf. Amos ix. 11 ; Hos. iii. 5 ; Ez. xlv. 8.
[3] Jer. xxiii. 5, 6 ; cf. xxxiii. 14 f.
[4] Haggai ii. 23 ; Zech. iii. 8, vi. 12. In the last two passages the Jeremianic term 'shoot' (E.V. 'branch') is referred by the present text to Joshua, the high priest, but the last clause of vi. 13 shows that there has been an editorial omission of another name, and iv. 9 makes it sufficiently plain that this was Zerubbabel.
[5] Is. ix. 6 f., xi. 1-5 ; Zech. ix. 9. The last of these belongs to the Greek period ; the first and second, according to the general trend of critical opinion, are thought to belong to the Exile, or shortly after it, but the question of their date is still open to discussion. The famous passage concerning 'Immanuel' (Is. vii. 14) 'speaks clearly of a Deliverance, but is silent as to a Deliverer' (Gray, Comm., p. 136) ; as a token of that deliverance, mothers will soon be naming their children, 'God with us'. But the other interpretation is as old as Micah v. 3, which seems to be a remark subsequently added to the Davidic hope of the preceding verse.

read too much into these enigmatic titles, but it is clear that they give to this ruler a unique position, through his judicial decisions, his superhuman powers, his protection of his people, and the unbroken stability and peace of his rule. In the second passage (Is. xi. 1-5), the character of the Davidic king, the 'shoot from the stump of Jesse', is described with greater plainness and detail. The Spirit of Yahweh will endow him with the full equipment of a righteous and efficient judge, viz. penetrating insight, upright standards, and the power to execute the sentence passed. In both these passages it will be noticed that the emphasis falls upon the government of the Kingdom of God, after it has been entrusted to the prince, rather than upon any acts of his own which acquire the position. Such government will be necessary, because the perfection of the kingdom is not conceived as absolute. 'The Messianic age is not to be an age free from sin (cp. lxv. 20, xxxii. 5); the conception is thus entirely different from the later conception of heaven. But the wicked will not as now sin on with impunity'.[1] The third passage (Zech. ix. 9) is that which bids Jerusalem rejoice at the coming of its king, 'righteous and granted victory, lowly, and riding upon an ass, even upon a colt the foal of an ass'. Here, also, 'the Messiah is described not as bringing victory or salvation, but as the passive recipient of it'.[2] He rides no war-horse, but comes in peace, and 'shares the character of the saved people'.[3] The same relation of the king to the kingdom underlies the messianic references in the Psalms.[4] Yahweh sets His king upon His holy hill of Zion, and says, 'Sit thou at my right hand, until I make thine enemies thy footstool'.[5] Exalted to this high place, and vested with unique powers that he may worthily discharge his office, the Messianic king of

---

[1] Gray (*Isaiah*, i. p. 218), whose exposition of these two passages has been followed.
[2] Driver, *Century Bible, ad loc.*
[3] Davidson, *D. B.*, iv. p. 123.
[4] See Additional Notes.
[5] Pss. ii. 6, cx. 1.

the Old Testament still remains a man supreme among men, rather than the equal, in any sense, of God. His figure results from the religious view of history in general, and of the kingship in particular, not from a philosophic theory such as that which gave rise to the Greek doctrine of the Logos. In fact, the nearest parallel in the Christian centuries to the Old Testament doctrine of the Messiah would be found in those ' heresies ' which thought of Jesus as raised to His divine authority by the Spirit of God which came upon Him at baptism.

5. *The Servant of Yahweh*

The national hope finds its most elaborate and remarkable expression in part of our present ' Book of Isaiah ', viz. chaps. xl.-lv., written by an unknown prophet of the Exile somewhere about 540 B.C. This illustrates, with exceptional vividness of style and thought, that interpretative idealism of the prophets which transformed the history of Israel. Not only is it the fullest statement of the national hope which the Old Testament contains, but it can be assigned, on the clearest evidence, to a definite historical setting. The immediate stimulus to this prophecy was the victorious career of Cyrus, the vassal of Media, a career which began about the middle of the sixth century B.C. He eventually became the ruler of Western Asia. Babylon fell before him in 539 B.C., and a contemporary inscription shows that he reversed its policy, and restored various deported peoples to their own countries. At some time previous to the fall of Babylon, the unknown prophet of the Exile acclaims Cyrus as the divinely appointed instrument for the restoration of Israel.[1] Nothing will hinder this, for Yahweh is behind him, and Yahweh is the one and only God, the creator and ruler of the whole world ; the heathen gods are naught but senseless idols. In the restoration of His people Israel,

[1] And, indeed, designates him ' his anointed ', Is. xlv. 1.

Yahweh returns to reign in Zion. Not only for Israel's sake, but for the sake of His own name, Yahweh works this deliverance, and through it He will be made known to all the earth. ' I am God, and there is none else . . . unto me every knee shall bow, every tongue shall swear '.[1] With this exalted faith, the prophet begins and ends on the keynote of comfort for Israel,[2] in marked contrast to the demand for penitence which characterises pre-exilic prophecy.

In the course of these chapters the nation is frequently described or addressed as ' the Servant of Yahweh ', a title already borne by distinguished individual Israelites and by the nation as a whole.[3] It is beyond dispute that the title, in some instances, here refers to the nation, e.g. in the words ' thou, Israel my servant, Jacob whom I have chosen, the seed of Abraham my friend '.[4] But there has been much discussion as to the reference of the title in the remarkable series of ' Songs of the Servant of Yahweh '.[5] The personality of the Servant appears to be distinguished from the nation as a whole,[6] and is described with such individuality of detail, that many have seen a reference to some distinguished Israelite, either of the past (e.g. Jeremiah) or of the unknown future.[7] Both these difficulties in the way of a collective interpretation seem to be met when due weight is given to that conception of ' corporate personality ' which has already been noticed,[8] a conception which goes so far beyond anything familiar to us in the way of personification. The national ' thou ' can include both the evil and the good,[9] and the prophet

---

[1] Is. xlv. 22, 23.   [2] xl. 1 f., lv. 12, 13.

[3] E.g., Gen. xxvi. 24 (Abraham) ; Jer. xxx. 10 ; Ez. xxviii. 25.

[4] Is. xli. 8.   [5] xlii. 1-4, xlix. 1-6, 1. 4-9, lii. 13-liii. 12. See Additional Notes.   [6] xlix. 6, liii. 8.

[7] In connection with this interpretation, the Songs are often ascribed to a different source from that of the rest of the prophecy. On this individualistic interpretation we might compare the obscure passage, Zech. xii. 10, where an unknown martyr seems to be meant.

[8] See chap. iv. § 3.

[9] For an instructive example, see Zeph. iii. 11-13.

can turn his gaze now on one and now on the other part
of the nation, in rapid transition, still employing the same
title.   Thus the prophet (outside the Songs) asks, ' Who
is blind, but my Servant ? or deaf, as my messenger that
I send ? ' whilst in the Songs themselves the Servant is
described as righteous.[1]   In both cases there is reference
to the actual nation, in the light of its past history ; in
the former, to Israel's unwillingness to realise its mission,
as taught by Yahweh's prophets ; in the latter, to the
realisation of that mission, at least through the truer part
of the nation.   Whatever may be Israel's shortcomings
in relation to Yahweh, still, in contrast with the world,
Israel is Yahweh's righteous servant, as the kings of the
nations themselves acknowledge.[2]

We have already noticed, in connection with the problem
of suffering, the way in which this mission of Israel to the
world is conceived.   For if Israel has received at Yahweh's
hand double for all her sins, then the surplus of undeserved
suffering belongs to the mystery of His dealing with His
people.   The veil of that mystery is partly lifted to reveal
His purpose, which is to bring the world to His feet.   That
purpose is accomplished through Israel's history, not only
because the nation is made a missionary prophet to the
Gentiles, but because its sufferings form a sacrificial offering[3] for the sins of the world—doubtless including the
unworthy within Israel.   The sight of these sufferings
moves the nations to penitence, when they are interpreted
in the light of Yahweh's redemptive purpose, and no
longer as the penalty of Israel's sin.   The whole description
implies that the suffering has been nobly endured, and
that there belongs to it a positive worth and intrinsic

[1] xlii. 19, liii. 11.
[2] liii. The peculiar reference to ' my people ' in verse 8 is either textually
corrupt, or a relapse into the writer's own standpoint within the nation.
[3] liii. 10 (āshām) ; cf. verse 12 : ' he bare the sin of many, and made
intercession for the transgressors '.   The sacrificial idea cannot be set aside
simply because the text of verses 9-11 is corrupt as it certainly is.

value, in virtue of which the nations find acceptance and forgiveness.[1]

It will be seen that we have here a hope of the nation very different in character from the expectations hitherto considered. It is true, in this case as before, that Israel is triumphantly vindicated in the eyes of the world, and that Jerusalem still remains the spiritual metropolis. But the path to this vindication is through defeat, not victory ; Israel, like Christ, rules the world from the Cross. The very nature of this ' hope ' explains why it has left so little trace on the subsequent religion of Israel.[2] The Old Testament has no doctrine of a suffering Messiah ; the conception of the suffering Servant of Yahweh belongs to the ' Messianic ' hope only in the widest sense of the word. The nearest parallel to these Songs of the Servant is supplied by the Book of Job, where Job also reaches a triumphant vindication after sufferings [3] that minister to Yahweh's mysterious purpose, receiving double for all his losses (cf. Is. lxi. 7), and making intercession for those who have misjudged him. In the 22nd Psalm, also, the sorrows of Israel are followed by the divine deliverance and the conversion of the world. But, for the most part, it was the brighter aspect of the prophecies of Deutero-Isaiah that left its mark on the subsequent religion and literature of Israel. The spiritual demand made by the Songs of the Servant on those who would share in their ideals was too great for the rank and file, especially in the atmosphere of narrowing nationalism which followed the Exile. The demand is still too great for the rank and file of the newer Israel which Jesus of Nazareth created.

---

[1] This 'objective' value of the sacrifice must not hastily be identified with much later theories of penal satisfaction ; it is rather a parallel to Job's disinterested piety. Israel has enabled the nations to make a costly gift to Yahweh. Cf. chaps. vi. § 2, vii. § 3.

[2] 'Jonah is a protest of the more Liberal Judaism in the spiritual succession of the Servant of Yahweh' (Bennett, *Post-Exilic Prophets*, p. 127).

[3] It is possible that both Job and the Servant were lepers, this being the probable meaning of ' stricken ' in liii. 4.

Yet Israel's sufferings, so interpreted, have entered into His Gospel, shaped His life and issued in His Cross. To those sufferings, coupled with this interpretation of them, are due the most characteristic ideas of the Christian faith and morality.

6. *Nationalism and Universalism*

We have already seen [1] that the Exile gave birth to two distinct ideals of the future of Israel—to the priestly ideal of Ezekiel, with a nationalism centred in the restored temple and its ritual, sharply separated from the outside world, and to the prophetic ideal of Deutero-Isaiah, which anticipated the conversion of all other nations to the religion of Israel, through the missionary work of the Servant of Yahweh. These two contrasted ideals, which we may call nationalism and universalism, run through the whole of post-exilic Judaism, but from the time of Ezra and Nehemiah onwards it is the former which gains in strength, and eventually issues in the post-Biblical Judaism, ' a nation, which could not live, and could not die, a Church which did not free itself from the national life, and therefore remained a sect '.[2]   On the other hand, the universalistic tendencies which sprang from the monotheism and morality of Old Testament religion were maintained through the propaganda of the Jewish Dispersion, and finally found their triumphant outlet in Christianity.

The peculiar intensity of Jewish nationalism springs ultimately from the consciousness of unique religious possessions, a consciousness fully justified by subsequent

---

[1] Chap. i. p. 14; cf. Stade, *Bib. Theologie des A.T.*, p. 309 : ' Whilst according to Ezekiel's idea of God there must be the most rigorous separation of Israel from the whole world, according to the idea of Deutero-Isaiah heathenism will be overcome '.

[2] Bousset, *Die Religion des Judentums*,[2] p. 110.

history, as well as by comparison with other religions. This consciousness goes back, as we have seen, to the deliverance from Egypt. It found political expression under David and Solomon, and in the subsequent divided kingdoms. Already, in the seventh century, it demanded religious separation from other nations : 'Thou art a holy people unto Yahweh thy God: Yahweh thy God hath chosen thee to be a peculiar people unto Himself, out of all peoples that are upon the face of the earth '.[1] This demand for a 'holy', *i.e.* a 'separated' people, corresponding to the 'holy' God, finds fullest expression in the later Priestly Code,[2] particularly in the ' Law of Holiness ' (Lev. xvii.-xxvi.), which is inspired by the principles of Ezekiel. These were the principles which the combined work of Ezra and Nehemiah enforced in the restored Jewish community. Because they could no longer find expression in political independence, their concentrated strength was poured into religious moulds. Already, in the Exile, the primitive practice of circumcision and the ancient Sabbath festival had acquired a new meaning and a greatly increased importance for Judaism. ' As substitutes for the sacrificial worship, no longer possible, the sabbath and circumcision became the cardinal commands of Judaism, and the chief symbols of the religion of Yahwè and of membership of the religious commonwealth '.[3] Ezekiel, in his description of Sheol, distinguishes the uncircumcised from the circumcised.[4] One of the things that shocked Nehemiah's stricter religious conscience was the sight of Jewish labour on the Sabbath.[5] The most important step taken by Ezra and Nehemiah, however, was the abolition and prohibition of marriage outside Judaism. Ezra was moved to the deepest sorrow and indignation when he found that such relationships existed, even in the case

---

[1] Deut. vii. 6 ; note the whole chapter.   [2] *E.g.*, Lev. xi. 44 f.
[3] Benzinger, in *E. Bi.*, col. 832.   [4] xxxii. 19-32.
[5] Neh. xiii. 15 f. ; cf. x. 31.

of priests; he called on the Jews to separate themselves 'from the peoples of the land, and from the strange women'.[1] He could appeal to the Deuteronomic prohibition of marriage with the Canaanites. But his justification, from the nationalistic standpoint, was deeper than any ancient law. 'The permanence of Judaism depended on the religious separateness of the Jews. . . . He fenced off the people against the subtler temptations to idolatry and averted the imminent danger of his time, the fusion of the Jews at Jerusalem with the semi-heathen "peoples of the land"'.[2] The result of the assertion of this rigorous principle of separation is seen in the rise of the rival community of 'Samaritans', the descendants of those northern Israelites who had not been deported, together with the colonists from abroad settled in these districts by Assyrian kings.[3] Towards this community the attitude of Nehemiah is unmistakable: 'Ye have no portion, nor right, nor memorial, in Jerusalem'.[4]

It is significant, both for the strength and for the character of Jewish nationalism, that the famous Maccabæan Revolt, more than two and a half centuries after the time of Nehemiah, was provoked by the Syrian attempt to Hellenise the Jewish religion, not by the Jewish desire to gain political liberty. It was in 168 B.C. that the general of Antiochus Epiphanes replaced the altar of Yahweh by an altar of Zeus, and forced the Jews throughout the land to worship idols. In the following year the revolt began through the priest Mattathias and his family. The Old Testament istelf provides a glimpse of the opening years of this revolt in the Book of Daniel. Its latter half,

---

[1] Ezra x. 11; cf. Neh. xiii. 23 f.; Mal. ii. 11.

[2] Ryle, in *Cambridge Bible, Ezra and Nehemiah*, pp. 143, 144.

[3] Jer. xli. 5; Ezra iv. 2, etc. The Elephantine Jewish community appealed for help to the Samaritans in 408 B.C. The foundation of the Samaritan temple is usually connected with Neh. xiii. 28, but cf. Moore, *Judaism*, vol. I. pp. 23 ff.

[4] Neh. ii. 20. This rival community was of real advantage to Judaism as a safety-valve.

though thrown into the form of a prophecy ascribed to the sixth century, is really an allegorical description of the external fortunes of the Jewish people in the hands of Babylonians, Medes, Persians, and Greeks.[1] Prophecy proper enters with the vision of ' one like unto a son of man ', *i.e.* the Jewish nation, whose kingdom follows that of the ' beasts ', and shall know no end. The interest of the writer naturally lies in the present conduct of Antiochus, and his desecration of the temple (viii. 11). The ' mighty king ' (xi. 3) is Alexander the Great ; the kingdoms of the north and the south (xi. 5 f.) are those of the Syrian and Egyptian rulers in whose hands the Jews were, throughout the Greek period, up to the time of the Maccabæan Revolt. The ' contemptible person ' (xi. 21) is Antiochus Epiphanes himself. The closing chapter moves in the realm of the future kingdom of God, which follows the fall of Antiochus. The Book of Daniel as a whole, it will be seen, really belongs to the apocalyptic literature which flourished so abundantly in the period between the Old and New Testaments. Its presence in the Canon forms a convenient landmark in the development of Jewish nationalism,[2] and illustrates the continuity of that development with both the past and the future. The nationalism which claimed political as well as religious independence in the Maccabæan period was again to enter the political and military arena in the events which led to the destruction of Jerusalem in A.D. 70, and to the Barcochba Revolt of A.D. 132-135. One of the keenest observers of men and manners, writing at the close of the first Christian century, was struck by the contrast between the inner and outer attitude of the Jew : ' Among themselves they are inflexibly honest, and ever ready to show compassion, though they

---

[1] See the vision of the four beasts in chap. vii. The empire of the Medes is an unhistorical insertion.

[2] The (unhistorical) story of ' Esther ' shows what this nationalistic spirit could become when divorced from that finer religious consciousness which usually redeemed it.

regard the rest of mankind with all the hatred of enemies '.[1]
That apparent inconsistency sprang from Jewish nationalism, which was so mighty a passion for good and for
evil, because it drank so deep at the fountain of national
religion.

Yet it would be quite unfair to the religious ideas of the
Old Testament if we judged them solely by such a narrow
and embittered nationalism. The broader outlook, even
of the post-exilic period, is manifest in not a few passages.
We have only to think of the two companion books,
' Jonah ' and ' Ruth '—both expressing, though in such
different ways, a noble universalism, a fine disregard
of the lower nationalism— to realise the heights possible
within that nation which could also descend to the level
of ' Esther '. The truth which ' Jonah ' and ' Ruth '
utter in story—that Yahweh can look beyond all the
barriers drawn around Israel—finds expression through
more than one unknown prophet. One of the most
remarkable passages is that which couples Israel with
Egypt and Assyria, as sharing alike the blessing of Yahweh.[2]
In another, almost startling by its catholicity, Yahweh
is pictured as removing the veil of mourning, and wiping
the tears from the eyes, not of the Jews alone, but of all
humanity.[3] Yet another seems to have taught that
the great world's altar-stairs slope, even through the
darkness of heathenism, up to the one true God.[4] The
spirit that underlies such utterances corresponds to the
practical relation of the Jewish Dispersion to the outside
world. The ' protected stranger ' (gēr) of the older nationalism was succeeded by the ' proselyte ' of the newer.[5]

[1] Tacitus, *Histories*, v. 5 (E.T. by Church and Brodribb, p. 195).

[2] Is. xix. 24, 25.

[3] 'One of the most catholic passages in the entire Old Testament, and one
of the tenderest presentations of Yahweh '(Gray, *Isaiah*, p. 429; on xxv. 6-8).

[4] Mal. i. 11. 'Malachi must have recognised a spirit of monotheism in
heathen religions, and allowed that offerings rendered to a God recognised
as one were rendered to Yahweh ' (Driver, *Century Bible, ad loc.*).

[5] Cf. Ps. lxxxvii. 5-7 ; Is. lvi. 6, 7.

Around the scattered groups of Jews within the Roman Empire we find larger circles of 'those that fear God', who were attracted to the moral monotheism of Judaism, and welcomed through its implicit universalism. And thus we come to the origins of Christianity, of which the ideas are so largely the ideas of the Old Testament interpreted through the Person and work of Jesus Christ.[1]

[1] On the liberation of these ideas from the narrow nationalism which fettered them, see Montefiore, *Hibbert Journal*, July 1912 ('The Significance of Jesus for His own Age').

CHAPTER IX

THE PERMANENT VALUE OF THE OLD TESTAMENT

FAMILIARITY is said to breed contempt, but much more frequently it is the parent of indifference. We are so familiar with the incorporation of the Old Testament in the Christian Bible that we seldom, if ever, reflect on the remarkable fact of its presence at all—one of the most remarkable facts in the history of religion. Here is the literature of an ancient people of the East, a nation of no great political importance, surviving into the crowded civilisation of the modern West, not simply as documents for the scholar, but as the common book of multitudes of common men. Here are writings in an Oriental speech, moulded throughout by Oriental modes of thought, and belonging to perhaps the most conservative of nations, which have passed from their unwilling hands into the thought and speech and very life-blood of Occidental religion. Here is an ancient book, of imperfect morality and anthropomorphic religion, still being offered to men as the living Word of God to their souls. A business man, harassed by the industrial problems of modern demo-cracy, drifts in to the service of an English cathedral. The majesty of his surroundings carries him back to the religion and art of the thirteenth century. The Creeds take him on a longer journey to the early centuries of the Catholic Church. But the First Lesson demands the longest pilgrimage of all, for he must listen, perhaps, to the story of Jezebel, of whose body was found no more than the skull, and the feet, and the palms of the hands.

It is worth while to try and realise the strangeness of the
history which has incorporated such flotsam and jetsam of
Semitic story into the ritual of an English cathedral in the
twentieth century after Christ.   But many at the present
day are concerned less with the wonder than with the
incongruity of it.   What has that Jehu who trampled
on the body of the murdered Jezebel to do with the religion
of Him who said ' Love your enemies ' ?   or, changing
the question from the particular to the general, how far
is the Christian use of the Old Testament based on un-
reasoning tradition, and how far on the recognition of its
permanent value to the Church ?

The question is not new, but it has been accentuated
by certain tendencies of modern thought.   From the very
beginnings of the Christian Church, so soon as it ceased
to be a Jewish sect and became a universal fellowship,
the inheritance of the Old Testament carried difficulties
with it.   That inheritance was indeed felt to be a
splendid one, and apostles in the first and apologists in
the second century made Old Testament prophecy the
main ground of their defence of Christ's claims.   To say
' Jesus is the Christ ', as Paul did, was to say ' Jesus is
that Messiah of whom the Jewish Scriptures speak '.
Justin Martyr dates his Christian life from the time when
a love of the prophets possessed him—men who spoke by
the divine Spirit, and foretold events which would and
actually did take place.[1]   More than this, it was plain to
any reader of the Gospels in the second century that the
life and teaching of Jesus were closely and vitally connected with the Jewish Scriptures.   Jesus Himself appealed
to them frequently for His own justification, as when He
said that mercy[2] was better than sacrifice, or when in the
synagogue at Nazareth He claimed the prophet's mission
as His own.   Throughout the whole New Testament
there ring the words, 'that the Scriptures might be fulfilled '.

[1] *Dialogue with Trypho*, chap. vii.
[2] Hebrew *hesed* ; see Additional Note to p. 49, line 22.

The prophecies they contain are traced back beyond the will of man to the influence of the Holy Spirit ; the Scriptures are ' a lamp shining in a squalid place until the daystar arise ' ; they are ' profitable for teaching, for reproof, for correction, for instruction which is in righteousness ' ; even if their testimony be fragmentary and varied, yet it is a true message from the same God who has now spoken in His Son.[1] The value of the Old Testament to the early Church was obvious and unquestioned ; it formed, indeed, the Bible of that Church before there was a New Testament at all.

At the same time, the difficulties attending its use were not less plain. The Old Testament, on the face of it, was primarily a national book, whilst Christianity soon became conscious of itself as a universal religion. The laws of the Old Testament gave little hint that they were intended for a season only ; indeed, the writer of the Epistle to the Hebrews must labour to convince Jewish Christians that the priesthood and sacrifices of the Old Covenant are but a provisional symbol, a passing shadow of the realities which belong to the New Covenant. A Christian writer in the second century [2] takes the more violent method of declaring that the Jews had completely misunderstood the Old Testament, which was meant to be throughout an allegory of spiritual realities. It was the allegorising method prevalent amongst Christians which enabled them to make the use of the Old Testament profitable for edification, and, in their own judgment, efficacious in argument. A yet more serious difficulty, however, arose from the moral teaching of the Old Testament. Jesus had Himself abrogated some of its laws as imperfect and now superseded, such as that which demanded an eye for an eye, a tooth for a tooth. Those who admit this principle of criticism, and use it intelligently, are

---

[1] 2 Peter i. 19-21 ; 2 Tim. iii. 15, 16 ; Heb. i. 1, 2 ; cf. Rom. xv. 4.
[2] In the so-called ' Epistle of Barnabas '.

faced by the same question in regard to every single precept of the Old Testament, ' Does this come up to the Christian standard ? ' The Jewish Law, indeed, seemed to contradict not only the Christian conscience, but even the Christian Gospel of grace ; [1] if God regulated His attitude and conduct towards men by strict justice, as the Old Testament frequently inculcated, what room could there be for the love which spared not His own Son ? In view of all these difficulties, there were not wanting Christians in the second century who boldly urged that the Old Testament should be rejected. A cardinal contrast was drawn by Gnostic Christianity between the God of the Old Testament and the God of the New ; by some the Old Testament was analysed into elements of varying value, on moral and other grounds. Yet, in spite of this searching criticism, the general Christian consciousness maintained its hold on the Old Testament, though often at the cost of forced and arbitrary exegesis. The heretics were often right in their explanations of the Old Testament ; yet the Christian religion would have been impoverished beyond measure if their conclusion had been accepted, and the Old Testament had been abandoned as an encumbrance, rather than a help, to the faith of Christians.

Modern objections to the Old Testament, so far as they appeal simply to its unscientific view of nature, its historical inconsistencies, its imperfect morality, its anthropomorphic representations of God, need not be considered. These are effective enough against those who still uphold a theory of verbal inspiration, but their effectiveness disappears when they encounter the critical view of the

---

[1] The contradiction is apparent rather than real, for behind the individual requirements of the Law lay the national covenant of grace, answering to the covenant with the new Israel, made in Christ's death. The legalistic detail of the Old Testament largely obscured this parallelism, and the Jewish emphasis on the 'Law' naturally led to the Pauline antithesis between 'Law' and 'Gospel'. The grace of the Gospel is more prominent partly because of its *individual* presentation.

history of Israel which regards it as a progressive development. Yet other difficulties arise as the result of the acceptance of this principle which do deserve serious consideration. The critical view of the Old Testament seems to many to exclude the reality of revelation, by surrendering the history to purely naturalistic, or, at any rate, purely human factors. The ideas themselves are thought to belong as a whole to a stage of thought now left behind, and to have lost their authority. The Old Testament, however interesting to the scholar, appears to become unsuitable for moral and religious instruction, when historical, moral, and religious perfection is no longer claimed for its contents. These are the difficulties now to be met in the light of the results of preceding chapters. It will be urged (1) that the history of Israel fulfils all the conditions we ought to expect in a divine revelation; (2) that the intrinsic worth and permanent value of the created ideas does prove them to be such a revelation ; (3) and that the literary record of this history has a service to render to morality and religion not less valuable in the future than in the past.

1. *Israel's History as a Divine Revelation*

The essential fact in revelation is the real activity of God. The highest conception of religion regards it as the fellowship of God and man, but there can be no real fellowship where the self-manifestation is all on man's side. Man often seems to speak into a measureless and unbroken silence, but if the silence of God were as real as it often seems to be, religion would be the most pathetic of all self-deceptions, and the highest experiences of human personality a cruel illusion within an irrational universe. The fact is significant that the three great theistic religions—Judaism, Christianity, and Muhammedanism—are all religions of revelation. From the standpoint of philosophy, divine personality is unthinkable without divine self-communication, resulting in human knowledge of God. The manner and the matter of such divine self-communication can be ascertained only by experience. Man must adjust himself to the divine method, and thankfully profit by the measure of knowledge he may attain. This knowledge will be of the truth, and truth will be self-consistent. But God will certainly not be dependent on external human methods of communicating knowledge. Fellowship with God implies that man is in the presence of One greater than himself, One who may make Himself known in subtle and unforeseen ways. The line of demarcation between man's approach to God and God's approach to man may be indecipherable. Indeed, the soundest philosophical position seems to be that ' revelation and discovery must be the same process viewed from different standpoints '.[1]

The revelation of God to Israel must be sought primarily in the life behind the literature. That literature came into existence largely, if not wholly, in unconsciousness of any claim to canonical inspiration. At the most, it was a *record* of revelation. Even the prophets, in whom the experience of divine revelation culminates, were not so much scribes as spokesmen of truth. The Jewish theory that the Law was dictated to Moses does not agree with the evidence of the Law itself, which clearly shows successive and slowly developed strata. The Old Testament, interpreted in the light it throws on its own origin, testifies to the reality of a divine revelation in the *life* of Israel. God was revealed not simply in words, but in a series of acts extending over a thousand years. At first sight, much more unity is apparent in the Kur'ān than in the Old Testament, for the Kur'ān reflects the life of a single generation as interpreted through the idiosyncrasies of a single individual. But how much more

[1] Gwatkin, *The Knowledge of God*, i. p. 156.

majestic, on any theory, is the revelation which needed a nation's whole history for its medium !

But to say that the divine revelation was made through the life of Israel is necessarily to admit its progressive character. The 'discoveries' made by the nation's leaders, in the realms of morality and religion, were, so far as true, divine revelation. In every step forward God and man were participating, and the pace was set by the needs and limitations of the weaker partner in this fellowship. In the whole of Israel's experience, and in every idea which arose to interpret it, there were these two factors of both human and divine activity. The fellowship would not have been genuine without man's co-operation as well as God's. The men through whom the revelation came were themselves being educated, and educational advance is necessarily from less to more. We may speak anthropomorphically of a divine accommodation on the part of the teacher to the limitations of the pupil, but this takes into account no more than the revelation *to* Israel. There remains the revelation *through* Israel to the world, the revelation through an experience in which error and truth necessarily mingled, because man was working as well as God. The reason for the divine patience in revelation is, therefore, not wholly stated, when we speak of the education of Israel as necessarily progressive. A deeper reason, which helps to explain the apparent limitations of that revelation, is that God's purposes are such that they can be achieved only through the fellowship of man. Just as God commits the practical regeneration of society to the Christian citizenship of to-day, so He committed the cardinal revelation of His purpose to the deepening consciousness of moral and religious truth in the national life of Israel. Not only, then, had the revelation to be progressive, for the sake of those who first 'discovered' it, but also for the sake of Him who gave it. In this, as in so much else,

He waits for the co-operation of His fellow-workmen, because the value of the result in His eyes depends on the reality of the fellowship between Himself and men.

The point of most intimate contact in this fellowship of revelation was the prophetic consciousness of Israel, and the unique aspects of the result are largely to be explained through this characteristic feature of the religion. There are three possible spheres of revelation, grouped as concentric circles around the central fact of the fellowship of God and man. The largest is Nature, taken in abstraction from man ; then comes History, in its broadest sense, as the record of man's development, individual or racial; and finally, at the centre, Consciousness, the direct personal experience of the individual. The Greeks began at the circumference of the largest circle, and worked inwards. The Hebrews began [1] at the centre and worked outwards. Within each circle they found themselves in contact with God. The innermost conviction of the prophetic consciousness is that the same divine Person who speaks to the prophet's heart is controlling the events of history, and upholding the phenomena of nature. From these two outer circles are drawn the necessary materials, the contemporary data, for the prophet to interpret. It is his task to find God *there*, as he has already found Him *here*. But the fact that he begins *here*, at the centre of personal communion with God, gives him new and far-reaching powers of insight. The prophet himself makes the claim that that insight comes from God. Certainly no other explanation is adequate to explain the results of the insight. Directly, or indirectly, it is the prophetic consciousness which gives to the Old Testament its peculiar quality and its historic influence. The claim of Israel to have received a divine

---

[1] *I.e.* in emphasis, not historical order, since the three 'circles' are separable only for such analysis as this. Moses, for example, interprets by his prophetic consciousness a physical event, which is part of Israel's history, as the act of God.

revelation stands or falls with the reality of such personal fellowship between God and man as may issue in a true knowledge of God within the human heart. In this way the philosophy of revelation passes into the philosophy of religious experience in general ; what reality underlies both ? This vital question ought not to be complicated by any of the alleged difficulties of inspiration within and of miracle without. These are questions of method and manner, and they are subsidiary to the fundamental issue of all religion—the reality of God's fellowship with man. It may be said that such a view of revelation, which traces it to the immanent presence of the transcendent God within the prophetic consciousness, is open to two objections. It does not distinguish that consciousness from the general religious experience, except in degree, and therefore it leaves us without a unique origin for admittedly unique results. Nor does it enable us to distinguish the false and the true, the human error and the divine truth, within that consciousness, by any external criterion or standard, and therefore it leaves us unable to decide what *is* divine revelation in any particular instance. Both statements are true, and both conclusions are false. There is no need to distinguish the prophetic consciousness from religious experience in general, except by its greater intensity. But greater intensity, or difference of degree, does insensibly pass into a difference of kind.[1] We do not dishonour prophecy when we lift human personality into such kinship with the divine as to make the prophetic experience possible to all men. 'Would God that all Yahweh's people were prophets, that Yahweh would put His spirit upon them !'   We

---

[1] This may be illustrated by the fact that the earth is large enough to have an atmosphere, and the moon is not. 'By simply piling atoms or stones together into a mighty mass there comes a critical point at which an atmosphere becomes possible ; and directly an atmosphere exists, all manner of phenomena may spring into existence, which without it were quite impossible ' (Lodge, *Life and Matter*,[4] p. 72).

must conceive God as seeking entrance into all human souls not less, but more, eagerly than the highest souls seek entrance into His fellowship. That one man, or one nation, should enjoy a closer and more intimate knowledge of God than others, presents no more difficulty than the fact that one man or nation may possess a finer artistic consciousness, or a deeper passion for freedom. They will all have their place in the embracing purpose of God, and 'all service ranks the same with God'. The problems of divine election, which re-state the problems of human experience, are very real, but they must not be exaggerated by ideas of partiality and favouritism. Where God finds men able and willing to receive Him, there He finds an instrument for His purpose. The prophetic consciousness is essentially human consciousness in fellow-ship with God. As for the second objection, that no adequate criterion of divine revelation exists unless truth be communicated to the prophets in some 'miraculous', *i.e.* abnormal, manner, such a view really dishonours truth. If God really imparts truth to man through inter-course with Himself, will not that truth have an intrinsic quality which will suffice to set it apart, sooner or later, from all that is untrue ? What higher test of revelation can there be than truth itself ? In one sense, indeed, history becomes the guide to truth. The prophets them-selves appealed to it in confirmation of their words. But we also saw that they appealed to a self-evidencing power in divine truth, which enforced conviction prior to the confirmation by history. The historic influence of Israel's ideas, and particularly their incorporation in the Christian faith, does confirm all that might be gathered from their intrinsic worth. But such evidence is subsidiary. The primary proof of revelation must lie in the character of the ideas which claim to be revealed. If they are unique in character and importance, and are able to secure a unique response from the human heart, then they have established their claim to be a divine revelation. The position in regard to the Scriptures as a whole has been tersely summed up by the words : ' There is impressed upon the writings which make up the Bible a breadth and variety, an intensity and purity of religious life, that are without parallel in any other literature of the world. That is the fact which we seek to express in the doctrine of Inspiration. We know no other explanation for it than a special action of the Spirit of God '.[1] ' This result and the relative history is not due to the inborn religious genius of this people, not to a dead law of necessary development, not to the fortunate concurrence of chance events, but, as our firm conviction is, to the real activity of God in the history and in personalities '.[2]

2. *The Ideas and their Intrinsic Worth*

' The great object in trying to understand history, political, religious, literary, or scientific, is to get behind men and to grasp ideas '.[3] That has been the chief aim of the preceding chapters, which have tried to penetrate through the literature to the history, through the history to the lives of the men who made it, through their lives to the dominant ideas which controlled their religion. It is there, if anywhere, that the self-evidencing results of divine revelation must be found. Israel's work and distinction in the general history of mankind is to have become the living embodiment of these ideas. If men want them, it is to the Old Testament they must go to find them most impressively expressed ; nowhere else will they be found set forth so thoroughly, so dramatically, and with such earnest conviction of their truth. But if they are to have the further claim upon our reverence and loyal obedience which belongs to divinely revealed truth,

---

[1] Sanday, *E.R.E.*, *s.v.* ' Bible ', ii. p. 579.
[2] Koeberle, *Sünde und Gnade*, p. 667.   [3] Lord Acton, *Letters*, p. 6.

the proof must lie in their own nature. It will be convenient, in the first place, to summarise the results that
have been reached.

The leading idea of Israel's religion, the characteristic
feature that alone sets it apart from all other religions
not dependent upon it, is its idea of God. He is the personal Creator, Upholder, and Ruler of the world, adminis-
tering its government in pursuit of a holy and gracious
purpose. Complementary to this, there is the idea of
man as wholly dependent upon God, and not able to
approach Him without moral holiness, yet drawn to love
Him in that gracious fellowship through which He gives
Himself to man. Through the moral demands of this
fellowship the problem of human suffering found characteristic interpretation, as penalty for sin, discipline of
character, opportunity for disinterested service and sacrificial offering. As a further result of the moral emphasis,
there came the vision of a future Kingdom of God, in
which His sovereignty would at last be fully displayed in
social righteousness.

These four ideas (of God, of man, of suffering, and of
the kingdom) may be said to epitomise the spiritual
religion of the Old Testament. They have become so
familiar to the religious thought of Western civilisation
that it is difficult to realise their greatness—until we
remember that our very familiarity with them is a spiritual
debt to Israel through Christianity, and the best proof
of their epoch-making significance. In the Old Testament they are usually found with the limitations of a
nationalistic setting, but in principle they are of universal
application. In the Old Testament, also, they are more
or less closely linked to a ceremonial religion that has
ceased to have more than archæological interest ; yet
they are essentially spiritual principles, of which no outward forms and ceremonies can ever be more than the
passing accompaniment. Moreover, Israel's ethical mono-

theism, its religious view of human nature, its moral philosophy of history, its divine Utopianism, are features unique in the history of religion, in respect of their vigour, intensity, and practical effects. Thus, the universality, the spirituality, and the uniqueness of these ideas prove them to be at least worthy to be made the contents of a divine revelation. But their intrinsic worth becomes most apparent when considered in relation to the New Testament, to the tendencies of modern philosophy, and to the ultimate test afforded by religious experience.

The New Testament, in the light of all it has done for the human race, is the clearest historical demonstration of the worth of the religious ideas of the Old Testament. The ideas indicated in the last two paragraphs are central also in the *New* Testament, and historically necessary for its explanation. The earliest form of Christianity may be regarded as a reformation of contemporary Judaism along the lines of the prophetic teaching of the Old Testament. The idea of God which is presupposed by the faith and teaching of the prophet of Nazareth is substantially that of the Old Testament. 'The New Testament', it has been said, 'had nothing further to add to the outline of the idea of God [in the Old Testament], but, on the contrary, is glad to employ its language '.[1] Children sometimes ask the naïve question whether the Jews have the same God as the Christians. The answer of history is surely in the affirmative, however true it be that the Person and work of Christ add a wealth of new meaning to the old idea. The Gospel of the New Testament, moreover, implies just that religious view of human nature which is the distinction of Old Testament faith. Men are assumed to be wholly dependent on God. No approach to Him is possible if moral holiness be not sought. No morality is adequate which is not due to the inner prompting of love for God. The central fact of the New Testament,

[1] Kautzsch, *Die bleibende Bedeutung des Alten Testaments*, p. 26.

the suffering of Christ on the Cross, gains its evangelical passion and power by being interpreted along lines already laid down by the Old Testament. Finally, the dominant New Testament idea in regard to human society is that of the kingly rule of God, realised amongst all sorts and conditions of men by moral obedience to Him. To say this is not, of course, to say that the New Testament makes no substantial addition to the Old. But the advance lies rather in the liberation of the highest Old Testament ideas from their limitations and lower accompaniments,[1] in their historic exhibition and enrichment through the life, death, and resurrection of Christ, and in their combination with the fresh and powerful dynamic created by personal devotion to Him.

Whatever degree of authority, therefore, may attach to the New Testament as divine revelation belongs, in its own measure, to the Old. The cardinal ideas of both are intrinsically and historically inseparable, and herein consists the organic unity of the Bible.[2] Its unity is one of the most convincing examples of divine purpose in history. This teleological argument, it should be noticed, is strengthened, not weakened, by the critical study of the Old Testament. The vision of its whole religious teaching as a divinely guided development supplies a broad-based argument from the Old Testament to the New, immeasurably richer and stronger than the ingenious application of obscure sentences. We may compare this change of general standpoint with that which has come over the teleological argument for the existence of God, the argument from design in the natural world to a designer.

[1] Cf. Montefiore, *Hibbert Journal*, July 1912, p. 767: 'the significance of Jesus for his age lay in this, that he caused fundamental beliefs of Judaism, and more especially fundamental religious relationships of the Jews to one another and to God, to flow over to, and become the possession of, the world at large'.

[2] That 'prophetic consciousness' which is central in New Testament revelation (cf. the work of the Spirit) is not less central in the creation of the Old Testament—a fact brought out more clearly than ever by critical study.

Paley could compare this or that detail of Nature's working to a watch, from which one might infer a watch-maker. The acceptance of natural evolution has destroyed the argument in its old form, because it has taught us the slow growth of each detail from the less to the more perfect. But it has given us a new form of the argument in the vision of Nature as a whole, ceaselessly striving onwards and upwards. We do not need to look for cunning details as examples of the designer's skill; the heavens declare the glory of God, and the firmament showeth His handiwork. So is it with the modern argument from the Old Testament to the New; it rests not on precarious interpretations of the text, ' Behold a virgin shall conceive ',[1] but on the whole course of Israel's history, and on the implicit prophecy of Israel's religion. There is a vital unity, a cumulative effect, a cosmic method, in the modern appeal to the Old Testament, which the older appeal never had.

In the second place, it may fairly be claimed that the tendencies of modern philosophy support the religious ideas of the Old Testament. Here we may seem to invoke a dangerous and unnecessary ally. It needs less thought and trouble to declare that religion is independent of philosophy, and to point to the warring philosophic schools as sufficient evidence of the futility of metaphysics. But philosophy is after all as much pledged to truth as is religion. Ultimately they must be different aspects of the one truth, and every true philosophy should issue in a religion, as every religion involves a philosophy. At the present day materialism is bankrupt, so far as competent thinkers are concerned; agnosticism is in little better case, save as a healthy moderating influence against easy dogmatism; only a spiritualistic interpretation of the universe has any chance of acceptance. But within this realm of thought the inadequacy of any uncompromising

[1] Isa. vii. 14 as translated by A.V. and R.V. (text; margin has ' maiden').

theory of immanence has become apparent to many. The facts of life are too complex to be traced so easily to the manifestation of the Absolute. Personality, in very different schools of philosophy, asserts its right to fuller recognition. The future of philosophy is seen to depend on its attitude to the great mystery of personality, whether in man or God. More attention is being directed to the moral and spiritual 'values' of personality than, perhaps, ever before. But this increasing emphasis on personality is itself an approximation to the religious emphasis of the Old Testament. Man and God are there brought face to face, with no impenetrable barrier between them. Man is conceived as a personality distinct from God, yet wholly dependent upon Him. God has imparted a life to man which, by its spiritual kinship with His, makes religious fellowship possible between them. God controls Nature no less directly, simply, and mysteriously than the human will controls the movements of the human body, and miracle can be interpreted as the operation of higher law (wherever there is adequate evidence for its occurrence), the higher law of higher personality. Is there not much more common ground between the tendencies of modern thought and the presuppositions of the ideas of the Old Testament than is often recognised ? May we not fairly claim that the truth, and therefore the divine source, of those ideas is confirmed by the testimony drawn not only from religious experience, but also from many centuries of philosophic inquiry ?

Thirdly, and chiefly, there is the evidence to the worth of these ideas offered by religious experience itself. That intimate fellowship with God, through which these ideas were generated in the Old Testament religion, and universalised in the New, is still necessary for the full proof of their truth. Their primal source is still their ultimate guarantee. That through which they first came is still the highest court of appeal. Conviction in religious

truth is religiously conditioned, as inevitably as conviction of artistic beauty is æsthetically conditioned, or as
conviction in the realm of natural phenomena is scientifi-
cally conditioned. Without a certain equipment in each
of these realms, a man lacks the data for proof. To say
this is not to surrender the highest proof of revelation
to mere wilful subjectivity ; it is rather to raise spiritual
discernment to the level of artistic and scientific insight.
In each case truth without is recognised through the
spiritual capacity for truth within, and all else that is
said is really the explication of the recognition, by appeal
to the ' doctrines ' of religion, the ' principles ' of art, the
' laws ' of nature. This may be more apparent if the four
fundamental ideas of the Old Testament be briefly considered as an interpretation of universal religious experience.

The idea of God which the Old Testament presents is
rich in just that wealth of personal attribute which religious experience demands.[1] All that makes the noblest
companionship between man and man is represented
here, whilst the divine attributes of perfect wisdom,
power and love are those which religious experience must
seek in order to find rest. Religion cannot be content
with anything less than this idea, when once it has reached
it, and no clearer proof of its *worth* can be given.[2] Similarly, at any rate, since Schleiermacher's time, the element
of dependence in the deepest religious experience has been
generally recognised. Man does find his highest powers
in the conscious surrender of himself to One higher than
himself. There is an implicit logic in the abandonment
of the soul to the mercy and love of God—' the right of
the weaker over the stronger, which is part of the moral

[1] The statement is obviously not true of certain types of Eastern religion,
but the issues between East and West are too large for discussion in this
place. The assumption here made is that the future lies with the religion
that develops, not with that which denies, personality.
[2] Cf. J. S. Mill's argument as to the worth of pleasures in *Utilitarianism*,
pp. 12 f. of 11th ed.

structure of the universe '.[1] In regard to the great
problem of all religions and all philosophies, the existence of moral and physical evil, the interpretation of the
Old Testament still leaves no inconsiderable margin of
mystery, but it can inspire adequate courage with which
to face the mystery. If this interpretation be true, it is
worth while to suffer, whether by way of penalty, discipline, or service. It is worth while, in a sense in which
the Buddhist escape by the denial of personality is not
worth while. Finally, the vision of the Kingdom of God
in social righteousness gives just that strength and
stimulus to humanitarian effort and social progress which
they need for permanent and vital success. Sooner or
later, the religious consciousness will raise the question
as to the source and the goal of those social duties which
the moral consciousness prompts. The Old Testament
lays the foundation of the only satisfying answer.

Ideas which thus continue to meet the deepest needs of
men must have an intrinsic worth, establishing their claim
to truth. They have received one convincing testimony
in the arena of history, a testimony supported by a multitude of lesser testimonies, but supreme and unique. The
life of Jesus Christ was based on faith in those ideas,
and that life, issuing in apparent defeat, is the clearest
example of victory history knows. The story of the
Cross is the most terrible indictment of the Providence
of God that experience can offer—till we penetrate to
the intrinsic worth of the Sufferer's self-surrender, and
see that the Resurrection is the crown of *a victory already
won*. We may apply to that story words written in
a very different connection, yet even more true here :
' the heroic being, though in one sense and outwardly
he has failed, is yet in another sense superior to the world
in which he appears ; is in some way which we do not
seek to define, untouched by the doom that overtakes

---

[1] Phillips Brooks, *The Influence of Jesus*, p. 131.

him ; and is rather set free from life than deprived of it
. . . an idea which, if developed, would transform the
tragic view of things. It implies that the tragic world,
if taken as it is presented, with all its error, guilt, failure,
woe and waste, is no final reality, but only a part of reality
taken for the whole, and when so taken, illusive ; and that,
if we could see the whole, and the tragic facts in their true
place in it, we should find them not abolished, of course,
but so transmuted that they had ceased to be strictly
tragic '.[1]

It is in this way that Jesus demonstrates the truth
of the Old Testament, rather than by the use He makes
of its literature. The ideas supply the one interpretation of life which the religious consciousness seeks. The
prophets and Christ declared certain things to be true of
God and human life. We cannot gain the ultimate proof
that they spoke divine truth, except by following their
footsteps up the peaks of spiritual fellowship with God,
along tracks which their feet have made possible. Is there
not a certain divine purpose apparent in the fact that
religion itself becomes the one test of religious truth ?
Here, as elsewhere, the co-operation of man is essential
to the result. If a man does not in some measure
share in the purposes of God, they will not convince him of
their ultimate reality. But, ' if any man willeth to do His
will, he shall know of the teaching, whether it be of God '.

3. *The Practical Value of the Literature*

There remains a final question of great practical importance, which to-day perplexes the minds of many who are
concerned with the teaching of Biblical religion. Suppose
the general contention of Old Testament criticism to be
admitted, viz. that the Old Testament is a progressive

[1] Bradley, *Shakespearean Tragedy*, pp. 324 f. (with special reference to
King Lear).

and not an absolute revelation of the fundamental Christian truths, containing much that is not history, much imperfect morality judged by a Christian standard, many statements about God which have dramatic rather than dogmatic value—how far can we continue to make use of it in public worship and private devotion, and especially in the teaching of religion to the young or the uneducated ? In rejecting such direct appeal to the letter of Scripture as would imply that this, and not the life behind it, were the primary revelation, have we not deprived it of its authoritative place and power ?

In answer to such questions, it is not enough to say that we must take the Bible as we find it, and that if the facts to which criticism appeals are indeed facts, we must make the best of the conclusions. Such an answer might imply that we have lost something by the newer interpretation of the Old Testament, whereas the argument of this book has been that we have gained immeasurably, so far as the vital and permanent elements of the Old Testament are concerned. The difficulty really springs from the inability of many to realise that Old Testament criticism attacks not the authority of revelation but only the supposed *externalism* of it. The great ideas still possess whatever authority they once possessed ; moreover, they are brought out more clearly, just as the light and shade of a country are brought out by the study of its contour lines. More intelligent study and a deeper spiritual response are needed in order that we may hear God's voice with full confidence, but are not these demands gain instead of loss ?

As for the supposition that a selective attitude to the letter of the revelation must of necessity weaken its authority as a whole, it is worthy of notice that the principle of selection as applied to Scripture is not new in practice. Whatever theory has been held as to the absolute value of revelation, men have, in practice, always been drawn to attach more importance to some parts than to others. The only authority worth the name exercised by Scripture has been that which is involved in the intrinsic worth of its ideas, the authority of truth over life. The Bible is written in invisible ink, until its hidden characters are brought out by the warmth of personal experience. The real argument for the authority of the written Word has always been the same, since the intrinsic worth of certain parts of Jewish and Christian literature was recognised and acknowledged. Men have accepted the Bible in the past, as they will accept it in the future, because they have been able to say with Coleridge, ' I have found words for my inmost thoughts, songs for my joy, utterances for my hidden griefs, and pleadings for my shame and my feebleness '.[1] The Bible, as he says, proves its inspiration because it *finds* us. But to admit this is already to recognise a selective principle. Life brings its test to truth, as the father says to his son, on visiting the school chapel :

> 'This is the Chapel : here, my son,
>   Your father thought the thoughts of youth,
> And heard the words that one by one
>   The touch of Life has turned to truth '.[2]

So far as the educational use of the Old Testament is concerned, the practical difficulties that spring from its critical interpretation can easily be exaggerated. In the case of young children—and this applies to all who occupy the position of children from the standpoint of instruction—difficulties will hardly arise in such passages as are chosen, and a wise selection of passages would have to be made in any case. Children ' should be familiarised early with the text of the Bible. . . . Whatever is to be added afterwards, a knowledge of the text is a primary

---

[1] *Confessions of an Enquiring Spirit*, p. 10 (ed. 1840).
[2] Henry Newbolt (*Clifton Chapel*).

essential'.[1] Nothing ought to be taught them, of course, in this or in any other field of instruction, which could not subsequently be accepted as *relatively* true. But it would be not less fatal to sound instruction to call attention prematurely to those less obvious features on which criticism fastens, and to suggest difficulties that have not yet been felt. The simple narratives of the Old Testament, such as the story of Joseph, and the simple statement of great ideas, such as the 23rd Psalm, can be taught to a child like any other story or poem within its range of comprehension. As questions concerning historicity arise, they must be frankly met. When the 'lower morality' of the Old Testament as compared with the New has become apparent, the time will be ripe for showing that the history of Israel was itself an educative process, for even a child notices that parents and teachers judge the same act differently when done at different ages. Indeed, such difficulties belong rather to the conventional view of Scripture as a verbally inspired text-book of morals and doctrine. It may fairly be urged that, even for a child, the interpretation of the Old Testament as a progressive revelation does away with more difficulties than it creates. The child who has never been taught an untrue literalism will never be handicapped by the necessity of unlearning it. The teacher can afford to neglect those difficulties which a child taught on modern lines will never feel. The teacher's aim is, firstly, to impart true and sympathetic knowledge of the Old Testament, simply as literature, and, secondly, to emphasise and bring into prominence those great ideas which are the true prophecies of Christ and His Gospel. If teaching on these modern lines does call for more skill, more patience in the teacher's own acquisition of truth, less easy dogmatism and parrot-like repetition of borrowed ideas, surely this should make us thankful for that new light by which God has called

[1] Driver, *The Higher Criticism*, p. 62.

us to devote ourselves with more whole-hearted application, and with greater expenditure of time and pains, to the study of His holy Word.

A closer study of the Old Testament, critical in method, yet devotional in spirit and aim, might well prepare men for the better understanding of the Gospel of Christ as the power of God unto salvation. Those who have escaped from the naturalism and agnosticism of a past generation, without yet finding firm anchorage in religious truth, might well ponder the words with which Herbert Spencer brings his autobiography practically to its close, words which have their own pathos in view of the prison-wall he built around himself and so many others : ' Largely, however, if not chiefly, this change of feeling towards religious creeds and their sustaining institutions, has resulted from a deepening conviction that the sphere occupied by them can never become an unfilled sphere, but that there must continue to arise afresh the great questions concerning ourselves and surrounding things ; and that, if not positive answers, then modes of consciousness standing in place of positive answers, must ever remain '.[1] Here, surely, the permanent value of the Old Testament is apparent. Its great ideas can train men in such ' modes of consciousness ' as will be transformed into ' positive answers ' by spiritual contact with Christ.

The Old Testament is more than ever the Word of God to man, when its religious ideas are seen in their true perspective, and its authority is recognised as not of the letter, but of the spirit. The literature which is the casket of these ideas is rightly to be called a divine revelation. It will still speak to the hearts of men, as with the living utterance of the God and Father of Jesus Christ. The truths it contains await our needs, not as pale and remote abstractions, but embodied in the concrete history of a national life, a history recorded in a literature second

[1] *Autobiography*, ii. p. 469.

only to that of the New Testament in the height of its religious experience. The ideas come to us wedded to striking phrase and vivid figure, which form the noblest part of the vocabulary of religion, in all the generations. They are accessible to all men, and comprehensive of all needs through the variety of their expression, which ranges from the simple story that a child can follow, up to the vision of unseen things large enough to be the goal of a life of saintly experience. They are the only vestibule by which we can enter with understanding into the palace of New Testament truth, prepared to reverence its greater glory.

ADDITIONAL NOTES

P. 8, line 28 : See H. H. Rowley, *From Joseph to Joshua* (Schweich Lectures), 1950, for a recent discussion of the settlement in Canaan. Very full bibliographical details are also to be found there.

P. 13, note 2 : Recent attempts to dissociate the book of Deuteronomy from the reform of Josiah, on the grounds that the book must be either very much earlier, or very much later, have not gained much support from scholars. H. H. Rowley has a penetrating study of the date of Deuteronomy in relation to the work of the prophet Jeremiah in his essay 'The Prophet Jeremiah and the Book of Deuteronomy' in *Studies in Old Testament Prophecy*, Ed. H. H. Rowley, 1950.

P. 49, l. 22 : The allusion here is to Hosea vi. 6. The Hebrew word translated 'mercy', *hesed*, 'is very difficult to render, for it expresses the moral bondage of love, the loving discharge of an admitted obligation, the voluntary acceptance of a responsibility' (H. W. Robinson, *Two Hebrew Prophets*, 1948, p. 47). The parallelism of phrasing in Hos. vi. 6 shows that the prophet has in mind man's obligation of *hesed* towards God. This would, of course, in turn affect his behaviour to his fellow men.

P. 56, l. 14 : For a recent treatment of the Ark, discussing its possible origin in the palladium of early Bedouin tribes and emphasising its military associations, see J. Morgenstern, *The Ark, the Ephod, and the 'Tent of Meeting'*, 1945.

P. 60, l. 14 : Another possible translation is 'Yahweh our God is one Yahweh' as in the R.V. This may well be a polemic against the use of the term Baal for Yahweh. There were many Baals but there cannot be more than one Yahweh.

P. 64, l. 1 : On the 'brazen serpent' and its possible connection with Jerusalem and the Zadokite priesthood see H. H. Rowley 'Zadok and Nehushtan', J. B. L., 1939, pp. 113 ff.

P. 69, l. 6 : The word here translated 'loving-kindness' is *hesed*, see the additional note to p. 49. In this instance it is Yahweh who will show *hesed* to his people. It is closely bound up with the love that Yahweh has for his people of which Hosea speaks in chapter xi.

P. 72, l. 17 : For a fuller recognition of the realism of the belief that man is in God's image just as Seth is in the image of Adam (Gen. v. 3) see H. W. Robinson, *Inspiration and Revelation in the Old Testament*, 1946, p. 19.

P. 105, l. 2 : These two types of media of manifestation, the human form and natural phenomena are not necessarily mutually exclusive. There were anthropomorphic features in all theophanies, even those which might be termed nature theophanies.

P. 106, n. 4 : For a short time the conception of the name of Yahweh seems to have played a similar role to that of the ' angel '. In Isa. xxx. 27-33 the name advances in all strength and majesty to punish the Assyrians. In a somewhat stereotyped form it appears in the Deuteronomic conception of the name of Yahweh dwelling in the central sanctuary. With the designation of Astarte as the ' name of Baal ' (in the inscription of Eshmun-'azar, Cooke, *North Semitic Inscriptions*, 1903, p. 30) we may compare that of the goddess Tanith as the ' face of Baal ' in Carthaginian inscriptions (*op. cit.*, p. 132). In Hebrew thought there was a time when the ' face of Yahweh ' was parallel in usage with that of ' name ' or ' angel ', cf. Exod. xxxii. 14 (' My face shall go with thee '), Deut. iv. 37 and Isa. lxiii. 9 (LXX).

P. 107, n. 1 : This paragraph scarcely represents the full vigour of Hebrew anthropomorphism. However veiled the language may have become through the use of terms like angel, name and face, there remains the vivid Hebrew conception of God in person making himself known to his people. In a later work (*Inspiration and Revelation in the Old Testament*, 1946, pp. 189 f.) Robinson wrote : ' In all simplicity of conviction they do not hesitate to use the most daring language of God, and to ascribe to Him what might be called a human constitution . . . The God of the prophets, . . . is no changeless and impassible being, but a living Person, revealed through His activities as sufficiently like man to be known by him '.

P. 109, line 1 : The word ephod is of uncertain etymology and we cannot readily determine from the few references to it in the O.T. what form or forms the object took. There are three possibilities : (i) a garment for ordinary use, apparently covering the loins, (ii) an image or other sacred object, and (iii) the special garment worn by the High Priest and associated with the Urim and Thummim. Whether, as a special development of the primitive loin-cloth it had phallic associations is not clear. There is almost certainly some constant association of it with divination. (See Foote in *Journal of Biblical Literature*, xxi. (1902), pp. 1-47, J. Morgenstern, *The Ark, the Ephod and the ' Tent of Meeting* ', 1945.)

P. 113, l. 29 : The ascription of independent psychical and moral qualities to the different physical organs should not be thought to imply a denial of the unity of self-consciousness, but rather a diffusion of functions *within* the unified self, see Ch. IV, 1.

P. 116, n. 3 : If Ezekiel was in Babylon from 597 onwards, then his knowledge of events in Palestine does involve some abnormal psychical conditions. If, however, it can be demonstrated, as Wheeler Robinson himself thought in later years (*Two Hebrew Prophets*, pp. 70 ff), that Ezekiel prophesied in Jerusalem until the fall of the city in 586, and only thereafter in Babylon, then some of the 'transporting' phenomena must be regarded as editorial.

P. 118, l. 4 : The 'diffusion' of consciousness, here implied, must not be pressed so far as to deny self-consciousness in the natural sense of the term.

P. 135, l. 25 : In the Old Testament the word *asherah* (translated 'grove' in A.V. and transliterated in R.V.) seems to be used both to refer to a goddess of that name and to the tree or pole that was a symbol of the goddess. For references to the goddess see Jud. iii. 7, 1 Kings xv. 13, xviii. 19, 2 Kings xxi. 7, xxiii. 4, 7 ; and to the tree or pole, Deut. vii. 5, xii. 3, xvi. 21, Jud. vi. 25 f., 2 Chron. xxxiii. 19. The occurrence of a similar name in the Ras Shamra texts suggests that the goddess *Asherah* is to be distinguished from Astarte (J. W. Jack, *The Ras Shamra Tablets*, 1935, p. 24). The *Mazzebah* was probably the symbol of the male deity.

P. 138, n. 1 : The story of Abimelech (Judges ix) shows that the Israelites and the Shechemites lived a common social life and possibly also a common religious life. There was a temple of El- or Baal-Berith, and it has been suggested that the covenant (*berith*) may have been between the Israelites and the Shechemites (although it might also be a covenant between the worshippers and their God).

P. 149, n. 3 : It is not at all certain that 'synagogue' is the right translation of the Hebrew word *moʻed*, the common meaning of which is 'meeting, assembly'. The synagogue therefore is probably not even named in the Old Testament.

P. 167, n. 1 : There is no doubt that the result of *kipper* is expiation or atonement, but it is not clear whether the Hebrews thought of the action as one of 'covering' the sins or of 'wiping' them away. The former draws on the meaning of the cognate verb in Arabic and the latter on the cognate verbs in Accadian and Syriac.

P. 188, n. 1 : Another view is that the word may be derived from the verb *barah*, 'to eat', 'to enjoy fellowship whilst eating', see Köhler and Baumgartner, *Lexicon in Veteris Testamenti Libros*.

P. 188, n. 4 : It is significant that W. Eichrodt presented the whole theology of the Old Testament around the idea of the covenant.

P. 190, l. 27 : A fuller treatment of the day of Yahweh will be found in Chapter X of Wheeler Robinson's *Inspiration and Revelation in the Old Testament*.

P. 195, n. 5 : Psalms xcv.-c., together with xlvii. and xciii., are commonly known as the 'Enthronement Psalms'. It is thought that Yahweh's kingship was celebrated by an enthronement ceremony of some kind at the New Year Festival. There was a corresponding festival held in Babylon, but the Israelite festival, while keeping alive some of the mythology of the past, went beyond the Babylonian counterpart not only because it celebrated the kingship of the 'living' God, but because it looked to the future, it was eschatological. Cf. A. R. Johnson, *Sacral Kingship in Ancient Israel*, 1955.

P. 197, n. 2 : The emendation 'in the furnace' is not strictly necessary ; the Hebrew word can be translated 'as with flux (or potash)' and refer to a natural part of the smelting process. In the following line the last word should be 'impurities' rather than alloy (which cannot be spoken of as removed).

P. 197, n. 3 : Perhaps also Isa. vi. 13, unless the phrase 'the holy seed is the stock thereof' be regarded as a gloss (since it is not found in LXX) and the verse then rendered : 'And if there be yet a tenth in it, then that shall be for burning, like the stump that is left when a terebinth or an oak is felled '.

P. 201, l. 29 : Messianic interpretation of the 'royal' psalms was made possible, and indeed inevitable, by the cessation of the Davidic dynasty during and after the years of exile.

P. 203, n. 5 : It should not be assumed that these 'songs', if detached from their context and joined together, would make a single and complete whole. Their fragmentary nature and uncertain limits have added greatly to the difficulties of interpretation.

BIBLIOGRAPHY

This bibliography is not intended to be exhaustive, but offers a selection for further study of topics that are discussed in the present volume.

I. LITERARY CRITICISM

BENTZEN, A., *Introduction to the Old Testament*, 1948.
CARPENTER and HARFORD-BATTERSBY, *The Hexateuch*, 1900.
DODD, C. H., *According to the Scriptures*, 1952.
DODD, C. H., *The Bible To-day*, 1946.
DRIVER, S. R., *An Introduction to the Literature of the Old Testament*, 9th Ed., 1913.
HEBERT, A. G., *The Authority of the Old Testament*, 1947.
HOOKE, S. H., *In the Beginning* (Clarendon Bible), 1947.
McFADYEN, J. E., *Introduction to the Old Testament*, New Ed., 1932.
PFEIFFER, J., *Introduction to the Old Testament*, 1948.
ROBINSON, H. WHEELER, *The Old Testament: Its Making and Meaning*, 1937.
ROWLEY, H. H. (Ed.), *The Old Testament and Modern Study*, 1951.
ROWLEY, H. H., *The Relevance of the Bible*, 1941.
ROWLEY, H. H. *The Unity of the Bible*, 1953.
SIMPSON, D. C., *Pentateuchal Criticism*, 2nd. Ed., 1924.
SMITH, W. ROBERTSON, *The Old Testament in the Jewish Church*, 2nd. Ed., 1926.

II. HISTORY

LODS, A., *Israel from its Beginnings to the Middle of the Eighth Century*. (E. Tr. by S. H. Hooke), 1932.
LODS, A., *The Prophets and the Rise of Judaism*. (E. Tr. by S. H. Hooke), 1937.
NORTH, C. R., *The Old Testament Interpretation of History*, 1946.
OESTERLEY, W. O. E., and ROBINSON, T. H., *A History of Israel*, 1932.
ROBINSON, H. WHEELER, *The History of Israel: Its Facts and Factors*, 1938.
ROWLEY, H. H., *From Joseph to Joshua*, 1950.

III. RELIGION

ALBRIGHT, W. F., *Archaeology and the Religion of Israel*, 3rd Ed., 1953.
CAUSSE, A., *Du Groupe Ethnique à la Communauté Religieuse*, 1937.
DAVIDSON, A. B., *The Theology of the Old Testament*, 1904.
DHORME, E., *La Religion des Hébreux Nomades*, 1937.

EICHRODT, W., *Theologie des Alten Testaments*, Vol. I, 1933, Vol. II, 1935, Vol. III, 1939.

OESTERLEY, W. O. E., and ROBINSON T. H., *Hebrew Religion : Its Origin and Development*, 1930.

ROBINSON, H. WHEELER, *Inspiration and Revelation in the Old Testament*, 1946.

ROBINSON, T. H., *Prophecy and the Prophets in Ancient Israel*, 1954.

SKINNER, J., *Prophecy and Religion*, 1922.

SNAITH, N. H., *The Distinctive Ideas of the Old Testament*, 1944.

WRIGHT, G. E., *God Who Acts : Biblical Theology*. 1952.

WRIGHT, G. E., *The Old Testament against its Environment*, 1950.

IV. SPECIAL TOPICS

ALBRIGHT, W. F., *From the Stone Age to Christianity*, 1940.

ALBRIGHT, W. F., *The Archaeology of Palestine*, 1949.

BERTHOLET, A., *A History of Hebrew Civilization*, 1926.

ČERNÝ, L., *The Day of Yahweh and some Relevant Problems*, 1948.

COWLEY, A., *Aramaic Papyri of the Fifth Century B.C.*, 1933.

GRAY, G. B., *Sacrifice in the Old Testament*, 1925.

GRESSMANN, H., *Der Ursprung der israelitisch-jüdischen Eschatologie*, 1905.

JOHNSON, A. R., *The One and the Many in the Israelite Conception of God*, 1942.

JOHNSON, A. R., *The Vitality of the Individual in the Thought of Ancient Israel*, 1949.

KRAELING, E. G., *The Brooklyn Museum Aramaic Papyri*, 1953.

MORGENSTERN, J., *The Ark, the Ephod and the ' Tent of Meeting '*, 1945.

MOORE, G. F., *Judaism*, 1927.

NORTH, C. R., *The Suffering Servant in Deutero-Isaiah*, 1948.

OESTERLEY, W. O. E., *Sacrifice in Ancient Israel*, 1937.

OESTERLEY, W. O. E., *The Evolution of the Messianic Idea*, 1908.

PEDERSEN, J., *Israel : Its Life and Culture*, I-II, 1926, III-IV, 1940.

PRITCHARD, J. B., *Ancient Near-Eastern Texts relating to the Old Testament*, 1950.

ROBINSON, H. WHEELER (Ed.), *Record and Revelation*, 1938.

ROBINSON, H. WHEELER, *Suffering, Human and Divine*, 1939.

ROBINSON, H. WHEELER, *The Christian Doctrine of Man*, 1911.

ROBINSON, H. WHEELER, *The Christian Experience of the Holy Spirit*, 1928.

ROBINSON, H. WHEELER, *The Cross of Job*, 1916.

ROBINSON, H. WHEELER, *The Cross of the Servant*, 1926.

ROWLEY, H. H., *The Biblical Doctrine of Election*, 1950.

SCHOFIELD, J. N., *Archaeology and the After-life*, 1951.

SMITH, W. ROBERTSON, *The Religion of the Semites*, 3rd. Ed., 1927.

SUTCLIFFE, E. F., *The Old Testament and the Future Life*, 1946.

WRIGHT, G. E., *The Challenge of Israel's Faith*, 1944.

INDEX